HISTORY'S MOST MAGNIFICENT RULERS

HISTORY'S MOST MAGNIFICENT RULERS

FROM RAMSES II TO NAPOLEON

Hywel Williams

FALL RIVER PRESS

Contents

INTRODUCTION

For thousands of years most human societies were ruled by aristocratic males who professed a religion, hunted wild animals for recreation and devoted most of their active lives to military campaigning. When not waging war or managing their landed estates, these powerful individuals spent much of their time at court immersed in the competitive politics, palace intrigues and prescribed rituals of an enclosed society which revolved around a central monarchical figure.

This supreme aristocrat exercised command on account of his lineage – a line of descent linking him with the founder of his family's power. That dynastic connection was the basis of his legitimacy – the title which gave him an exclusive right to raise taxes, to distribute patronage in the form of jobs and lands to key supporters, to exact personal homage and enforce obedience to the laws made in his name. Daughters, in most cases, succeeded to the throne only if there were no male heirs in the direct line.

The effective ruler enjoyed a monopoly of force: a unique and sovereign right to maim, kill and dispossess those who opposed him within his own territorial domain. The legitimacy of his title also allowed him to pursue glory by leading armies on campaigns of conquest into adjacent territories. Defeat in battle, weakness of character, mental feebleness, quarrels within the ruling family, religious disputes, natural catastrophes: these were among the many forces that might undermine the sovereign's power. Those who tried to run these aristocratic societies emphasized the theory of hierarchical order precisely because the social reality was so hard to control, and frequently vulnerable to both internal and external attack. Signs of weakness at the top of the political-military system invariably attracted the ambitions of restless warriors ready to contest authority and eager to establish their own dominance. Such rebels, however, rarely challenged the principles of aristocratic power and monarchical government: they simply wanted more of the fruits of office for themselves and, if successful in their revolts, were as keen on their rights as the rulers they had supplanted.

This is a world now lost to us largely as a result of the democratic and global impact of two documents: the US Declaration of Independence (1776) and the Declaration of the Rights of Man and the Citizen adopted by the French National Assembly in 1789. Monarchy is now reduced to a figurehead status in the few countries where it is allowed to survive, and the notion of its right to rule as an independent force has been widely rejected right across the continents, in both the developed and developing worlds. This is one of history's biggest shifts of attitude, separating as it does the history of the last two centuries from that of the preceding five millennia when societies and civilizations were governed by hereditary rulers able to command obedience to their will. Dynastic power may now seem exotic, secretive and 'unconstitutional', but the overwhelming majority of those ruled by it thought this was an entirely natural and obvious way of ordering human affairs, especially since various forms of sacred authority were also used to underwrite the ruler's legitimacy.

Kingship as an institution has a longer continuous history than that of any other system of power. The 'Sun Kings' are those individual rulers – whether holding the title of prince, sultan, queen, king, emperor or some other expression of supreme authority – who fulfilled their ambitions by exploiting a monarchical style that established a close identity between themselves and the countries, nations or territories they governed.

The phrase 'Sun King' (*le Roi Soleil*) was first used to describe Louis XIV of France since the king wished to be seen as the centre of the universe he created at his court in Versailles. Surrounded by his galaxy of courtiers, Louis was the embodiment of the state's central institutions and claimed to express the very essence of his subjects' collective identity. It is this ability which marks out all the rulers discussed in this book, which defines the basis of their authority and grounds it in a vision characterized by a majestic impersonality rather than mere egoism. The association between the charisma of kingship and the cosmological order had a long history even before Louis resorted to the symbolism of classical antiquity so that he might connect his power with that of Apollo, the god linked with the light of the sun. As early as the fourth century BC a series of 13 towers had been built along the ridge of a hill at Chankillo, the ceremonial centre in Peru's Casma Valley. Viewed from observation points on either side, access to which was reserved to the privileged few, the towers form a horizon spanning the arc of the sun which, according to the time of year, rises and sets at different points between the towers. These structures therefore constitute a solar calendar and if the sun was worshipped here then so possibly was the ruler who had, apparently, time itself on his side, since the buildings showed his control over the solar movement.

This book is concerned with the history of advanced societies in which the arrival of literacy means that the written record can supplement the material evidence of buildings and decorative objects. Certain key features recur in the history of kingship as it has evolved within such societies: an ability to unite its subject peoples by exciting their loyalty; the projection of the ruler's authority through acts of self-publicity and by aesthetic imagery; the building of temples and palaces which demonstrate the sovereign's authority; the association of kingly power with divine approval, military prowess and the maintenance of a national tradition; the idea of a dynastic succession which has to be maintained against foreign aggressors and internal rebels alike; and the importance of rituals, processions and festivals as part of the choreography of power.

It is in the Nile valley that these phenomena converge to greatest effect for the first time in recorded history and for that reason the story of the Sun Kings begins in the ancient Egypt of the pharaohs.

DATES
In the chapter headings 'R' indicates the reign dates of the rulers. Their birth and death dates are given in the Key Dates panels.

RAMSES II, Egypt's Defining Pharaoh

R. 1279–1213 BC

Thirty separate dynasties of pharaohs ruled over Egypt from *c.*2925 BC to 343 BC when the Persian army extinguished the country's independence. Egyptian culture demonstrated a profound identity between dynastic history and that of the civilization over which the rulers presided, and especially so in the case of Ramses II. The colossal statues of the ruler that were raised both in Egypt and in Nubia, just like his cartouches carved onto existing buildings, celebrated his achievements and enforced his authority.

On the site of a holy shrine built by his father Seti I, Ramses had built a magnificent funerary temple, known as the Ramesseum. At the centre of the complex was a hyppostyle hall supported by 48 columns, 39 of which still stand today. They are decorated with relief sculptures showing the pharaoh before various gods. The one above shows Ramses II before Horus and Thoth.

This was ancient Egypt's second longest reign, and the prodigious number of temples that were built shows the country's material prosperity under a ruler whose authority and munificent display supplied a standard by which later pharaohs were measured and inspired. Nine kings of the 20th dynasty which succeeded his own therefore named themselves after Ramses, and descent from the king was highly prized during the early first millennium BC when Egypt started to decline as a great power. For his subjects in his own lifetime and afterwards he was 'Sese', a nickname which showed the affection for a ruler who had become a national symbol.

Papyrus and Pyramids

The River Nile was the basis of a developed Egyptian civilization whose history extends into the pre-dynastic period of the fourth millennium BC. Flowing from Nubia, which lies to Egypt's south, with the arid Sahara to the west, it made its way to the Delta and the Mediterranean. Its annual flooding was the source of the river valley's exceptional agricultural fertility and the papyrus, which grew in the marshes, supplied Egypt's literate elite with writing materials. Papyrus, a major

Ramses's extensive programme of building works included six major temples in Nubia. The most famous are the two carved from a sandstone cliff at Abu Simbel. Four colossal statues of the great pharaoh himself (one of which is shown here) guard the entrance to the Great Temple.

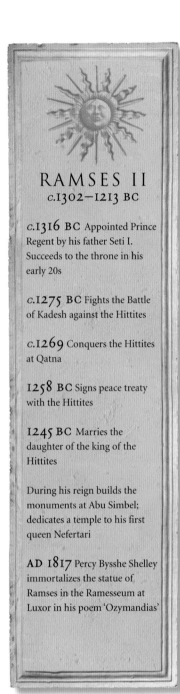

c.1316 BC Appointed Prince Regent by his father Seti I. Succeeds to the throne in his early 20s

c.1275 BC Fights the Battle of Kadesh against the Hittites

c.1269 Conquers the Hittites at Qatna

1258 BC Signs peace treaty with the Hittites

1245 BC Marries the daughter of the king of the Hittites

During his reign builds the monuments at Abu Simbel; dedicates a temple to his first queen Nefertari

AD 1817 Percy Bysshe Shelley immortalizes the statue of Ramses in the Ramesseum at Luxor in his poem 'Ozymandias'

export to the classical civilizations of Greece and Rome, formed part of Egypt's association with an august, if secretive, tradition of learning, especially in mathematics, astronomy and medicine. By *c.*3000 BC two forms of writing, hieroglyphs and the cursive script known as 'hieratic', had been invented in Egypt and both were used to develop a bureaucratic state by the mid-third millennium BC. Pyramid building (at its height between the Third and Sixth dynasties from *c.*2650–*c.*2150 BC) showed the centralized state's ability to mobilize an immense labour force, as well as its command of advanced technical skills – especially in surveying which was also used to ensure correct boundaries between fields after each annual flood. As a bridge joining life with death and the hereafter stood the various complexes of royal tombs, which included mortuary temples as well as the pyramids, and also the temples dedicated to the cult of the gods whose representatives on earth were Egypt's kings.

The Place of Egyptian Kings

The title of '*per'aa*' (and hence *pharaoh*) only became current by *c.*1400 BC and signified the ruler's association with the 'great estate' or royal palace. But the nature of the ruler's power had been established much earlier, and royal inscriptions show how the king was meant to uphold order or '*ma'at*' – an idea of creative stability, which was both social and spiritual, earthly and cosmic. Egyptian kings occupied a well-defined place in this hierarchy of being. Above them were the gods, while below them were the ever-present spirits of the dead and the persons of the living. The first element in the king's list of titles associated him with Horus, a god in the guise of a falcon whose form supplied the symbol for Egyptian kingship. Other kingly titles signified the unity of Lower Egypt centred on Memphis in the north with Upper Egypt centred on Thebes in the south.

A Leading Power in the Middle East

Widespread famine and violence marked the collapse of the Old Kingdom period at the end of the Eighth dynasty in *c.*2130 BC, possibly as a result of the Nile's repeated failure to flood. The 11th dynasty (2081–1938 BC) was able to assert its authority over Egypt from its base in Thebes and established the national importance of its dynastic god, Amon, who was also associated with the sun god, Re, and often represented by a ram's head. Occupation of lower Nubia in the 18th century showed Egypt's expansionist ambitions as it became the leading Middle Eastern power. The rule of the Hyksos dynasty (1630–1523 BC), a group of mixed Semitic-Asiatic invaders based in the Delta, was all-important in introducing western Asian technology into Egypt, especially the horse and the chariot, improved battle axes and advanced fortification techniques.

The period of the New Kingdom starts with the 18th dynasty whose first ruler Ahmose (1539–14 BC) expelled the Hyksos, reunited the country, regained territory in the south and penetrated southern Palestine. Ahmose was Egypt's first major imperial ruler and under the 18th dynasty the country acquired a large military establishment. Amon-Re was now a fully evolved state god sanctifying the expansionist missions of Egypt's kings and Babylonia, as well as Assyria and the Hittites, sent tribute to Egypt during the reign of Thutmose III (1479–26 BC). Garrisons were established to guarantee order in the Syrian and Palestinian city-states now ruled by Egypt's vassals and Thutmose also established systematic colonial rule in Nubia. The 18th dynasty's pronounced interest in Asiatic religion formed part of a new, typically imperial, cultural mingling and the cult of the Middle Eastern goddess of war and sexual love, Astarte, spread into Egypt where it would be assimilated with that of the local goddess Isis.

The Battle of Kadesh

The religious revolutionary Akhenaton (1353–36 BC) had attempted to introduce a monotheistic system by enforcing the sole worship of the sun god, Aton, and he had claimed to be the god's son as well as his priest. Akhenaton's persecution of the cult of Amon created national unrest and one of Ramses's first acts as ruler represented an affirmation of religious tradition. He visited Thebes for the religious festival of Opet, which marked the New Year, an occasion when Amon was taken ceremonially by a barge from his shrine at Karnak to the temple of

Wall painting from the Temple of Ramses II at Abu Simbel, showing Ramses at the Battle of Kadesh. Biased Egyptian accounts of the battle, whose outcome was indecisive, were recorded on numerous temples, claiming a splendid victory for Ramses.

Luxor. Egypt's authority also had to be reasserted in its Asian sphere of interest where imperial control had declined as a result of Akhenaton's religious preoccupations. Ramses's father Seti I (1290–79 BC) started the recovery by waging war on the rebel princes of Syria-Palestine; he also confronted the Hittites of Anatolia who nonetheless, by the end of his reign, had established their new southern frontier at Kadesh on the Orontes river in western Syria. In c.1275 Ramses led his army north into southern Syria where he quelled the local rebels before advancing on the Hittite stronghold. Four divisions of infantry and chariotry, some 5,000 strong each, advanced through Palestine and Lebanon before arriving in the plain extending in front of Kadesh. It was here that the main Hittite army, which Ramses thought was at Aleppo, now struck with its force of 2,500 chariots. Egypt's leading divisions broke up in disarray, though the arrival of a special Egyptian task force saved Ramses from total disaster and the engagement was drawn. The failure to take Kadesh was a serious blow to Egyptian prestige, but Ramses's propagandist gifts could still turn the battle to his advantage by portraying it as a heroic stand against the odds. Scenes and official accounts in this vein duly appeared on Egypt's temple walls and a narrative poem was commissioned to honour the king's valour.

A Diplomatic Marriage

Returning some four years later to southern Syria and Palestine in a major campaign, Ramses secured substantial victories over those city-states which had overthrown Egyptian overlordship after the battle of Kadesh. By c.1269 BC he had broken through the Hittites' defensive lines and conquered them in battle at the Syrian town of Qatna. The eventual peace treaty of 1258 BC concluded years of intermittent hostilities. Lengthy lines of communication with Egypt made it impossible for Ramses's forces to hold on to their territories in the face of unremitting Hittite pressure. But the pharaoh had nonetheless restored Egypt's role as a great power in the Middle East and the Hittites were themselves under pressure now from the Assyrians. Diplomatic relations were swiftly established between the two formidable military powers which recognized each other's might and in 1245 BC Ramses married the Hittite king's daughter. Having secured control of his imperial territories' Asian rim, Ramses could now concentrate on a major campaign against the Libyans to the west whose incursions into the Delta posed a serious threat to Egypt, and would continue to do so long after his reign.

I met a traveller from an antique land
Who said, 'Two vast and trunkless legs of stone
Stand in the desert. Near them on the sand,
Half sunk, a shatter'd visage lies, whose frown
And wrinkled lip and sneer of cold command
Tell that its sculptor well those passions read
Which yet survive, stamp'd on these lifeless things,
The hand that mock'd them and the heart that fed.
And on the pedestal these words appear:
"My name is Ozymandias, King of Kings:
Look on my works, ye mighty, and despair!"
Nothing beside remains: round the decay
Of that colossal wreck, boundless and bare,
The lone and level sands stretch far away.

OZYMANDIAS BY PERCY BYSSHE SHELLEY

Columns in the temple of Seti I at Abydos. The city of Abydos had been an important religious centre since early times, when kings built their tombs nearby. Seti's temple was erected partly to honour the early kings – a list of pharaohs of the principal dynasties, known as the Table of Abydos – was found carved on a wall of the temple.

Ramses's Building Frenzy

The Delta had always been important to Ramses because his family came from there. Seti I had built a palace at the family's home in the area's northeast, and Ramses moved his capital to the site partly because it was well placed for his Asiatic campaigns. He developed Pi-Ramesse (the House of Ramses) into a major city equipped with docks and storehouses, temples, gardens and orchards. This was now the administrative centre for the Egyptian bureaucracy as well as an important military base. Ramses's interest in merging Egyptian with Asiatic religion is shown in the city's division into four distinct areas each of which was allocated its own presiding deity: Amon and Buto (the royal cobra goddess) were local Egyptian gods while Astarte and Seth were Syrian arrivals.

The 19th dynasty's origins were non-royal since Ramses I (1292–90 BC), a general who was also the empire's vizier or chief minister, had been selected by the childless pharaoh Horemheb to succeed him. This comparative parvenu status may explain Ramses's building frenzy as he sought to imprint his reputation and that of his family on the Egyptian psyche. He arranged for work to resume on the great temple started by his father at the sacred city of Abydos. Its central long gallery contains a relief showing Seti and Ramses making offerings to the cartouches of 76 of their predecessors, starting with Menes in the early third millennium BC. Nearby stands Ramses's own temple and he also finished his father's funerary temple at Luxor. He built six temples in Nubia; two of them, carved out of the rock face at Abu Simbel, contain four monumental statues of Ramses. A smaller temple nearby was dedicated both to his first queen Nefertari and to the goddess of love, showing that even a king with a harem as large as Ramses's may be capable of marital affection.

His funerary temple at Luxor, the Ramesseum, contains the 57-foot statue of the seated king, which survives only in fragments. The poet Percy Bysshe Shelley was stirred to muse on how decay and failure must be the fate of all earthly powers by the monument's ruins that he associated with the vainglory of 'Ozymandias'. But Ramses had established a certain style of kingly rule whose inspirational appeal would outlast the history of his dynasty and that of his civilization.

SOLOMON, King of Israel

R. *c.*970–928 BC

The institution of a centralizing monarchy with its rights of dynastic succession had emerged among the tribes of Israel by the mid-tenth century BC. But it was a controversial development. Israel's 12 tribes were previously organized as a federation, and monarchy, although characteristic of their Middle Eastern neighbours, was alien to Israel's traditions. Many saw monarchy as undermining her status as a people chosen by God through covenant. Others thought it was a price worth paying if Israel was to survive.

David's slaying of Goliath and the resulting victory over the Philistines made him a hero among the people of Israel. Andrea del Verrocchio's bronze statue from about 1475 depicts the young David posing over the head of the slain giant.

Egypt's decline by the end of the second millennium BC had given the tribes of Israel an opportunity to consolidate but their further advance was checked by the aggressive power of the Philistines based in Palestine. Israel's reliance on the occasional tribal levy was no match for a military force commanded by a military aristocracy which was also expert in chariot warfare. The Israelites suffered a decisive defeat in *c.*1050 BC near Aphek on the edge of the Mediterranean coastal plain, and large tracts of their territory were subsequently occupied by the Philistines.

Biblical Stories

The biblical narratives composed by the mid-tenth century look back at these events of a century earlier, and mix the historical with the mythological, in accounting for Israel's recovery after this catastrophe. Their aim is to show how monarchy became a national focus of unity and how its organizational prowess helped Saul, the first king, to eject the Philistine army of occupation.

'The Judgement of Solomon' by the Italian artist Giorgione, painted c.1495–6. Solomon's legendary wisdom is popularly exemplified in the famous Judgement: two women, both claiming to be the mother of a child, asked him to settle their dispute. Solomon ordered the child to be cut in half; rather than allowing this atrocity, one of the women gave up the child, revealing herself to be the true mother.

SOLOMON
c.1000–928 BC

c.1000 BC Born son of King David and Bathsheba

c.970 BC According to some sources, Solomon becomes king of Israel around this time.

Makes alliance with Tyre. Queen of Sheba visits Solomon and brings him gold. Solomon's mines extract copper

960s BC Begins work on the temple in Jerusalem.

The biblical 'Song of Solomon', a celebrated work of erotic literature, is falsely attributed to the king. Solomon's supposed aphorisms are contained in the Bible's Book of Proverbs. The Seal of Solomon shows the Star of David

c.928 BC Dies in Jerusalem; his reign lasts for around 40 years

The two books of Samuel and the first book of Kings are inspirational literature containing tales of Samuel, the resistance leader in an occupied territory, and his anointing of Saul as the first king. David is shown resorting to guerrilla warfare against an unstable king during Saul's later years when the Philistine threat had returned. These were the Jewish equivalents of Achilles, Ulysses and Heracles.

But the biblical stories also show the precariousness of kingship in Israel. Samuel, disliking the powers of monarchy, is supposed to have repented of anointing Saul and to have disowned him. It is the popular acclamation of the people which is described as leading David to become king of the tribe of Judah. His rebellion against Saul and his heirs is regarded as being worthy of success because of his charismatic gifts – those signs of a prophetic power and a divine inspiration which Israel had always valued in her leaders. Saul's own display of charismatic frenzy, perhaps later degenerating into insanity, was what had qualified him to be king in the first place. David's career showed how a gifted charismatic, turned rebel, could undermine the dynastic rights of an incumbent.

David's Kingdom

Elements of other tribes became attracted to Judah's new dynamic king. As a result Judah in the south and the area in the north claimed by Saul's feeble son Eshbaal became united in the person of King David who secured the final defeat of the Philistines. Seizing a settlement in the centre of his new territorial holdings from the Jebusites, a Canaanite tribe, David renamed it Jerusalem. This, 'the city of David', was his own territorial holding, the site of his palace, and the new location for the Ark of the Covenant, housed in a shrine staffed with guardian priests.

David's legacy to Solomon, his son by his paramour Bathsheba, was therefore that of a sacral kingship, supported by a religious establishment of high priests and reigning over an empire which extended across most of Palestine. The Philistines had been confined to a narrow coastal strip and the Canaanite city-states had been absorbed. David's further victorious campaigns against neighbouring states, especially the Aramaeans whose centre at Damascus he turned into an imperial province, made Israel the dominant Middle Eastern power with southern and central Syria being governed from Jerusalem. The formal machinery of government borrowed heavily from Egyptian models. David's harem and guard of honour were very Middle Eastern in style. So also were the attempted coups by two other sons of David, Absalom and Adonijah, which almost denied Solomon his throne.

Solomon's Empire

Solomon's marriages, such as that with the daughter of Egypt's pharaoh, greatly expanded his harem and consolidated his empire's boundaries. The alliance with

Tyre, rebuilt and redeveloped by the Phoenicians in the 12th century BC, was especially important. Capital of a state controlling the whole of the southern Phoenician coastline in modern Lebanon, Tyre was engaged on a massive westward maritime expansion of Phoenician culture, power and wealth. By the end of the tenth century BC there were Tyrian colonies in Cyprus, Spain and North Africa as well as in Sardinia, an important centre of copper mining. Tyre could now import wheat and oil from Israelite-controlled Palestine while Solomon's big building projects used wood from Lebanon.

Solomon's military establishment included fortified cities and military bases along its boundaries. Chariot warfare, adapted from the Canaanites, was also a possibility along the plains of the new territories. Solomon's sole real military problems came in Syria. Here it was important for him to retain control of the Aramaean lands extending northwards from Transjordan, since they were the key to controlling the caravan routes that led towards the Euphrates.

The establishment of an independent ruler in Damascus imperilled, but never undermined, Solomon's command of the major north–south trade routes leading from Egypt into northern Syria. With foreign trade a royal monopoly he launched an expansion to the south by way of the Red Sea. Phoenician shipbuilders and sailors helped him to construct and man a merchant fleet whose voyages extended as far south as present-day Somaliland. Luxury goods from the coastal ports of the Red Sea now appeared back in Israel including gold and silver, ivory and jewels as well as monkeys – a regular feature of princely amusement.

According to legend, reports of Solomon's wisdom reached the queen of Sheba. The Bible tells of her arrival in Jerusalem bearing gifts including spices, gold and precious stones. The occasion is depicted in this painting of c.1452 by Piero della Francesca.

Fable, Gold and Trade

The queen of Sheba's visit to Solomon is the stuff of myth, but some such delegation would have made sense as a tribute from one great trading power to another. The Sabaeans' kingdom was centred in modern Yemen and it controlled the caravan routes which transported the spices and incense of southwestern Arabia towards Palestine and Mesopotamia. With Egypt no longer able to maintain a trade monopoly in Somaliland and Ethiopia, the Sabaeans probably extended their trading interests in those territories as well. Biblical sources emphasize how the queen was attracted by Solomon's celebrated wisdom but she is also described in the sources as bringing him gifts of gold – as much as 4.5 tons.

Solomon's interest in the overland trade routes to the south, his command of those routes in the north, his maritime ventures which were in direct competition with the Sabaeans' Arabian trade routes: all these factors made it necessary to

have good relations in order to protect Sabaean commerce. Trade agreements therefore ensured that Solomon's government received taxes and duties from Arabian trade.

King Solomon's Achievements

The most important exported cargo on Solomon's ships would have been copper extracted from the centuries-old mines in the Jordan valley and areas south of the Dead Sea, but the king also opened new copper mines, as well as establishing furnaces to smelt the ore. Solomonic Israel was also a middleman, importing chariots from Egypt, and high-quality horses from Cilicia, on the southeast coast of modern Turkey, before then exporting them along the trade routes to Syria. Agriculture also became vastly more productive with the introduction of the iron-tipped plough and a population boom ensued. Israel's population may well have doubled in size since the days of Saul.

Of all Solomon's building projects, which were run as a state monopoly and employed thousands, it was the temple which mattered most. Rectangular in shape, and designed by a Tyrian architect, it was begun in the fourth year of Solomon's reign and completed seven years later: 'the Holy of Holies' at the rear of the building was a small windowless cube containing the Ark.

The increased refinement of temple worship, a result of Solomon's expenditure, meant that both music and psalmody flourished. By the temple's side were two other buildings: the palace which took 13 years to complete and a structure which served as both treasury and armoury and was known as the 'House of the Forest of Lebanon' since it was supported by massive pillars made of cedar. Affairs of state were transacted in a separate judgement hall which contained a great ivory throne for the king. Israel's history and legends now took definitive shape and during Solomon's reign the 'Yahwist' – one of the authors who compiled the Hexateuch or the first six books of the Bible – constructed that great narrative account of God's dealings with his people and which forms a core element in those books.

Tax and Slave Labour

The 12 new administrative districts often disregarded the old tribal area boundaries. Integration was now the goal – especially since the new arrangements also covered the population of the old Canaanite city-states. Solomon personally appointed the area governors and each district had to supply enough revenue to cover the provision of the court for one month. Monarchy on this scale of magnificence was expensive and Solomon had to resort not only to tax, but also to slave labour. Slave gangs were levied and forced to work in Lebanon felling timber for his buildings. They would probably have been used in mining and smelting operations as well and, though drawn mostly from the non-Israelite and

A model of Jerusalem's Second Temple, completed in 514 BC and destroyed in AD 70 by Roman troops. It stood on the sacred site of Solomon's Temple, built in the mid-tenth century BC to house the Ark of the Covenant, and it became the central focus of the Jewish faith. Today all that remains is part of the western wall, which extends diagonally from the centre towards the lower right of the picture.

especially the Canaanite portion of the population, the novelty of a king of Israel running slave operations was viewed with resentment.

The tribes, surviving merely as a sacred order, were now politically marginal. Tribesmen were both taxed and liable for military conscription which could take the form of manual labour. An urban and commercial culture had, therefore, been grafted onto a pastoral and agrarian one, and in that process, an ancient egalitarianism had disappeared. In particular Solomon's Israel was much affected by its absorption of the Canaanites, the product of a centuries-old hierarchical order. Israel had evolved a new theology of power centred on a royal cult whose high feasts were celebrated at the temple: the king himself played a central role in the autumn one marking the start of the New Year.

For the purists Israel's new royal ideology was a dilution, even a paganization, of Judaism. This was particularly true of the north which, progressively disillusioned, seceded during the reign of Solomon's successor Rehoboam. But, if something was lost, much was gained. The cult stressed that it was Yahweh who had chosen David and his line to rule. It also maintained the centrality of Jerusalem as the holy city. This theology of kingship would inspire and console in future years of captivity and exile with its prophetic expectation of an idealized David who would return to restore the old order. Israel's expectation of this Messiah would be the most important legacy of the reign of Solomon.

NEBUCHADREZZAR II, King of Babylonia

R. 605–561 BC

Biblical writers among Jewish exiles recorded the sights of the imperial capital of Babylon which, partly because of their testimony, became synonymous with the decadent excesses of a world metropolis. In 597 BC the southern kingdom of Judah and the city of Jerusalem were invaded by the forces of Babylon under the command of Nebuchadrezzar II. The 18-year-old Jewish king Jehoiachin, the queen mother, senior officials and other leading citizens were deported to their famous 'Babylonian captivity'. A subsequent Babylonian attack on Jerusalem in 587–586 BC led to its capture after a siege and to another Jewish deportation, followed by a third in 582 BC.

The so-called Hanging Gardens of Babylon certainly exemplified the technical self-confidence of an advanced civilization and may have been built by Nebuchadrezzar to console his wife Amytis, a Median who missed the greenery and hills of her homeland in northwestern Iran. These roof gardens were built on a series of ziggurat terraces irrigated by pumps bringing water from the nearby River Euphrates. Reeds, bitumen and lead supplied the foundation of the terraces so that water would not drain away. But it was the ziggurat known as the 'tower of Babel' that caught the Jewish imagination as an example of Babylonian pride.

The Tower of Babel

This tower was a temple and the structure was an ancient one even in the time of Nebuchadrezzar who completed its reconstruction, begun during the reign of his father Nabopalassar. Babylonians called it Bab-ilu (the gate of God) and its Hebrew name was Babel. The phonetic similarity of Babel to the Hebrew verb *balal* (to confuse) was something of a gift to the Jewish authors who developed the powerful myth (described in Genesis 11, 1–9) of how God frustrated the Babylonians' projected goal – the building of a tower whose top would reach the heavens. He confused the workers by inventing the different world languages and, unable to understand each other, they had to down tools and leave the building unfinished. The myth may have consoled the captive Jews and it certainly reflects

*The Tower of Babel has become a symbol of humankind's rebellion against God
and the myth surrounding its construction has inspired many artistic
interpretations. This painting of c.1563 is by the Flemish Renaissance artist Pieter
Brueghel the Elder and is thought to draw parallels between the legendary tower
and his native Antwerp.*

the linguistic variety of Babylon's past but archaeology reveals a story of monumental achievement extending over at least 43 years and requiring some 17 million bricks, all of which had to be made and fired by Babylon's workers.

Erected on a vast terraced precinct in the city's centre, this ziggurat was the Babylonians' 'Foundation of Heaven and Earth' and it incorporated the remains of the earlier mud-brick structure dating back to the reign of Hammurabi more than a millennium earlier, in the 18th century BC. A new facing of baked bricks, laid in bitumen mortar, first of all provided a mantle for the old building whose height corresponded to the new ziggurat's first two stages. Above this level, four stepped terraces now rose and a temple was built on the topmost platform, with a series of rooms opening onto a central courtyard: these were the chapels of the Babylonian gods, foremost among which was Marduk, whose emblem was that of a hybrid creature with a lion's body and a snake's head and tail. Seated here on his throne, at a spot where heaven and earth came together, this supreme god of the national pantheon offered divine approval for the kings of a Babylonian empire whose roots lay deep in the soil of ancient Mesopotamia.

In this Kassite relief sculpture Marduk, the supreme god of Babylon, is shown in human form with a mythical dragon.

Early Cultures and Advanced Technology

The area between the Tigris and Euphrates extending from Baghdad to the Persian Gulf had developed a rich civilization long before Babylon's rise to prominence and domination over it. During the third millennium BC the land of Sumer, in the southeast of the territory, comprised a number of city-states. It was the Sumerians who developed the earliest known form of writing, the cuneiform, as well as civilization's first legal codes. Their advanced technology had led them to invent the sailboat, the potter's wheel and the seed plough. Internecine conflict among the Sumerian city-states however made them vulnerable to invasion by Akkad, a major Semitic civilization which was a more consolidated regional power in the northeast. The Sumero-Akkadian culture was assimilated by the Amorites, a great tribal federation of nomadic Semites which migrated to the east from Arabia at the beginning of the second millennium BC and which subsequently occupied the Mesopotamian region as well as Syria-Palestine.

The Amorites established a very diverse pattern of small kingdoms in Mesopotamia, including Babylon, which rose to imperial greatness under its ruler Hammurabi (*c.*1810–1750 BC). His conquests and alliances extended Babylonia's territories over the whole of southern Mesopotamia as well as parts of Assyria to the north. The cultural achievements of this first period of Babylonian greatness included Hammurabi's celebrated law code as well as the foundations of a sophisticated science including the astronomical observations for which the Babylonians became famous.

Babylon's Military History

Hittite incursions from Anatolia spelt the end of Babylonia's Amorite rulers in 1595 BC, and the line of Kassite rulers, a military aristocracy whose forces penetrated the region from the Caucasus in the middle of the second millennium BC, provided the second Babylonian dynasty which lasted for some 400 years. The horse, an animal sacred to the Kassites, was now introduced to Babylonia and helped to secure the dynasty's effectiveness. Their horse-drawn chariots ensured deep and fast penetration into enemy territory while communication systems generally became quicker and more reliable. Assyria to the north was nonetheless able to establish its independence of the Kassite dynasty and by the 13th century BC the state of Elam (southwestern Iran) threatened Babylonia from the east. Operating an unusual system of matrilineal succession, Elam's kings claimed their sovereignty by descent from a female member of the previous ruler's family. By the mid-12th century BC they had conquered Babylonia and destroyed the rule of the Kassites.

Both Elam and Assyria were now in contest for control over Babylonia. Nebuchadrezzar I (c.1126–1105 BC), the most successful of a new line of indigenous Babylonian rulers, was able to defeat Elam and keep Assyria at bay. But from the ninth century BC to the fall of the Assyrian empire in the late seventh century BC, Babylonia was predominantly under the control of Assyria which appointed sub-kings to run the country. Meanwhile, the arrival of further western Semitic tribes, especially the Aramaeans in northern Babylonia and the Chaldaeans in the south, contributed to the cultural mix of a now very cosmopolitan society. By the sixth to seventh centuries BC the Aramaic language, spread in part by Babylonian merchants, had supplanted Akkadian and become the Middle East's lingua franca. Ashurbanipal, the last Assyrian king, fell out with his brother, the sub-king in Babylon and embarked on a civil war which devastated large areas of Mesopotamia. Out of this chaos, however, arose the commanding figure of Nabopalassar, who formed an alliance with the Medes now established on the previously Elamite territories. Median assistance enabled him to defeat Assyria and establish the last dynasty to rule over an independent Babylonia.

Nebuchadrezzar Rules

Nabopalassar claimed no royal descent but his son decided to underscore his legitimacy by claiming that the third-millennium Akkadian ruler, Naram-Sin, was his ancestor. In 607–606 BC, while he was still crown prince, Nebuchadrezzar led operations against the traditional Assyrian enemy and he subsequently shattered the Egyptian army at Carchemish in 605 BC. Further campaigns in Syria and Palestine during 604–601 BC extended Babylonian power in these areas and also secured the initial submission of Judah. An Egyptian counterattack meant, however, that by 600 BC Judah and other vassal states were defecting from Babylonia's control. Nebuchadrezzar bided his time, repaired the chariots which

NEBUCHADREZZAR
II
c.630–561 BC

607–605 BC As crown prince Nebuchadrezzar leads campaigns against the Egyptians occupying Syria

605 BC Battle of Carchemish in which Nebuchadrezzar defeats the Egyptians, expelling them from Syria. In the same year, his father dies; Nebuchadrezzar returns and ascends the throne

597 BC Invades Judah and Jerusalem

568/7 Invades Egypt

During his reign, Nebuchadrezzar plants the Hanging Gardens of Babylon, reconstructs the ancient ziggurat, 'the tower of Babel', and builds a great temple dedicated to the god Marduk

were fundamental to his military technology and then regained the offensive by attacking the Arab tribes of northwestern Arabia as a prelude to his attack on Jerusalem in 597 BC. The port cities of Tyre and Sidon, after prolonged sieges, were forced to acknowledge Babylonian suzerainty and an invasion of Egypt in 568–567 BC, while not designed to conquer, nonetheless stopped any further Egyptian interference against Babylonia's interests. Nebuchadrezzar's claim that Marduk had granted him a universal kingship appeared vindicated.

Nebuchadrezzar's Reconstruction Programme

These campaigns meant that Nebuchadrezzar gained control of the major trade routes to the Mediterranean, as well as vast amounts of tribute and booty, while his control over the southern Anatolian provinces of Cilicia and Lydia gave him access to those regions' supplies of iron and other metals. He was able to embark on an ambitious reconstruction programme which would ally his own fame with that of a city intended to rival and surpass the celebrity of Nineveh, the Assyrian capital. Thousands of bricks were stamped with his own written identification and hundreds of commemorative plaques were inserted into the walls of his new buildings. Public ceremonies and religious rituals orchestrated on a grand scale reinforced the personal nature of his kingship and aimed to ground it in popular support. Departing and returning armies, as well as processions of the great gods' statues, made their way along the central Processional Way paved with limestone slabs. This started at the religious precinct which was the centre of the city, and which included not just the fabled ziggurat, but also a separate building, the great temple dedicated to Marduk. It then extended to the gate in the city walls which, named after the goddess Ishtar, was covered with coloured glazed tiles decorated with sacred animals on a deep blue background.

The palace built by Nabopalassar and extended by his son lay near the Ishtar Gate and Nebuchadrezzar built a second royal palace adjacent to it. The palaces' interior walls and ceilings were decorated with a rich wood panelling inlaid with ivory, lapis lazuli, silver and gold, while the walls of the throne room were glazed with more blue tiles. Lintels and thresholds were cast in bronze and doorways were set in walls several metres thick. This monumental scale was entirely novel in the history of architecture, while the lime and bitumen mortar which bound the baked brick and masonry together was designed to ensure the buildings' durability. In order to protect the temples and palaces from erosion and flooding Nebuchadrezzar diverted the Euphrates farther west by constructing a huge bulwark with walls up to 25 metres (83 feet) thick. A great moat, also built at the king's command, provided further protection for the city.

Plus Ça Change …

What the Jews saw as pride may well have been a concealed form of Babylonian anxiety. The architecture of vastness tried to bury the fear that this kingdom and

Northwest of the Ishtar Gate in Babylon Nebuchadrezzar built his royal palace. The main thoroughfare of the city, the Processional Way, was

lined with glazed bricks decorated with reliefs of animals such as this bull, symbolizing the god Adad.

empire, so recently restored, might yet again disappear. And so it proved. Babylonia fell to the Persians in 539 BC and the country lost its independence. Babylonianism nonetheless survived as a cultural style favoured by the ruthless. Alexander the Great died, appropriately enough, in Nebuchadrezzar's palace and the walls of the reconstructed early 21st-century Babylon contained special bricks bearing inscriptions that read: 'Rebuilt in the era of the leader Saddam Hussein'.

CROESUS, The Last King of Lydia

R. 560–546 BC

It was the Greeks of the classical age, and especially their historian Herodotus (484–c.425 BC), who first established the reputation of Lydia as the home of a commercially minded people. Lydia was a major military power from c.680 BC until the defeat of Croesus in 546 BC. Herodotus travelled widely throughout this area of western Anatolia during the mid-fifth century BC while gathering the information he would later use in his classic *Histories* of the Graeco-Persian wars.

In general Herodotus was struck by the similarity between the Lydians and his own people in their social customs and patterns of belief. This is hardly surprising given the range of cultural contacts, as well as the military campaigns that had been waged, between the Lydians and their neighbours in Asia Minor – the Ionian Greeks who had settled on the western coast of modern Turkey in cities such as Halicarnassus (Bodrum in modern Turkey) and Ephesus, Smyrna (now Izmir), Erythrae and Miletus.

Ionian Pioneers

The northern Greek tribes who had migrated eastward across the Aegean in the tenth century BC had extinguished the earlier Mycenaean culture but, by the early part of the eighth century, the Ionian cities had emerged to become pioneers of Greek civic development. The Ionic dialect had now become the established language of the Greeks and, from about 700 BC, the Ionians would also be adventurous explorers, establishing daughter settlements on the Black Sea coast and along the French and Spanish coasts of the Mediterranean. Much of this activity was a reaction against the Lydian territorial advance and as many as 90 such colonies are meant to have been established by Miletus alone.

As usual, with colonies came trade and Ionia became an important centre for the production of ceramics, metalware and textiles. But despite these developments Herodotus was struck by the unusual vitality of Lydian commerce and business life, something which for him marked the real difference between Lydian society and that of the Greeks wherever they were to be found.

*The legendary visit by the Athenian statesman Solon to the court of
Croesus at Sardis is depicted here by the 16th-century Flemish artist
Frans Francken the Younger.*

Lydia's Advanced Economics

As a native of Halicarnassus, Herodotus was finely attuned to the cultural variety of Hellenic civilization as lived away from mainland Greece. This was not the Greece of Athens or Thebes, of Sparta or Corinth. For centuries Ionian Greeks had been open to the influences of their neighbours as the cultural milieus of other Middle Eastern civilizations, especially those of Syria, Babylonia and Persia, spread to the west. If Herodotus was struck by how the Lydians' commercial acuity separated them even from the Ionian Greeks with all their cultural openness, then the difference must have been sharp indeed.

Mainland Greece with its rocky terrain and sparse cultivation produced little in the way of agricultural surplus and this made for a profound difference compared with the rich farmland of Anatolia whose produce, bought and sold, took the Lydians to an altogether more advanced economic level. The retail shops of the Lydians were a complete novelty to Herodotus and far removed from the occasional and seasonal markets he would have been familiar with as the basis of Greek commerce. Gold and silver coins were minted at the Lydian capital of Sardis while the use of such coinage as tokens of trade transactions, a practice which the Lydians may well have invented, had already been adopted by the Greeks of Herodotus's time and was the basis of the Greek-speaking world's substantial trade expansion in the seventh and sixth centuries BC. The historian's journeys, extending over many years, would take him beyond Lydia to Egypt and Libya, to Susa (now in Iran), Phrygia (now in modern western-central Turkey), Syria and even to Babylon, then the capital of the richest satrapy within the Persian empire. But he never had cause to revise his judgement that the Lydians' interest in money and profit was of an exceptional order, something which distinguished them from all the other societies he visited.

The Rise of Lydia

It was the destruction of Phrygia which had first given the Lydians their chance to develop as a major power in the Asia Minor of the seventh century BC. Located to the north of Lydia, in west-central Anatolia, Phrygia had its own reputation for commercial prosperity in the period following the 12th-century-BC collapse of the Hittite empire which had been previously dominant in the region. Although their supposed ruler Midas of *c*.700 BC is a legendary rather than a historical figure, the Phrygian

Gold and silver coins were probably invented by the Lydians and their use spread from Sardis to other parts of the Near East and Europe. The silver coin pictured above was minted in Athens.

cities of Gordium and Midas City were well-established centres of the eighth century BC. The Phrygians had developed an expertise in woodcarving, metalwork and embroidery, and their exported carpets became especially highly valued. This level of craftsmanship may explain why the Phrygians of a later period would be so highly regarded as slaves by the Greeks.

On the slopes of Mount Parnassus to the northwest of Athens lies Delphi. People travelled from all over Greece and further afield to ask questions of the priestess, known as the Pythia. Below is the temple of Tholos at the sanctuary of Athena Pronaia, gateway to the sacred site.

Towards the end of the eighth century BC, a wave of Cimmerian invaders, pushed south by Scythians, had spread from their southern Russian base across the Caucasus into Anatolia where, in 696–695 BC, they conquered Phrygia. In the ensuing power vacuum, Lydia's dynasty of Mermnad rulers established their hegemony in western Anatolia and the reign of Gyges (c.680–652 BC) saw Lydia emerge as a major military power. Gyges's alliance with the Assyrians enabled him to push farther west and invade Ionia: the Greek city of Miletus was attacked and that of Colophon was seized. But this campaign of conquest is also part of the story of the Hellenization of the Lydians since at its conclusion Gyges travelled to the oracle at Delphi in order to make an offering to the gods. His military campaigns against Egypt, where he despatched troops to aid an internal rebellion, made him vulnerable to another wave of Cimmerian attacks, in the course of which he was killed.

Lydia Controls Ionia

But the military power of the dynasty was now proving very resilient and King Alyattes (c.610–560 BC) was able to repel the Cimmerians, keep the Medes of Iran at bay, and also to advance the Lydian control of Ionia by taking Smyrna, a massively fortified city. The conflict with Miletus was particularly significant and Alyattes's five years of campaigning destroyed the agricultural hinterland supporting the city's economy. At the time this was the greatest Greek city of the east, and it was important not just economically, but also culturally, on account of its flourishing literary, scientific and philosophical traditions. In c.600 BC Miletus was the home of the mathematician and philosopher Thales, as well as of his pupil, Anaximander, whose work in astronomy and geography formed the basis of the first developed cosmological view of the world. By the mid-sixth century BC the city had acknowledged Lydian overlordship.

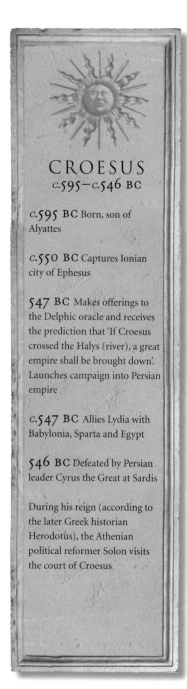

CROESUS
c.595–c.546 BC

c.595 BC Born, son of
Alyattes

c.550 BC Captures Ionian
city of Ephesus

547 BC Makes offerings to
the Delphic oracle and receives
the prediction that 'If Croesus
crossed the Halys (river), a great
empire shall be brought down'.
Launches campaign into Persian
empire

c.547 BC Allies Lydia with
Babylonia, Sparta and Egypt

546 BC Defeated by Persian
leader Cyrus the Great at Sardis

During his reign (according to
the later Greek historian
Herodotus), the Athenian
political reformer Solon visits
the court of Croesus

The Rise and Fall of Croesus

Croesus succeeded to the throne of Lydia following a dynastic struggle with his
half-brother but his military prowess had already been demonstrated during his
father's lifetime when he had acted as viceroy and commander-in-chief. Just like
Gyges before him, Croesus both campaigned against the Ionians and respected
the Greek gods. Ephesus was a comparatively recent foundation of the Ionian
Greeks (c.600 BC) when Croesus captured it in c.550 BC and this event meant
that Lydia was now in control of the whole of the Ionian mainland – although
Croesus's lack of a naval force meant that he could not take the battle to the
offshore Greek Ionian islands such as Chios and Samos. The fact that he made
so many offerings to the oracle at Delphi was used by the Greeks to demonstrate
the king's wealth. In a typically Greek style however they would also have
appreciated the nemesis that lay in wait for Croesus as the gods turned against
him at the very height of his prosperity.

Confronted by the sudden rise to power of Persia's Achaemenid dynasty,
Croesus resolved on an alliance with Nabonidus, the ruler of a Babylonia
which was then in the last stages of its independence and was also threatened
by the Persians. Further Lydian alliances with Sparta and Egypt were intended
to protect Croesus's position to his south and west. Accordingly he made the
first move against the Persians and advanced into the eastern Anatolian terrain
of Cappadocia, where he fought an inconclusive engagement in 547 BC. By
now Cyrus had persuaded the Babylonians to break their alliance with Lydia.
He had also taken the southeast Anatolian region of Cilicia, a territory whose
land routes supplied Anatolia's sole link with Syria: as a result the Lydians were
cut off from any possible military support which might come from the east.

Because it was late in the campaigning season, Croesus assumed that military
operations had ended for the year and he retreated to Sardis, having disbanded
the army he had raised by a national levy. He was subject however to a surprise
lightning attack since Cyrus and his forces had pursued him right up to the city
walls. First besieged and then stormed, Sardis fell in 546 BC and Croesus himself
was captured. In Ionia the Greek cities fought against their latest takeover by an
external power but were overwhelmed by Persian military superiority. Lydian
culture would continue, but the independent rule of the Mermnad was at an end,
and with the dynasty's demise, a century and a half of Lydian political and
military dominance in western Asia Minor had passed.

Athenian Influences and Attitudes

The supposed visit of the Athenian political reformer and lawgiver Solon
(630–560 BC) to Croesus represents Greek propaganda and myth-making of
a later age. Herodotus recounts it as historical fact, but was merely recirculating
a fable which had become popular among the Greeks as they, rather gleefully,

contemplated the fate of Croesus and his Lydians. Solon is meant to have counselled the Lydian king that recognition of good fortune, rather than possession of wealth and power, was the key to whatever happiness might be available to mortals. Moreover, while alive, no man could be regarded as being truly happy. This pious piece of triumphalism may have been particularly appealing to the Athenians of the mid-fifth century BC, the period of their greatest political self-confidence after the defeat of the Persians. The fact that they believed and enjoyed the story of Solon's encounter with Croesus is, nonetheless, revealing of Greek attitudes towards monarchy and dynastic rule in the period between Solon's reforms and the time of Herodotus.

Solon's measures had diminished the powers and privileges of the aristocratic factions that had dominated Athenian politics in the early sixth century. His institution of a sovereign general assembly attended by all citizens, the law-making ecclesia, became the basis of Athenian democracy's later development. And the entire citizenry, except for the very poorest, also served on an annual basis in the Council of Four Hundred which prepared assembly business. Served by such institutions and fortified by their cultural achievements, as well as their military advances, the Athenian democracy came to regard the palace societies of Middle Eastern monarchy as hopelessly reactionary, part of humanity's primitive past rather than of its future. A certain amount of gloating at the fate of Croesus who could not be saved from an ignominious defeat despite all his riches was surely appropriate.

Ruins of the temple of Artemis at Ephesus, one of the Seven Wonders of the Ancient World. The original temple was badly damaged during fighting when the Lydians attacked the city in c.550 BC. Magnanimous in victory, Croesus contributed to the building of a new temple, including financing most of the columns, some of which still stand today.

DARIUS I, The Great King of Persia, Founder of Persepolis

R. 522–486 BC

The tone of the *shahanshah* was exultant as this 'king of kings' listed the materials used in the construction and adornment of the palace he had built at Susa, his capital. Lebanese cedar, Egyptian ebony and silver, Ethiopian ivory: all had arrived from his westernmost territories. Turquoise came from his northern frontier province of Chorasmia lying on the Aral Sea's southern shores. Sogdiana, in modern Uzbekistan, had produced lapis lazuli and two other eastern regions of the empire had supplied gold: Bactria lying between the Hindu Kush mountains and the River Oxus, and Gandhara in the vale of Peshawar.

The palace workmen showed the same imperial breadth. The stonecutters were Ionian Greeks from the coastal city-states of Asia Minor and Lydians from western Anatolia, while it was Babylonians who had baked the palace bricks. Egyptians had cut the timbers and, as goldsmiths and decorators of the palace walls, their workforce had been joined by Medes, a people whose hegemony in Iran preceded that of Darius's own Achaemenid dynasty.

Both Medes and Persians were among the Indo-European peoples who had established themselves in Iran by the beginning of the first millennium BC and the rise to power of the Median kingdom of northwest Iran is a seventh-century-BC phenomenon. By the mid-seventh century BC the Median kingdom had absorbed the threat of nomadic warriors, including Scythians, who had entered western

Detail from a painted pottery vase depicting Darius I. It is the most famous work by a fourth-century-BC Greek artist, subsequently known as Darius Painter. The red-figure technique, in which figures and patterns are left unglazed on the red clay, was the dominant style of Greek vases during the fifth and fourth centuries BC.

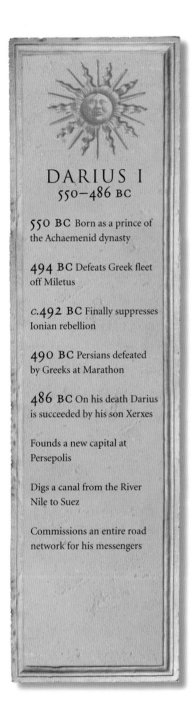

550 BC Born as a prince of the Achaemenid dynasty

494 BC Defeats Greek fleet off Miletus

c.492 BC Finally suppresses Ionian rebellion

490 BC Persians defeated by Greeks at Marathon

486 BC On his death Darius is succeeded by his son Xerxes

Founds a new capital at Persepolis

Digs a canal from the River Nile to Suez

Commissions an entire road network for his messengers

Iran from across the Caucasus. The Medes formed a Babylonian alliance and the Median army's specialized units of spearmen, archers and cavalry destroyed Assyria to the west, with the city of Nineveh falling in August 612 BC. The arc of Assyrian-controlled territory extending from Mesopotamia, through Assyria and the Zagros mountains to Syria and Palestine, now fell to the Babylonians while the Medes gained the highland areas, including eastern Anatolia. A peace treaty of 585 BC ended conflict between the Medes and the Anatolian-based Lydians, then western Asia Minor's leading power, and the Medes' Iranian kingdom extended from its eastern Anatolian boundary to cover western Iran, including the southwest in which was located the province of Persis (modern Fars) centred on Susa.

The Rise of Darius and the Persian Empire

The dynasty, which ruled Persis as a Median vassal state, traced its origins to Achaemenes in the seventh century BC. Cyrus II (r.559–529 BC) was the Achaemenid ruler whose alliance with the Babylonians helped him to defeat the Medes in 550 BC and establish a Persian empire with astonishing rapidity. Conquest of the Lydians in 546 BC gave him control of the Greek Ionian city-states and, turning against his erstwhile ally, Cyrus captured Babylon in 539 BC. Persia now ruled all the Babylonian territories seized from Assyria and its power extended to Egypt's boundary. Cyrus's son and successor, Cambyses II (r.529–522 BC), probably murdered his own brother Bardiya, and took Memphis during the Egyptian campaign launched in 525. He died while returning to reassert authority in Persia where an impostor, claiming to be Bardiya, was leading a rebellion. Darius was the general in charge of the core unit of the Achaemenid standing army, the 10,000 'immortals' whose privileged status was shown by their wearing of jewellery and decorated robes. They included an even more elite group, that of the 1000 who, distinguished by the gold pomegranates on their spears, formed the king's personal bodyguard. Command of the 10,000 was central to regal control and Darius, a prince of the Achaemenid dynasty, now raced home from Egypt to Persia to seize his moment.

The inscription that Darius caused to be carved on the precipitous rock face of Mount Bisotun in the Zagros mountains, to the west of the Iranian plateau, asserts his dynastic legitimacy and describes how six Achaemenian aristocrats killed the false Bardiya. The revolt however had spread to most of the imperial provinces, especially Media in the northwest, and it took most of 522–521 to suppress the rebellion, after which Darius's expansionist policy helped to assert his authority. Eastern campaigns added large areas of the northwestern Indian frontier to his empire and in 516 BC Darius started a Greek offensive. Having established a bridgehead across the Hellespont he was able to attack Scythians located on the western and northern shores of the Black Sea – an important goal since the area was a major corn exporter to the Greek city-states. The revolt of the

Ionian city-states in 500 BC was a major challenge but in 494 BC Darius's navy defeated the Greek fleet off Miletus. Mardonius, the king's son-in-law, was named a special commissioner to Ionia. By *c.*492 BC he had suppressed the local 'tyrants' who had led the Ionian rebellion, restored the cities' Greek-style democracies and recovered Thrace and Macedonia, lands gained during the earlier anti-Scythian campaign but lost to the Persians during the Ionian revolt.

Athens and Eretria had sent a small naval force to support the Ionian revolt, a fact used by Darius to justify the major offensive which, launched against the Greeks in 492 BC, included the Persian defeat on land at Marathon in 490 BC and the Greek naval victory at Salamis ten years later. The peace eventually concluded in 449 BC however recognized the Greeks' limited success in attaining their central objective, the liberation of the Ionian cities.

Imperial Persepolis

Pasargadae, the new city Cyrus II built in Persis, illustrated the new dynastic authority complete with the columned halls which were now a distinctive feature of Persian architecture. Persepolis, built by Darius nearby, was a similar civic testimony elegant in its symmetrical layout, rich in its buildings' ornamentation and a setting for the Median court ceremonial now adapted by the Persians for their own use. Persians were also excelling in the decorative arts, in metal tableware, fine jewellery – especially gold work – and decorated pottery.

A glazed brick relief from Darius's palace at Susa represents Persian guards in their distinctive dress, carrying spears and shields. This form of ornamental brickwork was used extensively in Persia.

Darius's Bisotun inscription represented a major evolution in the national identity since the king had decreed that a script be invented so that Old Persian, a southwestern dialect of Iranian – just as Median was the northwestern dialect – could be transcribed for the first time. Bisotun also established the tradition that Achaemenid royal inscriptions should be trilingual as there were also versions of the text in Elamite and Babylonian. Elam, located at the head of the Persian Gulf, had been an important conduit transmitting Babylonian culture to the Iranian plateau from the mid-third millennium until the country's Assyrian destruction in the first half of the seventh century BC. Aramaic, the language used by the imperial bureaucracy, was yet another element in the distinctive cultural diversity of the Persian empire, the largest yet seen in world history.

Persian Tolerance

Darius's light touch in imperial administration and respect for national identities was a distinctly Persian tradition, as Mardonius's pro-democratic policy in Ionia illustrated. The very title *shahanshah* echoed the dynasty's origins in the imposition of a tribal levy and its continuing exercise of power through subordinate layers of authority. Cyrus had ruled Babylonia in accordance with local traditions and also allowed the Jews to return to Palestine, a policy maintained by Darius. Xerxes, Darius's heir, was a rougher imperialist: he suppressed an Egyptian rebellion in his campaign of 484 BC and then imposed direct Persian control just as he did in Babylonia after its uprising in 482 BC. Salamis, followed in 479 BC by another naval defeat at Mycale in the eastern Aegean and on land at Plataea, represented Xerxes's nemesis. He retreated into the harem whose intrigues led to his assassination in 465 BC. Subsequent imperial history was marked by an increase in the powers of the satraps – the provincial governors who came to assume both civilian and military powers with some of them becoming subordinate, and often dynastic, sub-kings.

Darius Asserts His Kingship

The rise of a national religion associated with a prophet named Zoroaster (c.628–551 BC) from the Iranian plateau's northeast helped Darius to assert his style of kingship. Zoroastrianism, a monotheistic faith with fire as its symbol of truth's purity, elevated the god Ahura Mazda as an ethical force opposed to lying and injustice. Achaemenid political theology asserted that Ahura Mazda had granted the dynasty its empire and the Zoroastrian concern with equity is reflected in the

Ruins of the city of Persepolis. Darius began to build the city in c.518 BC; his son Xerxes continued the work and his grandson Artaxerxes completed it nearly 100 years later.

inscriptions which emphasize Darius's juridical role. Troops raised by an imperial levy supplemented the standing army, but Darius respected the customary laws which, administered in the local courts, were supplemented by the body of imperial law proclaimed in the king's name.

Persis itself as a non-conquered territory was tax free, but there were agricultural tax reforms for the imperial provinces and vassal states following Darius's land survey: taxation was now levied on a fixed percentage of the average yield estimated on the basis of several years' information rather than being a fixed amount regardless of the harvest fluctuations. Land and agriculture formed the basis of imperial military might and Darius therefore introduced the measurement of the 'bow' – the amount of land calculated able to support one bowman whose military service then constituted his land duty.

A Major Boost to Trade

Standardization of weights and measures, as well as of coinage, proved a major boost to trade whose expansion was also aided by state-organized voyages of exploration in search of new markets. Rapid communications were key both to trade and government and Darius completed the originally Egyptian project of a canal linking the Red Sea with the River Nile. Naval routes across the Arabian Sea and into the Persian Gulf, whose coast saw significant port development, thereby linked the empire on an east–west axis. An advanced network of state-maintained imperial highways was crucial to imperial peace and prosperity: the famous road running from Susa to Sardis was serviced by another government business, the postal service with its relay stations – separated from each other by a day's journeying – supplying fresh riders and mounts. Such speedy communications were also central to the king's intelligence system as officials from the central government, based mostly at Susa, travelled the country to keep an eye on the satraps.

Fall of the Empire

The Greeks must have seemed mere pinpricks on the western periphery of his empire when Darius launched his Hellenic offensive. Greek mercenaries, far from being a threat, were eager for Persian gold and silver and were regularly used by the Persian army. But the Greek leadership's military and political hostility to the Persians proved a tough nut to crack, largely because their typical political structure, the city-state, was so alien to the Persian kingship system. Crucially, the Persian empire failed to ally itself with the Athenians in common opposition to the expansionist ambitions of the northern Greek Macedonian dynasty. Alexander would reduce the Persepolis of Darius to ruins. But the age of Hellenistic civilization that Alexander inaugurated in all its cultural pluralism was, nonetheless, built on the Persian respect for variety right across the empire bequeathed to posterity by Darius.

ALEXANDER III, 'The Great', King of Macedon

R. 336–323 BC

How did Alexander persuade his army of 30,000 footsoldiers and 5,000 cavalry to follow him on that great march of conquest which started in Macedon's highlands and plains, crossed the Hellespont in the spring of 334 BC and then struck deep into Persia and Babylonia before reaching the Hindu Kush and eventually crossing into northwest India? The fact that for most of that journey Alexander's men were on one of the great winning sides of history is, of course, part of the answer.

His military genius adapted to the strategic demands of different terrains and he beat armies whose fighting techniques varied from the cavalry assaults of the Persians to the attacking guerrilla styles of tribesmen in the north Indian hills. But authority at this level of success invariably needs an inspirational cause, something which endows the leader with an aura of magnetic symbolism.

A Homeric Hero

Alexander found his mythos in the poetry of Homer and presented himself as a Homeric hero. He followed that warrior code of honour and competitive valour, of loyalty to friends, horror of shame and respect for the gods which inspires both the *Iliad* and the *Odyssey*. This creed accompanied Alexander as he left the Greek mainland and inspired his establishment of Greek-style cities in the areas he conquered. He always carried with him that special edition of the *Iliad* prepared for him by his tutor, Aristotle, and he consistently acted in conscious imitation of Achilles whom he also claimed as an ancestor. To the Athenian democrats and intellectuals of his own day, both Alexander and his Macedonians would have appeared anachronistic and provincial, uncouth even with their

Although no authentic images exist of Alexander, a Roman mosaic discovered at the House of the Faun in Pompeii portrays him as the young heroic leader that he undoubtedly was. The so-called Alexander Mosaic celebrates the Battle of Issus in 333 BC, in which Alexander defeated the Persian king Darius III.

funny northern Greek accents and dialects. Macedon's system of kingly rule with a royal house boasting of its descent from Zeus was far removed from the urban values of the democratic *poleis* with their debates and assemblies.

Alexander had embraced the Greek past of King Agamemnon's campaign against the Trojans rather than the civilization which produced Plato and Euripides. But it was those deep roots which provided Macedonian Hellenism with the strength to endure and then to flower under Alexander, especially since the Greek city-states were so bent on self-destructive quarrels. Alexander's empire did not survive his death, but Greece, along with the western part of Asia Minor which he conquered, re-emerged as Byzantium, and Alexander's notion of supreme kingship is reflected in the authority claimed by Constantinople's emperors.

Homer wrote half a millennium before the age of Alexander, and the works attributed to him purport to describe the reality of an even more archaic Greece. But the aristocrats and kings of fourth-century-BC Macedon were distinctly Homeric in style with their feasts and hunting expeditions, their toasts of loyalty, drinking bouts and wrestling competitions. This was a frontier society right on the northern fringes of Hellas and its Greek culture was correspondingly intense because the despised 'barbarians' were so near. But the Homeric insights also mattered right across the Greek-speaking world. The *Iliad* and the *Odyssey* were simultaneously poetic narratives, ethical guides and religious handbooks showing how to deal with the gods whose favour and anger shaped human life. Alexander's regular habit of extensive quotations from these works often sought to illustrate the co-existence of the human with the divine; he habitually wore the lion-skin cap associated with Heracles, son of Zeus, and he was much influenced by his mother Olympias, an enthused mystic and Bacchante who rejoiced in the snake-handling rites associated with Dionysus's worship. The career of such a king mingled prophecy with fact since the gods favoured him with success on earth. That was reason enough for some Greeks to follow him. Yet others might think that this was a god.

The Delphic Prophecy

Keen to protect her son's claim to the throne after her divorce from Philip II of Macedon, Olympias was possibly implicated in the king's assassination in 336 BC. Elimination by death of all possible rivals to the throne followed, and Alexander was swiftly acclaimed as king by the army. He then travelled south to meet the League of Corinth, an alliance of Greek states, which elected him to head a major military offensive against the Persian empire.

Respect for oracles took him to Delphi where he was gratified to be informed by the Pythian priestess of his invincibility. This attribute was tested almost immediately when local democrats in the city of Thebes rebelled against his

overlordship. Alexander had been to the fore in the Battle of Chaeronea (338 BC) when Philip had crushed the combined army of the Greek states and stood ready to re-assert Macedonian power. Thebes was razed to the ground, 6,000 of its citizens were killed and the rest sold into slavery. The brutality cowed all other Greek states into renewed obedience.

Alexander's Persian campaign illustrated his characteristic combination of culture with bloodshed. Historians and architects, scientists and surveyors accompanied his army and, having crossed the Hellespont, he went to Ilium, supposedly the site of Troy, to pay his Homeric respects. He honoured Athena by sending 300 suits of armour, captured from the enemy, to Athens where they were dedicated as an offering to the city's goddess. After he had crushed the Persian army on his first engagement he took 2,000 prisoners and sent them, chained, to Macedon.

A painting by André Castaigne from about 1898 depicts the story of Alexander and the Gordian Knot. It was prophesied that the person who untied the impossible knot would eventually rule over all Asia. Legend has it that, unlike many others who had tried simply to unravel the knot, Alexander sliced it cleanly through with his sword, and went on to fulfil the prophecy by conquering much of the known world.

His victory at the Battle of Issus was decisive and Darius III, the Persian king, was forced to flee. The cities of western Asia Minor capitulated and, in striking contrast to his Greek mainland policy, Alexander imposed democratic regimes on them although he retained ultimate control since the cities were answerable to his own local governor. Turning south to Syria and Phoenicia, he then took Damascus and seized its great treasures, including Darius's war chest: this mattered greatly since he was heavily in debt and owed some 500 talents because of the scale of his campaigns. His army would pay for war by waging war, a material fact which explains his onward thrust. Alexander refused Darius's offer to cede all his lands west of the Euphrates, as well as the stupendous ransom of 10,000 talents for the captured Persian royal family, since he calculated that his eventual gains would be even greater.

A Man of Divine Origin

Egypt, conquered by November 332 BC, provided crucial propaganda because of its priestly-religious traditions. At Memphis Alexander sacrificed to Apis, the Egyptian god in the form of a bull, and was then crowned with the pharaoh's double crown. Travelling inland he visited the celebrated oracle of the god Zeus-Amon, a mixed Graeco-Egyptian-Libyan deity. Here the priest hailed him as 'son of Amon' although the circumstances are shrouded in calculated ambiguity since no one was allowed to accompany Alexander into the shrine. This, though, was the moment when Alexander came to believe that he was an adopted son of Zeus and it explains his conviction that he was of divine origin.

On a more concrete level of authority, by the end of 330 BC, Alexander was undoubtedly the 'great king', having succeeded to that Persian title on Darius's

death as well as seizing some 50,000 gold talents at the city of Susa. The subsequent sack of Persepolis was a notorious affair but Alexander's burning of the city's palace of Xerxes may well have been a ritual gesture, signifying the end of the campaign's phase as a war of Hellenic revenge.

From now on the campaign was personal and the king accordingly sent back his troops from non-Macedonian Greece and Thessaly. Subsequent inscriptions refer to him as 'lord of Asia' and Alexander's fondness for an Asiatic and absolutist style of kingship was increasingly apparent. He not only adopted Persian dress, but also tried to impose *proskynesis* or prostration, a custom common among the Persians when entering the king's presence. To all Greeks, including Macedonians, this was a degrading act and Alexander had to abandon the experiment.

Alexander's Army Mutiny in India

In the summer of 327 BC Alexander's army left Bactria, crossed the Hindu Kush into India and was divided into two components: one force went through the Khyber Pass while the other half, led by the king, travelled through the northern hills of India and had crossed the Indus by the spring of the following year. By the banks of the River Beas in the Punjab Alexander erected 12 altars to the Olympian gods. It was a culminating Greek cultural moment but it was here too that his exhausted troops refused to go on any further, and Alexander had to accept their mutiny.

His retreat through a waterless desert in Gedrosia (modern Baluchistan) was a nightmarish experience and he chose to relax after it by staging a week-long drinking festival in celebration of Dionysus with Alexander dressing up for the central role. There were other signs of mental strain too. Mistrusting the officials he had appointed to run his empire, Alexander sacked a third of his satraps and executed a further six. By now his thoughts concentrated on the establishment of a fused Macedonian-Persian ruling class and when he returned to Susa in 324 BC he staged a great banquet at which he and 80 officers took Persian wives. But the admission of Persians soldiers into his army on equal terms led to a further mutiny, which was only healed by a thoroughly Homeric touch – a vast banquet of reconciliation.

Death of a God

Megalomania had now set in and some of the delegates Alexander received from the Greek cities were dressed as if they were honouring a god. When his lover Hephaestion died in the autumn of 324 BC, Alexander gave him a royal funeral in Babylon with a pyre costing 10,000 talents. After another prolonged drinking bout the king fell ill and died at Babylon in his 33rd year. Both in Egypt and in the Greek cities, he received full divine honours in death.

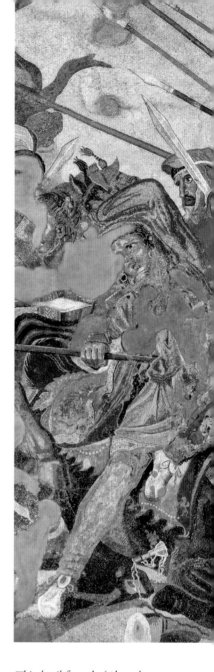

This detail from the 'Alexander Mosaic' shows Persians fleeing from the Battle of Issus. Although heavily outnumbered, the Macedonians succeeded in breaking Darius's defences, forcing his army to break ranks and retreat in disarray.

One final journey had to be made. Alexander's generals divided his empire into various kingdoms and Ptolemy, reigning (323–285/3 BC) as the first of Egypt's Ptolemaic dynasty, secured the transfer of the embalmed body from Babylon first to Memphis and then to Alexandria. Here the city's founder was buried in a gold coffin that was probably destroyed in the third century AD during one of Alexandria's notorious riots. The location is both ironic and appropriate. Ptolemy had pushed hard for the imperial division and thereby frustrated Alexander's goal of a fused European-Asian empire. It was the Seleucid kingdom to the east, centred in Babylonia and extending towards Syria and Anatolia, which would be the centre of a Hellenistic civilization that transmitted Greek culture within a wider world.

Nonetheless the museum that Ptolemy built in Alexandria endured, along with its celebrated library, for over 500 years as a witness to Greek culture's curiosity about the world and its resolve to expand the boundaries of human knowledge: qualities that had marked Alexander's character and elevated his kingship above the brutal facts of conquest.

SHIH HUANG-TI, The First Unifier of the Chinese Empire

R. 221–210 BC

Apprehension about his own death had dominated the great Chinese emperor's thoughts in his later years, and especially so after at least three assassination attempts had been made on his life. Concern for the gods and thoughts of the hereafter had always mattered to Shih huang-ti and he had been scrupulous in his performance of sacrifices at the traditional sacred sites.

Life-sized soldiers from the 'terracotta army' that guarded the burial site of Shih huang-ti in Shensi province. The lower part of each figure is solid, while the upper part is hollow.

Earthly power in China imitated heavenly hierarchies and the detailed regulations which governed his subjects' lives and jobs mirrored the pantheon of the national gods, who were also categorized in hierarchies and allocated their specialized functions. Imperial rhetoric maintained that the dynasty was destined to last '10,000 generations' but the boast masked the insecurity of a ruler isolated in his vast palaces and suspicious of conspiracies. The emperor had therefore resorted to magic and alchemy in the belief that these forces might protect him against death and even, perhaps, guarantee his immortality. Magicians who might produce an elixir of life were therefore consulted by the messengers dispatched by Shih huang-ti across his empire, and some had even been summoned to court. The emperor had himself met and talked to many magicians during his extensive official tours of imperial inspection.

The Terracotta Army

It was in the middle of one such expedition that he had died suddenly. In his burial place in Shensi province, his 43-metre- (140-foot-) high tomb was guarded by some 7000 life-sized terracotta soldiers, each with their own individual facial features, and accompanied by the figures representing their horses. Organized in the military formations used by Chinese army commanders, this silent host of warriors had also been arranged to look towards the east, just as Shih huang-ti's

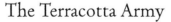

A painting dating from c.221–206 BC, during the Ch'in dynasty, depicts the 'First Emperor'. Shih huang-ti's reign was short but his reforms and public building projects transformed China.

army had often done in the past when advancing towards his rivals for supremacy among the Chinese kingdoms.

The funerary compound, which surrounded the emperor's mausoleum, extended over some 0.75 square miles (2 sq km) and was enclosed within the double walls with their gates and towers. Contemporary observers, suitably awed, described the large chart of the heavens which decorated the mausoleum's vaulted dome and below which there was a three-dimensional representation of the earth complete with mechanically powered streams of liquid mercury representing the Chinese rivers. The subterranean chamber in which the terracotta soldiers had been placed also included some 400 model chariots made of wood and bronze as well as spears and swords, silks, linen and precious objects made of jade and bone. Three other such chambers contained some 1400 ceramic figures representing foot soldiers, chariots and cavalry.

The Emperor's Monumental Palaces

Imperial building projects had invariably been designed to make a political point. Replicas of the pavilions and palaces once occupied by the emperor's rivals among the other Chinese royal families, had been built along 11 miles (7 km) of the Wei river, and were now occupied by noble

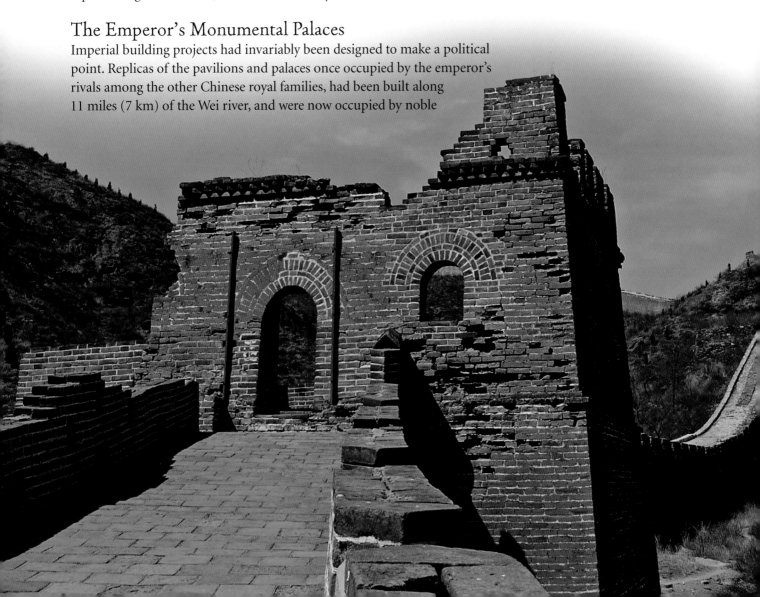

families transplanted from the conquered states. The emperor's own vast palace of A-fang made a similarly monumental point about supremacy with its main hall designed to accommodate 10,000 guests on its upper story alone. But it was the hundreds of thousands of workers required to build the great city of the dead in Shensi who provided the most emblematic testimony to the powers of command exercised over an immense population by the 'first sovereign emperor of Ch'in' or Ch'in Shih huang-ti, the title he first claimed for himself in 221 BC.

The Conflict of the Warring States

The Shang dynasty (1766–1122 BC), originally centred on the north China plain, included the earliest historically verifiable Chinese monarchs. Their written records were the earliest in Chinese history, and worship of the royal ancestors, a defining characteristic of Chinese civilization's continuity, first emerged during Shang rule. The Chou dynasty ruling to the west in Shensi province rose to predominance over the rest of the Chinese territories from the mid-11th century onwards and built a capital in the east in order to maintain its authority over a feudal structure of states that owed allegiance to the dynasty as its vassals. This order began to lose its cohesion during the 'Spring and Autumn' (Ch'un-ch'iu) period (770–476 BC) and the inter-state squabbles degenerated into the conflicts of the 'Warring States' (Chan-kuo) period (475–221 BC).

The more centralized nature of authority within the Chinese kingdoms had led their rulers to reject external vassalage to the Chou and also to abandon feudal arrangements within their own territories. Such an effective organization of state resources also contained within itself the seeds of a solution to the anarchy which had overwhelmed large parts of China. The emergence by about the sixth century BC of a class of educated bureaucrats drawn from the class known as the *shih* (or 'gentlemen') promoted social mobility as rulers competed for the services of this new ruling elite's cleverest members. Kingly power in China had thereby acquired intelligentsia support and especially so in terms of the doctrines associated with the philosopher Confucius (551–479 BC), the most celebrated of the *shih*.

Confucianism had modified the feudal notion that duties, power and status should be prescribed by inherited rank. The philosopher had elevated instead family relationships, such as those between fathers and children, as the basis of a well ordered society and also, crucially, had made intellectual ability and virtue of character the chief criteria in allocating powerful positions within the state.

Ch'in Rulers Become China's Kings

The state of Ch'in, located in the mountainous west, had evolved its own highly distinctive belief in impartial executive authority. The administration headed by Shang Yang (361–338 BC) had enabled the monarchy to establish the principle that noble rank should only be allocated to those who had rendered service to the

Snaking for almost 4000 miles (6350 km) across the Chinese landscape, the Great Wall of China is one of the world's most famous monuments. The original wall was built on the orders of Shih huang-ti as a barrier against the nomadic horsemen of the northern steppes, but the sections that stand today were largely the work of the later Ming emperors.

47

state. Localities within the kingdom were now grouped as counties which then
formed the constituent parts of prefectures supervised directly by the royal court.

From 325 BC onwards the rulers of Ch'in were claiming to be China's universal
kings and the greatly enfeebled Chou court was unable to contest this assumption
of its previous authority. Its geographical position meant that Ch'in had
concentrated on conquering and absorbing the non-Chinese tribes and states
which had originally surrounded it, and the kingdom was therefore seen as
something of a 'barbarian' state by its opponents. But by means of bribery,
espionage and diplomacy as well as outright war Ch'in disposed of its rivals. The
eastern state of Ch'i was absorbed by stages during the third century and that
of Chao based in the north was defeated in a great battle of 260 BC which led to
some 50,000 Chao losses and the slaughter of most of the 400,000 troops who
had surrendered. The elimination of the southern power of Ch'u in 223 BC was
a prelude to the ultimate Ch'in unification of the whole of China two years later.

The Early Achievements of the Ch'in Dynasty

The ensuing extension of Ch'in administration was detailed in its centralism.
Chinese law and language alike were standardized, as were weights and measures.
A network of imperial highways facilitated troop movements, while along the
northern border a 'Great Wall' emerged to keep the Hsiung-nu at bay. These
nomadic warriors of the steppe had been attacking northern Chinese states since
the fifth century BC and had now become a great confederation dominating most
of central Asia. Shih huang-ti consolidated and linked the pre-existing structures
to form a complete wall which, with its garrisons and watchtowers, extended
some 4000 miles (6350 km) from east to west. The wall marked the northernmost
limits of that process of Sinicization by means of which non-Chinese 'barbarian'
elements elsewhere had been assimilated within the newly powerful centralized
states, and especially those of the south and west, from the Spring and Autumn
period onwards. Local cultures had therefore been melded into a common
Chinese civilization even before the Ch'in dominance.

Attaining his majority in 238 BC, the man who had been born Chao Cheng started
to rule as king of Ch'in. Many of the stone inscriptions, which he later had raised
across China to record his achievements, claimed that he had ensured peace and
prosperity by abolishing past corruption. Nonetheless, his successes were built on
the corpses of hundreds of thousands of Chinese who died while working on the
construction projects and on the forced marches that transported a workforce of
millions to those same building sites. Behind the steely governmental and kingly
determination lay a consistent political doctrine which became the ideological
underpinning of Ch'in rule. 'Legalism' was a school of philosophy which had first
emerged in China during the Warring States period and was marked by an
extreme authoritarianism and a profound pessimism about human nature.

Humanity was selfish, myopic and incapable of detecting its own true interest. Human harmony could only be attained through the unconditional obedience of the ruled and by the elevation of the ruler's authority as the basis of state power. This supreme governor's effectiveness had to be maintained regardless of his moral virtues – or lack of them.

Book Burning and the Rejection of Confucianism

Legalism became particularly influential in Ch'in and the movement's greatest philosopher, Han Fei (*c.*280–233 BC), was much admired by Shih huang-ti. The emperor's chief minister, Li Ssu (?280–208 BC), used legalist opinions to justify the government's brutal efficiency and was a central figure in the notorious 'burning of the books' in 213 BC, when the administration ordered the destruction of most copies of the Confucian classics. Books dealing with agriculture, law, herbal medicine and prognostication were allowed because they were deemed socially useful, and the records relating to Ch'in history were kept for the same reason.

To enforce political and social unity Shih huang-ti attempted to wipe out dissent among his people. When Confucian scholars criticized his destruction of the old feudal order, the emperor responded by ordering the burning of all books not deemed to be of any practical use, together with histories of all the Chinese kingdoms preceding the Ch'in.

But other forms of literature were not allowed to circulate and intellectuals who criticized the policy were killed in their hundreds. Confucian scholars had been consistently critical of the Ch'in state's methods and especially scornful of the emperor's credulity about magic. The Confucian reliance on precedent and past authority was explicitly rejected in Han Fei's essays which had emphasized instead how political institutions necessarily changed in response to circumstances and especially in relation to economic change. From the mid-fourth century onwards, Ch'in economic development policies had been undermining the extended family, an institution basic to Confucian piety, by imposing double rates of taxation on any male subject who was not master of his own household.

Confucian orthodoxy returned to dominate Chinese intellectual life during the Han dynasty's extended period of rule (206 BC–AD 220), a fact which ensured the posthumous blackening of Shih huang-ti's reputation as a tyrant. After his death the Ch'in dynasty's authority collapsed in a welter of conspiracy, treachery, rebellion and civil war. But it was Shih huang-ti's institutional and doctrinal legacy which enabled the Han to restore and maintain a Chinese imperial authority. The first Ch'in emperor had defined those centralist goals and bureaucratic means which would be enduring features of Chinese government.

AUGUSTUS CAESAR, The Saviour of the Roman Empire

R. 27 BC–AD 14

For three days and nights starting on 31 May, 17 BC a series of festivities staged in the city of Rome marked the arrival of a 'new age'. Horace's specially composed hymn praising the new ruler and traditional Roman values was sung by choirs of youths and girls, first to Apollo at his temple on the Palatine and then to Jupiter at his temple on the Capitol.

Legislation passed in the previous year had made adultery a crime and started an official campaign promoting public morality. But there was much else to celebrate in a city growing ever safer and more comfortable, with its new public baths and a novel stability in the supply and sale of grain. Soon Rome would also have its own fire and police service and the city was starting to live up to its new ruler's claim that he had turned a city of brick into one of marble.

Coloured marble arrived to cover the Forum, whose redesign and embellishment had already been commissioned by Julius Caesar, and colonnades were raised here to contain statues of heroic Roman figures. But it was the living hero in charge of Rome who mattered most and his name, Augustus, was carved on the central blocks just below the pediment of the Forum's Temple of Mars. The *Ara Pacis*, a sculpture voted by the Roman senate in 13 BC, was public art in figurative form: Rome's chief priests, joined by the imperial family, are delineated as they prepare for a ritual sacrifice and the scene may record Augustus's assumption of Rome's supreme priesthood (*Pontifex maximus*) in 12 BC.

Augustus Becomes Central to Rome

Augustus restored over 82 temples in all and the claim that he was returning Rome to its ancient customs was central to his rule. But he also transformed those old ways, since he ensured that he himself became their central focus.

'Maecenas Presenting the Arts to Augustus' by Giovanni Battista Tiepolo, c.1743. Gaius Maecenas was a trusted adviser to the court of Augustus and a wealthy patron of the arts.

Accordingly, he moved the ancient books recording the Sibylline prophesies to Apollo's temple on the Palatine but that was a new building deliberately raised next to his own house. Rome had its ancient *lares*, or protective spirits, but it was Rome's chief spirit, the *genius* of Augustus, which was worshipped at the shrines built at the new crossroads after the city's division into 14 districts in 7 BC.

The emperor, Augustus Caesar, whose original name was Gaius Octavius, was born in 63 BC in Velitrae to the southeast of Rome. His father was a senator and his great-uncle on his mother's side was Julius Caesar. Augustus was therefore well connected, but his success owed much to the fact that he was a boy from a small town, fond of the Italian countryside's traditional religion, its rites and its gods. This piety was shared by most of Italy's population and Augustus's revival of religious festivals was correspondingly popular. Giving the poor new rights of appeal in the law courts was yet another populist element in his legislative programme. Augustus's conviction that Rome's empire had to be an

From the seventh century BC Rome's political and economic centre was the Forum, where many of the city's most significant political, religious and judicial buildings were erected, including the Regia, the residence of the 'Pontifex maximus'. Little remains of that building today; the photograph shows the ruins of the temple of Saturn (centre), and the temple of Antoninus and Faustina (right).

enterprise centred in Italy and run mostly by Italians, unsurprisingly, made him immensely appealing to the peninsula's population.

Virgil, Horace and Livy shared his traditionalist views and their artistry helped to set the tone of general appreciation for the Augustan revolution. But though the tributes paid him by Horace and Virgil are poetically sublime, they also endorse Augustus's central and brutal insight: the preservation of the best of ancient Italian and Roman civilization required the subversion of Rome's republican institutions. Elite squabbling had condemned Rome to civil war and 'republican virtue' seemed a mere platitude mouthed by oligarchs on the make. Rome had outgrown its past and the global perspective of its responsibilities made republicanism look provincial, antiquated and boring as well as vicious in its effects.

Augustus's Grasp of Politics

Caesar's will made Augustus his son and heir. Mark Antony's refusal to hand over the dictator's assets forced Augustus to raise as much money as he could in order to honour the will's personal bequests to the people of Rome. This was an early demonstration of Augustus's grasp of the politics of patronage and further credibility came to him when he resolved to continue the public games instituted by Caesar. Suetonius describes Augustus as short and well proportioned, with hair which 'was slightly curly and inclining to golden – his complexion was between dark and fair'. His most striking features were his 'clear, bright eyes, in which he liked to have it thought that there was a kind of divine power'. In all of this there was something of Alexander, and the finest sculptors of the age paid tribute to those wide eyes. The fine features of the portrait busts were then copied on the Roman gold and silver coinage which, mass produced by the mints in an age of economic expansion, established Augustus's profile as that of the ideal imperial visionary.

Rise and Fall of the Triumvirate

Loyal troops forced the senate to make Augustus consul and he obtained official confirmation as Caesar's adopted son. Reconciled to Antony, he then formed a triumvirate in 43 BC, which included his fellow Caesarian, Marcus Aemilius Lepidus. The three proclaimed that the state had to be 'reconstituted'. This meant the execution of their political enemies and 300 senators along with 2000 members of the class of *equites* or knights were accordingly dispatched. By 42 BC Augustus could rejoice in his new prestige as 'son of a god', Caesar having now been named a god of the Roman state.

Following the suicides of Brutus and Cassius after their defeat at the Battle of Philippi, Antony was allocated the eastern empire with Augustus controlling the west including Italy, and Lepidus was placed in charge of Africa. This

arrangement was meant to last until 33 BC after the triumvirate had been renewed for another five years. It foundered because Augustus decided to wreck it. Lepidus was deprived of his office and Antony had lost prestige after the failure of his campaigns against both the Parthian empire and that of the Medes. Augustus now turned to artful propaganda associating himself with the god Apollo as his patron. The contrast between that god of order and Brutus's chosen, very un-Roman, deity of Dionysus was deliberate. By now he was also using the title of *imperator* before his name.

Augustus whipped up public outrage in Rome against Antony's grants of territories to Cleopatra and, at the naval Battle of Actium (2 September, 31 BC), fought off the western coast of Greece, he defeated Antony and Cleopatra's fleet. He then proceeded to occupy Egypt in 30 BC, by which time the lovers had committed suicide.

Augustus's Finances

Having annexed Egypt as his personal fiefdom and seized Cleopatra's treasury, Augustus could pay off his veterans – and therefore count on their loyalty. He reduced his legions from 60 to 28 and henceforth relied on a core army of some 150,000 legionaries who were mostly Italians. This force was supplemented by the same number of auxiliaries based in the Roman provinces. More money meant more roads which, in turn, boosted trade and a newly organized fleet brought maritime security to the Mediterranean. Augustus's officials and troops, the enforcers of his *Pax Romana*, could therefore move quickly around the empire. The government of Rome as city and empire grew out of all proportion to its past – and so did the taxation that paid for it all. Augustus introduced the central treasury which collected two innovations: a poll tax and a land tax.

A Supine Senate Supports Augustus

This though was a tactful autocrat and one who appreciated how Romans, being conservative, wanted to preserve constitutional appearances. Augustus kept the senate but made himself its president, and eventually reduced its numbers from 1000 to 600 senators whom he could rely upon. From 31 to 23 BC the basis of his power was his election to a series of consulships by a supine senate. In January of 27 BC he said disingenuously that he had 'transferred the state to the free disposal of the senate and people'. But he was also granted a ten-year title allowing him to govern Spain, Gaul and Syria. Since his army's greatest numbers were concentrated in these areas the title's effect protected his power base.

Augustus claimed the right to rule by virtue of his *auctoritas* – a blend of personal prestige, experience and proven success which was impossible to define but unmistakable in its effect. It was also in 27 BC that he added the name Augustus to that of Caesar (which he had adopted under his great-uncle's will). This ancient term implied a connection with religious powers of prophecy. *Auctoritas* and *augustus* conjoined, placed this ruler far beyond any possible constitutional definition of his role. In 23 BC he ended his series of consulships and said that he had a form of supreme power (*imperium maius*), which elevated him beyond any particular office. He also now enjoyed an automatic superiority over the proconsuls governing the provinces and whose appointments he had, in any event, been engineering for some years. His constitutional package included the antiquarian gesture of becoming tribune – the officer who, historically, had been elected annually to represent the *plebs* (the general body of Roman citizens). Augustus though was tribune for life.

Imperial Challenges

Military successes confirmed his aura: in 20 BC Parthia recognized Rome's right to rule over Armenia and in the following year Agrippa completed the conquest of Spain. In 2 BC Augustus was given the title *pater patriae* but this 'father of the fatherland' continued to face imperial challenges. Judaea was annexed in AD 6 but the revolt in the same year of Pannonia in central Europe, joined by that of the Illyrians, was the greatest threat to Rome since Hannibal and took three years to suppress. The subsequent attack of the German tribes, led by Arminius in AD 9, destroyed three Roman legions and put paid to plans for an expansion into Bohemia and western Germany. But Augustus's care for his power base was undiminished and a military treasury was established to ensure that tax revenue was handed out to soldiers as retirement bonuses.

A God at Last

In AD 13 Augustus's powers were renewed for another ten years. This, like all such previous renewals, was a mere formality. Within a month of his death on 19 August, AD 14 the senate, obliging as ever, enrolled him among the gods of the Roman state. Tiberius, his stepson, succeeded him and added, in dynastic style, the name 'Augustus' to his own. The fact that Augustus's title as 'first citizen' was meant to be personal and not inheritable mattered not at all. His structures kept the eastern and western halves of the empire together for over 300 years, a period in which Rome successfully resisted the onslaughts of barbarian tribes from the north and east. The central question to be asked about Rome therefore, as both empire and civilization, is not why did it fall but why did it last so long? The answer is Augustus.

Statue of Augustus in a general's uniform, aged about 45. The breastplate shows a defeated barbarian and a Roman officer.

CONSTANTINE I, '*The Great*', Rome's Christian Emperor and Founder of Constantinople

R. AD 312–337

Sun worship had become popular in the Roman army of the third century AD, and the devotion of Flavius Valerius Constantinus to *Sol Invictus* – 'the Unconquered Sun' – was unexceptional. Constantine shared the Roman conviction that earthly success was a reward for personal piety and had therefore declared that this chosen god of his was a personal comrade. But his conversion to Christianity, previously a minority and persecuted sect, first of all upset and then destroyed traditional Roman religion, its ritual sacrifices and acts of divine favour.

Constantine's drive for church unity and explicit doctrinal creeds gave Christianity a new identity and purpose at a time when it could easily have disappeared as just another mystery religion of the late Roman world. The conversion also changed Roman imperial history since Christianity's cause now became closely associated with that of the survival of Rome's order and government. Early Christians had been persecuted and killed because of their refusal to worship Roman emperors, and the belief that it was sacrilege to worship any being other than the one true God remained fundamental to Christian monotheism. But the idea of a sacred political order, one that was blessed by the church, involved an immense new axis of power for the Christian

Hagia Sophia (the Church of the Holy Wisdom) in Constantinople was dedicated by Constantine in c.325. Nothing remains of the original building, but the structure that was rebuilt on the site is one of the greatest surviving examples of Byzantine architecture. The Deësis Mosaic dates from the 13th century, and the detail shown opposite depicts Jesus Christ.

rulers who came after Constantine. From then on disobedience could be judged heretical as well as treasonous. A style of governmental majesty, preoccupied with unity and prepared to persecute, is a long-lasting consequence of the Constantinian revolution.

Birth of the Byzantine Empire

Constantine was the son of Flavius Valerius Constantius, an army officer who became Caesar or deputy emperor in 293 and then served the co-emperor Maximian in the west. Following Constantius's separation from Helena, Constantine's mother, their son was raised in the east at the court of the senior emperor Diocletian in Nicomedia (now Izmit in modern Turkey). Christianity as a problem of public order would have been familiar to him here, and from about 303 onwards, Diocletian embarked on a systematic persecution of Christians in the eastern provinces, areas whose towns were major centres of the faith.

Nicomedia's cultural milieu was Greek but the language of the court, and of Constantine's education, was Latin. Despite his own uncertain command of Greek, Constantine as emperor would take the momentous decision to build his empire's new capital and centre of government in the Greek east. Constantinople's dedication in 330 therefore marks the start of the history of the Byzantine empire which evolved out of the eastern Roman empire. Its position on the Bosphorus separating Asia from Europe symbolizes the Roman order which renewed itself by looking east after a prolonged period of instability in the third century.

A bronze statue of Constantine stands at York Minster in the north of England, near the place where he was first proclaimed an emperor in 306.

Constantine Is Acclaimed Emperor at York

Imperial disunity broke out on a major scale in 305 when the two emperors, Diocletian and Maximian, abdicated and were replaced by their deputies, Galerius and Constantius. Constantine's claims to succeed his father as a Caesar were ignored: instead Flavius Valerius Severus succeeded to Constantius's former role in the west while Galerius Valerius Maximinus succeeded to his uncle Galerius's authority in the east. Constantine removed himself from the centres of power, joined his father on a British campaign and was acclaimed emperor by the army after his father's death at York in 306. In the wars that followed, the key rivalry was that between Constantine and Maxentius, the son of the former emperor Maximian. In 312 Constantine invaded Italy and defeated Maxentius at the Battle of the Milvian Bridge near Rome. He was now emperor of the west while Licinius emerged to become sole emperor of the east and a period of intermittent conflict between the two rulers ensued. In 324 Constantine defeated Licinius in battle and became thereby sole ruler of both east and west.

Divine Inspiration

Constantine claimed to have experienced a religious vision while leading his troops south to Rome in 312. A late form of the story as written up by his court historian, Eusebius, describes the vision as a Christian cross accompanied by the words 'In this sign, conquer'. This may be an apologist's enthusiasm at work but it is certainly the case that Constantine decided to fight the Battle of the Milvian Bridge as a Christian soldier and that he ordered his troops to paint the Christian monogram on their shields. From that moment on he interpreted his successes as examples of God's providence shaping history. The triumphal arch raised in Rome to mark his victory over Maxentius declared therefore Constantine's indebtedness to the 'inspiration of the Divinity' while also glorifying the emperor's genius. A statue of Constantine raised at the same time showed him holding a cross and was inscribed with the words: 'By this saving sign I have delivered your city from the tyrant and restored liberty to the Senate and people of Rome'.

Constantine's Edict of Milan (313) extended toleration to Christians at the same time as restoring to them property which had been confiscated during the persecution. But it was the emperor's special favour and gifts which really gave Christianity its new authority: Constantine gave to the bishop of Rome the imperial property known as the Lateran and it was here that a new cathedral, later known as St John Lateran, was built. He also issued decrees giving the clergy financial and legal privileges while freeing them from performance of civic duties. Later in the reign he introduced measures banning crucifixion and the branding of certain classes of criminals. Observance of Sundays and saints' days was officially encouraged.

His decisive victory over Maxentius at the Battle of the Milvian Bridge in 312 resulted in Constantine becoming sole ruler of the western Roman empire. The event is portrayed in the painting The Battle of Constantine and Maxentius by Rubens from c.1620.

Conflicts in Christianity

Church unity was an aspect of the empire's unity. A divided church would displease God and endanger Constantine's special status in the divine plan. He therefore treated schism both seriously and personally. North African Christianity had always been especially intense, and the region's Donatist movement was splitting the church with its claim that lapsed Christians could not be readmitted. Castigation of this rigorous position was well within the imperial remit. Constantine's declaration that he was 'bishop of those outside the church' protected the rights of the excluded and he urged their readmission. Abstruse theology in the form of Arianism however proved an intractable problem. Again the issue for Constantine was one of order and discipline. The followers of Arius of Alexandria emphasized God's unique status and denied Christ's divinity. Constantine cared little for the theological niceties of Trinitarian doctrine. But he underestimated the passions involved and the Council of Nicaea, convened in 325, failed to resolve the controversy which continued to plague him for the rest of his reign.

The Conversion of Emperor Constantine the Great, a sketch by Rubens. This central event in Constantine's life established a precedent for the role of subsequent emperors as protectors of the church.

Constantine Turns to the East

By 326 Constantine had to deal with more personal problems of disunity within his own family and, in mysterious circumstances, he ordered the death of both his eldest son Crispus and his wife Fausta. The family slaughter of 326 happened while Constantine was away in Rome, where he was attending the celebrations marking the 20th anniversary of his reign. While there he gave offence by refusing to take part in a pagan procession and he left the city, never to return. By now his thoughts concentrated on the east, naturally enough since in the fourth century that was where the empire's greatest concentration of intellectual resources and economic power were to be found, while the city of Rome itself, though still a focus of emotional loyalty, looked increasingly provincial. The pilgrimage made by his mother Helena to Jerusalem and the Holy Land took place immediately after the family murders, and perhaps constituted a penitential act. But its consequences led to a further enlargement of imperial horizons and ambitions since Helena caused churches to be built on the reputed sites of the Nativity and of the Ascension.

New Churches in Jerusalem, Rome and Constantinople

In 336 Constantine dedicated the Church of the Holy Sepulchre in Jerusalem, built on the supposed site of the Crucifixion. Legends would later claim that the True Cross had either been discovered by Helena herself, or been recovered during the excavation work on the site. These developments were used to show how God was still intent on confirming the Christian emperor's power. A similar policy of architectural display was followed in Rome, where work began on the building of St Peter's on the Vatican hill in the late 320s and, in Constantinople, it was marked by the foundation of Hagia Sophia and the Church of the Apostles. Yet other church foundations, in Antioch and Alexandria, Trier and Nicomedia as well as in Gaza and Alexandria showed the breadth of Constantine's vision of an imperial Christian style.

The emperor's decision not to be baptized until just before his death shows both the sincerity of his faith and his awareness of the fact that, as a ruler, he necessarily had blood on his hands. It was best therefore to meet God without having reneged on the promises involved in baptism. Accordingly at Nicomedia, and just before he died, Constantine put aside the imperial purple and put on the white robes of a neophyte as he prepared for baptism. From there his body was carried back to Constantinople and buried in the Church of the Apostles. As a ruler he had claimed to be *isapostolos* or the equal of the apostles and that status was reflected in the statues of the 12 disciples which were placed on either side of his tomb.

The End of Classical Antiquity

Constantine's suppression of paganism was the single act which, more than any other, signified the start of the end of classical antiquity. Nonetheless, he still had to move cautiously given the innate conservatism of Roman culture. Roman emperors were expected to uphold tradition, not undermine it and the magnitude of his revolution had to be masked. He tolerated traditional country magic and the provincial priesthoods, basic to civic life, outlasted his reign. Nonetheless, the pagan gods disappeared by stages from Constantine's coinage and the new gold coin that he introduced, the *solidus*, became for centuries the stable basis of Byzantine currency. He was a notoriously high-spending emperor and his looting of the old pagan temples enabled him to bestow lavish gifts on his supporters. But the major expenses of government were met by Constantine's innovation of a five-yearly tax on business, the *collatio lustralis*, a much resented and onerous measure.

Constantine's administrative division of Roman government between its fiscal and military branches was a major development and one that built on Diocletian's reforms. In the same way, Diocletian's development of Nicomedia as a major city of the east pre-figures the establishment of Constantinople. But Constantine's establishment and patronage of a Christian and imperial governing class, based on his new city, was a cultural revolution in a class of its own.

A Christian and biblical culture now took its place beside the traditional classical culture of aristocratic society. Partly by law but mostly by acts of personal favour and example, Constantine had made Christianity socially fashionable. This climate of opinion was his greatest legacy and became the basis for the idea of a Christian state.

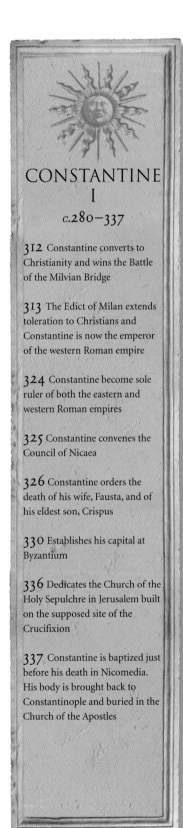

CONSTANTINE I
c.280–337

312 Constantine converts to Christianity and wins the Battle of the Milvian Bridge

313 The Edict of Milan extends toleration to Christians and Constantine is now the emperor of the western Roman empire

324 Constantine become sole ruler of both the eastern and western Roman empires

325 Constantine convenes the Council of Nicaea

326 Constantine orders the death of his wife, Fausta, and of his eldest son, Crispus

330 Establishes his capital at Byzantium

336 Dedicates the Church of the Holy Sepulchre in Jerusalem built on the supposed site of the Crucifixion

337 Constantine is baptized just before his death in Nicomedia. His body is brought back to Constantinople and buried in the Church of the Apostles

AL-MANSUR, Second Caliph of the 'Abbasid Caliphate of Baghdad

R. 754–775

In 762 al-Mansur, second caliph of the 'Abbasid dynasty, began to see the fulfilment of his vision of a new city when workmen started to build the foundations of Baghdad at a point where the rivers Tigris and Euphrates flow close to each other. The caliph had first arrived here in high summer. He had slept overnight and 'awoke the next morning', according to the ninth-century Iraqi historian Al-Tabari, 'having passed the sweetest and gentlest night on earth'.

But it was economic and political strategy, rather than a good night's sleep, which made Baghdad an ideal location for al-Mansur's new city. Canal networks had created a fertile countryside, which could produce food for Baghdad's population and trade revenues for its government. The city's foundation was intended to demonstrate the 'Abbasid dynasty's permanence and also to assert the eastward thrust of Arab civilization away from its original heartlands in the Arabian peninsula and Syria.

Early Islamic power had been shaped by the simplicity and nomadism of the Arab tribesmen who had formed the army, inspired by the prophet Muhammad, on its great wave of conquest out of the Arabian peninsula during the seventh century. The subsequent geographical shift involved a major change to a more elaborate style of government. Baghdad lay on the main route to Iran, whose bureaucracy influenced al-Mansur's administrative methods, and the city's palace ceremonial would borrow heavily from the ancient traditions of Near Eastern kingship which emphasized the awesome distance between ruler and people.

The attack on Baghdad by the Mongol army in 1258 and the subsequent destruction of the city marked the end of the 'Abbasid dynasty's 500-year rule. The Mongol invasion also brought changes to the artistic traditions in the region, with an emphasis on calligraphy and illustrated manuscripts. This late 15th-century Mongol School manuscript illumination shows scenes from the life of Muhammad.

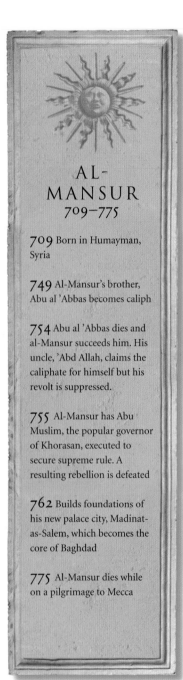

AL-MANSUR
709–775

709 Born in Humayman, Syria

749 Al-Mansur's brother, Abu al 'Abbas becomes caliph

754 Abu al 'Abbas dies and al-Mansur succeeds him. His uncle, 'Abd Allah, claims the caliphate for himself but his revolt is suppressed.

755 Al-Mansur has Abu Muslim, the popular governor of Khorasan, executed to secure supreme rule. A resulting rebellion is defeated

762 Builds foundations of his new palace city, Madinat-as-Salem, which becomes the core of Baghdad

775 Al-Mansur dies while on a pilgrimage to Mecca

Baghdad – a Panoply of Magnificence and Wealth

Baghdad's quarter of the 'round city' consisted of the palace, government offices and army barracks: residential areas and the city markets were consciously separated from it. Islamic rule now acquired a panoply of magnificence with chamberlains, pages and eunuchs thronging the palace courtyards, corridors and parks. Baghdad's palace would eventually contain a Room of the Tree – that artefact of gold and silver on whose branches were perched the mechanical birds whose sight and sound astonished visitors. Al-Mansur's palace and city became material symbols of a system of absolutist government whose power was demonstrated by its ostentatious wealth.

The Caliphate

From its very beginning, the institution of the caliphate, uniting religious with political authority, aimed to consolidate the empire gained by Arab conquest as a result of the seventh-century fragility of its neighbours, who had been undermined by plague and long military campaigns. By the mid-seventh century the whole of Arabia, along with large parts of the territories ruled by Iran's Sassanian dynasty, as well as the Byzantine provinces of Syria and Egypt, had all been conquered. Barely 30 years had passed since the prophet Muhammad had first fled from Mecca to Medina in 622 and thereby established the first community of believers loyal to his message of submission to a single, transcendent God. The caliph (*khalifah* or successor) was Muhammad's heir as civilian and religious leader of the Arab alliance and, though not himself a prophet, he could claim to be the interpreter of Allah's will.

The first caliph was Abu Bakr who had been Muhammad's closest companion, his chief adviser in Medina, and initiator of the military expansion. He and his three successors, 'Umar I, 'Uthman and 'Ali, the prophet's son-in-law, were chosen by the community leaders and became known as the *rashidun* or 'rightly guided' caliphs. But the murder of 'Uthman in 656 led to a major Islamic sectarian divide. The members of 'Uthman's clan, the Umayyads, demanded that his murder be avenged and disputed the legitimacy of 'Ali's succession. The partisans of 'Ali (or *shi 'at 'Ali*), who was himself murdered in 661, became known as the Shi'ites and regarded Ali's close family connection with Muhammad as the source of his authority. Mu-awiyah, the governor of Syria, was an Umayyad clan member and, having seized the caliphate from Ali and his supporters, he introduced the dynastic principle into the institution's government.

The Umayyad Dynasty Faces Rebellion

Urban life now replaced some of the old tribal loyalties and, from its base in Damascus, the Umayyad dynasty exercised control over the eastern Mediterranean coast. But, with Mecca and Medina dwindling in importance, Islam's real strength was now emerging further east. The cities of Iraq were

growing in size and importance while the traditional
Iranian elite was increasingly merged with the Arab ruling
class. Umayyad control was precarious in these areas to the
east and the rebellion which first broke out in the Khorasan
region of northeast Iran spread rapidly from 747 onwards.

The 'Abbasid family claimed descent from Muhammad's
uncle al 'Abbas. Their agent, Abu Muslim, leader of the
Khorasan revolt, had been intriguing for many years against
the Umayyads. In 749–50 Arab rebels and dissident Iranians
united in protest against the heavy burden of Umayyad
taxation and defeated Marwan II, the last Umayyad caliph.
Shi'ites were to the fore in the rebellion although the
'Abbasids frustrated the sect by claiming the caliphate for
themselves rather than transferring it to 'Ali's descendants.
Marwan had arrested the leader of the 'Abbasid clan, al-
Mansur's brother Ibrahim, who died in captivity, and it
was another brother, Abu al-'Abbas, who became the first
'Abbasid caliph, with al-Mansur succeeding him in 754.

Al-Mansur and the 'Abbasids

The 'Abbasids had rewarded Abu Muslim with the governorship of Khorasan
and al-Mansur used him to defeat the rebellion of 754 led by the caliph's uncle,
'Abd Allah. But subsequently, fearful of the victorious Abu Muslim's influence,
al-Mansur sacked him and then had him put to death in 755. A major Shi'ite
rebellion had to be suppressed in 762–3 and during al-Mansur's reign the sect
became the irreconcilable opponents of Sunni Islam, the orthodoxy of the
political-religious establishment.

The 'Abbasid restoration of authority involved a conscious policy of intimidation
and splendour, both of which were designed to impress and thereby enforce
obedience. A haphazard collection of disparate interest groups had gained
the upper hand for the 'Abbasids and they therefore decided to create an
unambiguously loyal governing elite to serve their interests. Iranian families
with a tradition of state service, who were now converted to Islam, proved
a particularly fertile source of recruitment to this new ruling class.

The 'Abbasid System of Control

Court officials controlled access to the caliph, and the presence of an executioner
hovering at his side was a constant reminder of the ruler's ability to administer
justice and enforce judgement at will. The office of vizier (*wazir*) emerged to head
the civilian administration, which was divided into its component *diwans*: the
treasury collected revenues and controlled spending, a chancery was concerned

*The Umayyad caliph Hisham
(691–743) built a fortified
palace in the Syrian desert
37 miles (60 km) west of
Palmyra. Completed in c.727,
the palace of Qasr al Hayr al
Gharbi was constructed of
baked mud brick on stone
foundations. The original
front façade, seen above, was
taken from the desert site and
reconstructed at Syria's
National Museum
in Damascus.*

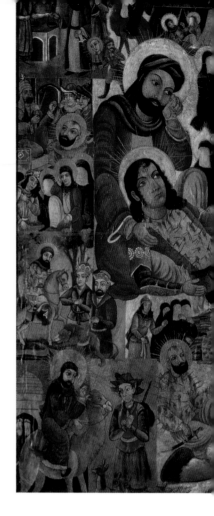

with official records and documents, while the army had its own *diwan*. Permeating the whole structure was a highly developed intelligence system which gave the caliph information about what was happening across his territories. Much of this intelligence gathering was designed to guard against the danger of local officials becoming over-mighty and abusing their powers since they operated over such vast distances far from Baghdad. Both the caliph and his provincial governors therefore held public meetings at which complaints against officials could be aired and recompense given.

It was the 'Abbasid dynasty which was also responsible for systematizing the taxation system in order to pay for their army and bureaucracy. The tax on land and its produce, known as the *kharaj*, had originally favoured Muslims by levying a rate lower than the one paid by the adherents of the officially tolerated religions, Judaism, Zoroastrianism and Christianity. This distinction now became increasingly theoretical but the poll tax (or *jizyah*) paid by these non-Muslims, which was graded according to their wealth, continued while new duties were introduced on imported and exported goods.

Eastern-facing Internationalism

Instead of concentrating on North Africa, the Mediterranean and southern Europe as the 'Umayyads had done, the caliphate of al-Mansur and his successors looked towards Iran and Transoxania – modern-day Uzbekistan, Tajikistan and southwest Kazakhstan. As a result of this detachment, local dynasties in Spain, Egypt and North Africa would in time claim caliphate status for themselves. The eastern-facing internationalism of the 'Abbasids was increasingly based on Islamic religion, since it was that idea of a community of believers (including non-Arab converts), which now gave their empire its identity rather than Arab ethnicity. The caliph in Baghdad was a remote figure for most of his subjects but his right to rule over them, and his hold over their loyalty, could be strengthened by showing that he shared their Islamic framework of belief and morality. It was therefore fitting enough that al-Mansur died while on a pilgrimage to Mecca.

A Centre of Arab Law and Scholarship

Al-Mansur's claims to legitimacy, just like those of his descendants, laid emphasis on a continuity of lineage with the prophet's family, and the caliphate of Baghdad allied itself with the Sunni theology's evolution of those traditions of belief and conduct attributed to Muhammad. As part of the same process the dynasty encouraged the development of Islamic law that was acquiring its first systematic expression. Under 'Abbasid rule the judge or *qadi* emerged as a distinctive and independent figure qualified to give an authoritative legal judgement. Ninth-century Baghdad also became a major centre of Arab scholarship. Greek mathematical, scientific and philosophical texts were translated into Arabic by the scholars who worked at the Bayt al-Hikmah (House of Wisdom), the library and

The Battle of Karbala in 680 was a key event in the history of Shi'ite Muslims. Muhammad's grandson Husayn, unwilling to swear allegiance to the Umayyad caliph Yazid, led 72 soldiers and a handful of family members against Yazid's 4000-strong army. Outnumbered, Husayn and most of his supporters were killed. This early 20th-century painting by Abbas al-Musavi shows the fall of Husayn (left of picture).

research institute established by the caliph Ma'mun in 830. Islamic civilization developed into a prodigiously bookish culture and Baghdad's paper mill produced the material that replaced parchment and papyrus.

End of the 'Abbasid Caliphate

The civil war waged between al-Mansur's descendants in 809–13 showed that the caliphate's chief problem was the lack of a loyal army. Mercenaries consisting of non-Muslim Berbers, Slavs and especially a large number of Turkish tribesmen from central Asia, were therefore recruited to form part of the caliph's personal army, but produced in turn their own challenges. These soldiers, drawn from the frontiers of settled government, might convert to Islam but their very presence undermined al-Mansur's doctrinal aim of an empire governed in accordance with Islamic law and precept. Their officer class was also ready to assassinate any caliph who disagreed with its demands and the Turkish component, in particular, was unwilling to assimilate culturally.

The Buyid dynasty of Iranian rulers first established their rule in western Iran during the 930s and then invaded Baghdad itself in 945, reducing the 'Abbasids to puppet status. Following their victory over the Buyids in 1055, the tribe of Seljuk Turks stripped the 'Abbasid caliphate of its residual temporal power but restored its character as a religious institution and focus of Islamic unity. The history of the caliphate ended in 1258 when the Mongols sacked Baghdad, disposed of the 'Abbasids, and wrecked the irrigation system fundamental to the city's prosperity. The last remnants of the vision which had first inspired al-Mansur on a summer's morning almost 500 years previously had been destroyed.

CHARLEMAGNE, King of the Franks, Lombards and *Imperator Augustus*

R. 768–814 (774–814, 800–814)

For some 500 years before Charlemagne's reign, Europe had been the scene of a westward movement of migrating tribes from the east. This had been the major source of external pressure on the decaying body politic of ancient, imperial Rome. Under Charlemagne this pressure was relieved and the Christian warrior aristocracy of western Europe started a push back towards the centre and east of the continent.

Charlemagne's ideas of kingly rule were fundamental to the new European confidence, for this revival of ancient Roman and imperial notions of government and conquest proved to be both an inspirational idea in cultural terms and an effective way of organizing military might.

The Frankish Kingdom

Between 500 and 800, Roman Gaul became the kingdom of the Franks. These Germanic people had first established themselves in the region of the Meuse-Moselle valley before extending their authority towards the south and the Pyrenees as well as into Provence. The kingdom had also spread eastwards beyond the Rhine and into Germania with the defeat of the Alamani by Clovis, the Franks' first Christian ruler. These had been successes enjoyed during the period of the Merovingian dynasty's rule. But the absence of primogeniture, along with the persistence of the ancient Germanic belief that all the king's heirs shared in his charisma and could therefore reign simultaneously, led to civil wars. As a result, during the seventh century, the Frankish kingdom was divided into two halves: Austrasia in the northeast and Neustria in the northwest.

This painting from c.1512 by the German artist Albrecht Dürer represents Charlemagne in his coronation robes. Charlemagne was crowned emperor of the Romans by Pope Leo III on Christmas Day, 800.

Effective control in each area had now passed to the court official known as the Mayor of the Palace, while the Merovingian kings had become merely titular rulers. The Austrasian Mayor of the Palace, Pippin of Herstal, emerged as victorious in the contest between the two regions and also in the aristocratic conflicts which plagued them internally. It was his family with its extensive estates in the Frankish heartlands which would eventually be termed Carolingian after its most famous member, Charlemagne or Carolus Magnus.

Charles Martel Wins a Crucial Victory

Succeeding him as Mayor of the Palace, Charles Martel, Pippin's illegitimate son, also continued the extension of Frankish authority over the Germanic peoples to the east. He secured a crucial victory over the Arab invasion force at the Battle of Tours after the beleaguered ruler of Aquitaine, Eudo, summoned the Franks to assist him. Pippin III, Martel's son and Charlemagne's father, took the decisive step in 750/1 of deposing Childeric III, last of the Merovingian kings. The Carolingian line was already effective. After being blessed by the pope and duly anointed, it could boast a legitimate title to kingship as well.

Charlemagne's Early Achievements

Ascending the throne in 768, Charlemagne's major early achievement was the defeat of the Lombards, the last of the Germanic tribes to invade, who were now settled in northern Italy. They were expert horsemen at a time when the Franks were only just beginning to learn about cavalry techniques. The stirrup, a fourth-century-AD Chinese invention, had now travelled west and was key to the Lombards' successes. But they never developed a royal dynasty and fell victim to the greater unity of the Franks. Pavia, their centre on the plain of Lombardy, was taken in 774. The Franks seized the famous Iron Crown of Lombardy and Charlemagne became king of the Lombards – much to the relief of the papacy for whom the Lombards had been a major threat.

The Palace at Aachen

In the 770s and for much of the 780s Charlemagne's court remained itinerant though its centre of gravity was moving steadily towards its northeastern territories. As a strong swimmer the king had always been attracted to the hot springs at Aachen, and by the late 780s he had decided that the palace there should be embellished as his permanent residence. This was a large one-storeyed building and its main room was a rectangular reception hall, 46 metres long and 20 metres wide (138 by 60 ft), opening on to three apses. In one of these apses were to be found the steps leading up to the royal throne, modelled on Solomon's in Jerusalem. In front of the palace was a courtyard with porticos and containing accommodation for the king's attendants. Caged bears and lions in the precincts along with, in the 800s, an elephant (a gift from the 'Abbasid caliph of Baghdad), symbolized kingly authority. The courtiers included Charlemagne's concubines:

Charlemagne's court was characterized by a lack of pomp and ceremony. His simple throne, consisting of slabs of marble, can be seen in the cathedral at Aachen.

four were officially acknowledged as such, while a larger number constituted a more floating population available to gratify kingly desires. Charlemagne's canonization would require some turning of blind eyes by church authorities.

The chapel, begun in the 790s, was the centrepiece and was emblematic of the Franks' conviction that they were a chosen people. Their kings were custodians of the cloak (*cappa*) of St Martin of Tours torn in half by the saint in order to relieve a beggar's need. And this *capella* (chapel) of theirs, along with its clergy of *capellani* or chaplains, was so called because it housed this precious relic. The octagon inscribed in a 16-sided polygon was, and is, austere from the outside but its interior would have been sumptuous in Charlemagne's day.

There were bronze doors and coloured paving along with antique columns which, imported from Ravenna, contained shafts of marble and porphyry. The cupola contained mosaics portraying Christ surrounded by 24 Elders of the Apocalypse. Ravenna's church of San Vitale is very similar to this building and Charlemagne's visits to the town in 786 and 787 may have inspired him architecturally. But in 774, 781 and 788 he had also been to Rome and would have seen another octagonal building – the Lateran baptistery in which the emperor Constantine was supposed to have been baptized. Little wonder then that the court poets called Aachen not just *Roma Nova* but also the Rome of the future – *Roma Ventura*.

A Modest Court

Charlemagne's court ceremonial was modest just like his dress. His biographer, Einhard, says that he only wore his bejewelled sword on the great liturgical feast days and when receiving foreign envoys. There is no mention of any other regalia. The palace's reception hall was a place for feasting after the hunt and for the transaction of business. It was not a setting for elaborate ceremonial in the Byzantine tradition. But it was the substance of power that was important here – not its superficial pomp. The profusion of his official documents show the scale of the king's ambitions as he set about imposing an oath of loyalty on the upper ranks of Carolingian society; while the detailed nature of his personal rule is seen in edicts such as those prohibiting the treading of grapes by foot during the production of wine (deemed to be an unhygienic practice), and in the measures he took against clerical incest and sodomy.

Defeat of the Saxons

Campaigning against the pagan Saxons started in 772, lasted until 804 and was the central concern of Charlemagne's reign, involving ethnic cleansing and mass extermination before the region was Christianized. Saxon magicians and soothsayers were enslaved and given to the territory's newly established churches as part of their servile labour force. One-tenth of the moveable income and wealth of the local free population was to be paid to the church and is the earliest example of the Medieval tithe.

The Carolingian Renaissance

Charlemagne lends his name to the Carolingian renaissance – that movement in the arts and scholarship which, centred on the palace at Aachen, saw the revival of classical learning. It was not however just a hankering after the classical past – this was to be a forward-looking *renovatio*. Charlemagne therefore commanded that the ancient folk tales and songs of the Franks be compiled and written down; while the Carolingian minuscule provided, through precise spelling and clearer orthography, a more accurate expression of the ruler's intentions than the messy script of the Merovingians. The visual arts that survive in the decorations of gospel books and psalters show a similarly profound change. Human figures become animated and expressive with their flowing and elongated forms replacing the two-dimensional and Byzantine-influenced decorations of earlier manuscripts in the west.

Such glories were not just confined to Aachen's palace workshops with their specially imported foreign craftsmen, especially Italians, who had retained a command of the ancient skills. The cathedral school at Metz was celebrated for its music, Orléans was a major centre for the production of illuminated manuscripts, while Salzburg's bishop, Arno, established a great library and arranged for the copying of some 150 texts both classical and literary, as well as Christian and theological.

Charlemagne's Treasure Chest

New money gained through conquest paid for new culture. Huge amounts of treasure were seized at Pavia from the Lombards and at the Irminsul, the central area of pagan Saxon worship. But the biggest booty was that seized from the Avars. This pagan and Mongolian host established in modern Hungary were nomadic killers on horseback who for almost a century had terrorized Byzantium into paying 80,000 gold *solidi* a year in order to stay away from Constantinople. This stupendous treasure was hoarded in their central encampment, a vast fortified ring, and after their defeat in 796, was removed to Aachen in 15 wagons. Existing European quarries of gold and silver had been mined out of existence during the later Roman empire. Charlemagne's loot enabled him to overcome Europe's chronic shortage of bullion, to pay his sculptors, architects, artists and scribes, and also to provision his army.

A Roman Coronation

In November 800 Charlemagne travelled to Rome as he had refused to accept the deposing of Pope Leo III by the Romans. Subsequently he was crowned *Imperator Augustus* (Emperor of the Romans) by Leo on 25 December 800,

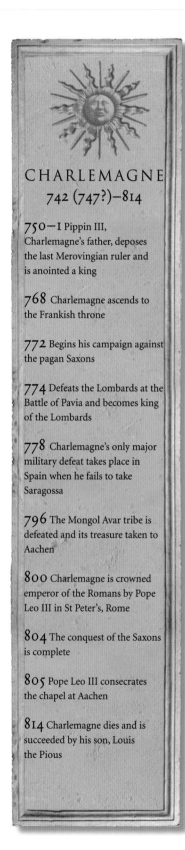

CHARLEMAGNE
742 (747?)–814

750–1 Pippin III, Charlemagne's father, deposes the last Merovingian ruler and is anointed a king

768 Charlemagne ascends to the Frankish throne

772 Begins his campaign against the pagan Saxons

774 Defeats the Lombards at the Battle of Pavia and becomes king of the Lombards

778 Charlemagne's only major military defeat takes place in Spain when he fails to take Saragossa

796 The Mongol Avar tribe is defeated and its treasure taken to Aachen

800 Charlemagne is crowned emperor of the Romans by Pope Leo III in St Peter's, Rome

804 The conquest of the Saxons is complete

805 Pope Leo III consecrates the chapel at Aachen

814 Charlemagne dies and is succeeded by his son, Louis the Pious

making Charlemagne the first emperor to appear in western Europe since the disappearance of the ancient Roman title. Charlemagne's quarrelsome grandsons fought each other after his death and divided his empire into eastern Francia (largely modern Germany) and its western component which corresponds to latter-day France. But the Carolingian renaissance was itself reborn. In the late ninth century Alfred, king of Wessex, was inspired by a king who, like himself, united military genius and a capacity for government along with a taste for literature and the arts. The Solomonic ideal of the king as a declaratory lawgiver had been basic to the Carolingian order and it now lived on in Wessex where it would be fundamental to English kingship's development.

Carolingian Imperialism Survives

In France the Capetian dynasty acclaimed Charlemagne as its great forebear, the preserver of Gaul and of Gallic civilization. And it was the German part of the old Carolingian empire, with its centre now in Saxony, which ensured the return of Carolingian imperial force. In 936 Otto I, duke of the Franks, was elected, consecrated and enthroned as king of the Germans at Aachen in a series of ceremonies which were thoroughly Carolingian. In 962 he was crowned an emperor in Rome by the pope – just as Charlemagne had been. Otto's coronation marks the official start of the Holy Roman Empire, an institution which lasted until 1805 and whose rulers, like so many believers in European unity, acclaimed Charlemagne as their inspiration.

Cast in gold and encrusted with gemstones and enamel, this 14th-century reliquary bust of Charlemagne stands near the great king's tomb in the cathedral at Aachen.

KAMMU, Fiftieth Emperor of Japan
R. 781–806

It was on a site in the centre of Honshu, the largest of Japan's four main islands, that the emperor Kammu decided to build the city which became the greatest symbol of Japanese civilization's traditionalism, authority and seclusion. Kyoto, the country's capital and imperial residence for over a millennium (794–1868), bore the imprint of a precise design, with its streets laid out on a grid pattern. Protective mountains guarded the city towards the north, the traditional location of evil spirits in Japanese mythology, while the Kamo and Katsura rivers provided the city with its eastern and western boundaries.

Japanese courtly and aristocratic culture would attain its most refined expression within this urban rectangular enclosure. Formalized tea ceremonies and methods of flower arranging, exquisite calligraphy and painting, the ritualised aesthetic of Noh drama: all evolved in the city during its long centuries of glory.

Between the 11th and 16th centuries, politically ambitious Buddhist monks regularly launched raids on the city from their monastery complex on Hiei-zan mountain in the northeast, and Kyoto would be largely destroyed during the Japanese civil war of 1467–77. But restoration of the original civic design followed every act of devastation, for Kammu's city had come to define the very essence of a civilization.

The First Japanese
Ethnically the product of a fusion between migrants from the Asian continental mainland and the South Pacific, the Japanese make their first historical appearance in the Chinese chronicles of the Han period (206 BC–AD 220). There they are described as a people 'who are divided into more than 100 states, and who bring tribute at fixed intervals'. A degree of unification was achieved from the third century onwards by the court established at Yamato on the Nara plain in central Honshu. By the end of the fourth century a substantial Japanese force had been sent to fight Koguryo, the largest of Korea's three independent kingdoms.

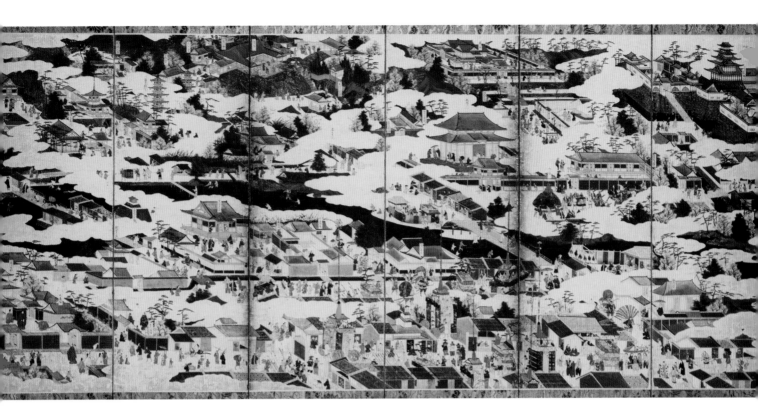

Yamato allied itself with the Paekche kingdom on the southwestern tip of the Korean peninsula and against both the Koguryo and the Silla kingdoms.

With the Korean involvement came also a Chinese political influence as both Yamato and Paekche looked towards the southern Chinese states, while the two other Korean states looked towards those of northern China. Silla's military predominance however drove Yamato forces from the Korean peninsula in the sixth century. Thereafter the court's central authority declined as the leaders of the Soga clan acquired power, partly through intermarriage with the royal family, and also on account of their mastery of specialized financial techniques. They were also active sponsors at court of Buddhism, a faith which had spread into Japan from China through Paekche.

Prince Shotoku – A Learned Prince

Prince Shotoku (574–622) was a Soga clan member and the emperor Yomei's second son. When his aunt Suiko become empress (r.592–628) he subsequently became crown prince and regent. Shotoku was an enthused and learned Buddhist while also being versed in Confucianism and he resumed the practice of sending envoys to China which was now governed by the Sui dynasty (581–618). Chinese artists, craftsmen and clerks were encouraged to settle in Japan and Shotoku's compilation of governmental chronicles, a very Chinese practice, is the first book known to Japanese history. The system of 12 court ranks he adopted in 603 was characteristically Confucian in its rewards for ability: courtiers' different ranks were marked by the wearing of differently coloured caps.

The regent's blend of Buddhism with Confucianism supplemented the folk beliefs of Japan's traditional Shinto religion and the nation's previously simple

Kammu's fine capital at Heian (Kyoto) would inspire a new genre of painting, known as Scenes in and around the Capital (rakuchu rakugai zu). These colourful, highly detailed panoramas depicting everyday life in and around Kyoto were usually mounted on six-panel screens, as in the above example, which dates from c.1625–50.

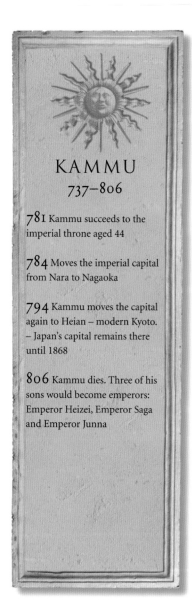

architectural tradition was transformed by the consequences of his patronage: Buddhist temples in the Chinese style were erected, built of wood and covered with enormous tiled roofs. Shotoku re-established control over the feudal lords and the royal house's authority was given a further boost by his 17-Article Constitution, with a clear distinction drawn between emperor and ministers.

Conflict and Anarchy

Anarchy followed Shotoku's death and his entire surviving family was wiped out by other Soga clan members in 643. Conflict was spreading in east Asia too, with the Koguryo forces marching towards Korean dominance and defeating two armies sent from an enfeebled Sui China. But the T'ang dynasty's rigorous restoration of Chinese order proved a decisive inspiration for Japan's own imperial arrangements. In 645 a coup intended to place Iruka, son of the head of the Soga clan, on the throne seemed imminent. Nakano Oe, a prince of the imperial house, and Nakatomi Kamatari, of the powerful Nakatomi clan, resolved on pre-emptive action. Their own coup annihilated the Soga and led to Japan's first experience of absolutist government.

An edict of 646 abolished private ownership of land and people by the *uji* or heads of regional clans. Former *uji* territory now became state property and, allocated among subjects of the crown, was to be cultivated in return for a fixed sum of taxation. Provincial governors were appointed and the entire Japanese population was registered in central records. The imperial prince, Karu, was placed on the throne as the emperor Kotoku and Nakano Oe, having been named heir apparent, succeeded to the throne as Emperor Tenji in 662.

In 669, as a reward for his ministerial services, Kamatari was given the new family name of Fujiwara and for centuries the clan would be a dominant force in Japanese politics. Prince Shotoku had effected Japan's Sinicization in cultural terms but the 'Taika' (great reforms) period amounted to a political imitation of T'ang China's methods in restoring national cohesion.

A Succession Struggle

Tenji's death in 672 sparked off a massive succession struggle between his uncle and younger brother, the future emperor Temmu, supported by their respective followers. The victorious Temmu ordered the compilation of official histories which enhanced dynastic prestige, and the myth would emerge that Jimmu, a supposed ruler of the seventh century BC and child of the sun goddess Amaterasu, had been the first emperor. Temmu also used the Shinto shrine ceremonies at Ise to assert dynastic legitimacy. But even more central was the Asuka Kiyomihara code which codified the Taika reforms. From this emerged the *ritsuryo* political structure with its close definition of the civil, criminal and administrative systems.

The emperor remained both head of the bureaucracy and high priest, in charge of the Council of State and also of the Office of Deities which systematized the worship of the gods. But the idea of the state ultimately owning all Japan's land, introduced by the Taika period, was proving unworkable. Land of a certain annual yield was now being given to high officials as their stipends and also as revenue to both Shinto shrines and Buddhist temples.

A growing population needed more paddy-field development and, in 743, the government allowed for the permanent private possession of land by those cultivating it for the first time. A defining feature of the regime had therefore been undermined and by now some of Japan's Buddhist priests were also causing problems.

Rising some 15 metres (49 ft) from the ground, the colossal statue of Buddha at the Todai temple in Nara is the largest gilt bronze structure in the world. Completed in c.752, the figure has been restored several times over the centuries following damage caused by battles and earthquakes.

Buddhist Influences

Japan's imperial capital from 710 to 784 was settled at Nara, a city where the emperor Shomu introduced a strongly Buddhist component to his government. It was here that he raised the Todai temple and placed within it the huge bronze figure known as the Daibutsu (the Great Buddha), a divinity intended to be the nation's guardian. But the large number of provincial Buddhist temples that he built amassed substantial riches and their monks acquired a degree of political influence that was resented by many Japanese aristocrats.

The Fujiwara were supreme examples of the new breed of bureaucrat-nobles who had risen to prominence at court and the emperor Shomu's own wife belonged to the clan. The Buddhist priest Dokyo had become a chief minister under Shomu's daughter, the empress Koken. On her death in 770 the Fujiwara moved into action against the priestly domination of their country's politics and court. They ousted Dokyo, who may well have been plotting to gain the throne for himself, and set on the throne Emperor Konin who was less of a Buddhist political partisan. They also established the principle, following their unhappy experience under Koken, that no woman could succeed to the throne.

Emperor Kammu Restores the Old Order

Kammu was Konin's successor and shared his distrust of Buddhism as a political force. He therefore moved the imperial capital from Nara, a city crowded with priests and temples, to Heian (modern Kyoto) where he re-established government according to the *ritsuryo* system. The geographical move reflected

An illustration of a coronation ceremony outside Taikyokuden temple, one of the buildings of the imperial palace at Kyoto. Even after the capital moved to Tokyo in the late 19th century Taisho and Showa emperors held their coronation ceremonies at Kyoto.

a dynastic shift. Kammu stood in the line of Tenji rather than of Temmu, and Yamashiro province, site of the new capital, was the home of Tenji's other descendants. Kammu was restoring what he took to be the old order but he also modified it by making it more practical.

Rice fields were allocated every 12 years instead of every six. Kammu abandoned the old system of raising conscript troops from among the peasantry and local officials now provided the army with sons whose military abilities had been reliably attested. Armies were sent to quell the Ezo tribal group of northern Honshu and those who submitted were assimilated by being settled throughout the country. Buddhist priests no longer played a political role in government but the emperor still found the religion useful as an aspect of the national culture. Kammu's patronage encouraged the development of a more distinctively Japanese version of Buddhism, one that was less obviously drawn from the original Chinese inspiration.

The Decline of Imperial Authority

The system of *ritsuryo* government as modified by Kammu continued for over 150 years after his death with the minting of coins, the compilation of histories, and additions to legal codes all following carefully defined precedent. This administration eventually came under great strain: census registers could not catch up with population changes and the system of land allocation became chaotic as a result. Corruption emerged, since provincial governors were allowed to administer devolved systems of tax assessment and gathering. Two new offices, created outside the *ritsuryo* regime, would undermine Kammu's legacy: that of *sessho* or regent (held during an imperial minority) and of *kampaku* or chief councillor. The regency was restricted to those whose daughters had married into the imperial family and produced a child emperor. It soon became an established practice that the Fujiwara family should hold both the regent's post and that of *kampaku*. A long-term decline in imperial authority ensued.

But it was the cultural distinctiveness of Japan which was the profoundest legacy of the age of Kammu. At the end of the ninth century Japan decided to cut off formal relations with China partly because of the political unrest which had spread at the dissolution of T'ang dynastic authority. A more substantial reason lay however in the fact that Japan's culture no longer needed to look to China for its inspiration. A country had come of age and from now on would stand on its own, assertive two feet.

'ABD AL-RAHMAN III, Emir and Caliph of Cordoba

R. 912–961 (929–961)

The Great Mosque at Cordoba is the most important historic mosque in the West and one of the best examples of Islamic art in Spain. After the fall of Cordoba in 1236 the building was consecrated as a Christian cathedral.

In the middle of the tenth century Cordoba's Great Mosque, the architectural apotheosis of Andalusian Spain's Islamic civilization, was nearing completion. Two centuries had passed since the caliph's ancestor, fleeing from the slaughter in Damascus, had first arrived in the city. Back in the east, victorious 'Abbasid forces were in full pursuit of his Umayyad relatives. But Spain had witnessed intense tribal rivalry among its Arab leaders ever since the original Muslim invasion of 711.

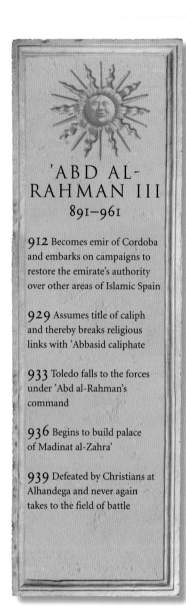

'ABD AL-
RAHMAN III
891–961

912 Becomes emir of Cordoba and embarks on campaigns to restore the emirate's authority over other areas of Islamic Spain

929 Assumes title of caliph and thereby breaks religious links with 'Abbasid caliphate

933 Toledo falls to the forces under 'Abd al-Rahman's command

936 Begins to build palace of Madinat al-Zahra'

939 Defeated by Christians at Alhandega and never again takes to the field of battle

In that fact lay 'Abd al-Rahman I's opportunity. Enlisting mercenaries, in 755 he had defeated the governor of al-Andalus, whose capital of Cordoba was seized, and the further arrival from Syria of Umayyad partisans and officials ensured the dynasty's survival in its new base. A site had been bought from the Christians, the cathedral that stood there was demolished and work on the mosque that emerged to take its place had rarely ceased from then until now. By 976 it was finished in all its grandiose proportions: the prayer hall was in place with its 19 aisles whose roofs were supported by more than 850 columns made of porphyry, jasper and coloured marble; a two-tiered system of arches consisting of white stone and red brick linked the aisles and columns; domes were covered with mosaics, floral decorations arose from their base of stucco, and alabaster panels were engraved with Quranic texts. The horseshoe arch and the ribbed dome became the 'Cordoban style' much imitated across the world of Islam, and the city's glories were the only possible rival to the magnificence of 'Abbasid Baghdad.

Cordoba was tenth-century Europe's largest city with a population approaching 100,000. The refinement of its exported goods in the form of leatherwork and jewellery, silks and brocades, was acclaimed in European, North African and Middle Eastern markets. This was a showcase for a distinctively Islamic notion of the city, a cultural ideal which had revived Mediterranean civilization. But this southern Spanish site by the banks of the River Guadalquivir had its own history of refinement, trade and power long before the Umayyads arrived

Early History of Spain

Originally a Carthaginian settlement, Cordoba was conquered by the Roman army in 152 BC and under Augustus this commercially prosperous city became capital of the imperial province of Baetica. During the years 415–18 Germanic Visigoths, a tribe that had embraced Arian Christianity, made an initial foray into Spain following their leader Alaric's sack of Rome in 410. Another Germanic tribe, the Vandals, had established themselves in southern Spain (including Baetica) in 409. They, too, were Arians and gained notoriety as persecutors of Catholic Christians. Gaiseric, the Vandal leader, transported his people en masse in 429 to North Africa, where they were initially Rome's federated allies and then its foes. But the memory of that brief southern Spanish sojourn lived on in the Arabs' description of the region as 'al-Andalus' or Vandal land.

The Visigoths became imperial allies in 418 and were resettled for this purpose in Roman Aquitania, between the Garonne and Loire rivers. But during the fifth century an increasingly independent Visigothic kingdom expanded from this Gaulish base, spread across the Pyrenees to most of Spain and moved its capital from Toulouse to Toledo. Clovis found the Visigoths' Arian associations a useful pretext to declare war and dislodged them from Gaul following the Frankish victory of 507 at the Battle of Vouillé near Poitiers.

Muslim Invaders

Visigothic Spain, increasingly Catholic in Christianity, had been intolerant of its substantial Jewish population, who therefore welcomed the arrival of Muslim invaders in 711. The Visigothic nobility had recently elected Roderick, in all probability Baetica's military governor, to the throne, and dissidents who supported the claims of the previous king's two sons joined the ranks of defectors.

The 7000-strong force which had left Tangier was led by the city's Arab governor Taiq ibn Ziyad, and consisted mostly of the non-Arab Berber tribesmen along with a number of Syrians and Yemenis. Toledo and Cordoba fell to Islam and the arrival in the following year of another invading force of some 18,000, again mostly Berber, meant that by 714 Islamic control was effective over most of Spain, a country which became collectively known as al-Andalus.

New Arab Rule in Spain

Immense religious and ethnic variety emerged as the new Arab ruling elite established its rule over a population consisting of Hispano-Romans and Visigoths. Cultural Islamicization and political control were aided by the policy that allowed the peninsula's large number of serfs to become freed men as long as they converted. Spanish Christians who kept their religion but adopted the Arab language and customs were termed Mozarabs. Descendants of the pre-invasion population who converted to Islam were called Muwallads. Berbers arriving in successive waves of immigration had a major impact on population patterns. In 741 there was a major uprising of those Berbers who were garrisoned as troops in Spain after their fellow tribesmen in North Africa rebelled against Arab rule. The subsequent arrival in the peninsula of a large army of Syrians in order to reassert Arab control ensured an even greater ethnic mix. Berber settlement had been especially strong in the northwest and the 741 rebellion gave the Christian kingdom of Asturias, a northern outpost established in 718 by fleeing Visigothic nobles and officials, a chance to incorporate Galicia.

Arab tribal rivalry in Spain did not diminish the desire for northern expansion and this thrust was maintained until 732 when Charles Martel defeated an invading force near Tours in 732. Defeat by Byzantium in Anatolia during 740 suggested that Islam was reaching its territorial limits in the east as well as the west, and the caliphate of Syrian rulers was about to pay the price. Muslims who wanted a continuous and consistently Islamic expansion had always thought them too secular and dismissed the Umayyad domain as merely 'the Arab state'.

The tenth-century court of 'Abd al-Rahman at Cordoba is depicted in this painting, from about 1885, by the Spanish artist Dionisio Baixeras-Verdaguer. During 'Abd al-Rahman's reign Cordoba was the Islamic capital of the Iberian peninsula and competed in splendour with some of the most important cities in the world.

Nonetheless, it was the Umayyads who had broken with the
Arab custom of allowing tribal leaders to elect their leader
or caliph and established the new principle of hereditary
rule within a dynasty. Following major revolts in Iran, Iraq
and Khorasan, the Umayyad forces were defeated in 750 at
the Battle of the Great Zab River in Mesopotamia.
Surrounded by their ruination in the
east, the dynasty and its adherents now looked west.

Arab Dissidence

As emirs instead of caliphs, Cordoba's first Umayyad rulers
claimed political rather than religious independence from
the 'Abbasids and confronted major challenges. In 778
Charlemagne's army was defeated at Roncesvalles and
Barcelona's seizure in 801 contained the Frankish Christian
advance. But the emirate faced major bouts of dissidence
among the Arab nobility, lasting for a generation from the
end of the eighth century. Mozarabs protesting against their
co-religionists' increasing Arabization were a major public-
order problem of the mid-ninth century. Embracing
martyrdom, they embarked on a systematic campaign of publicly reviling the
Prophet's name, an offence punishable by death from 850 onwards.

During the second half of the ninth century there were also several major revolts
among the Muwallads. Asturias with its capital at Oviedo emerged to become a
strong Christian frontier state, especially after the discovery in 813 of St James's
supposed tomb at Compostella. With its expansion to the south the territory
became known as the kingdom of León from 910 onwards, and Mozarabs flocked
there in increasing numbers.

'Abd al-Rahman III's Rule

The emergence by 909 of the new and independent caliphate of the Fatimid
dynasty based in Tunisia changed Islam's international power alignments. As
caliph of the west 'Abd al-Rahman III established his religious independence of
the 'Abbasids and in 929 he adopted the caliphal title of Al-Nasir li-Din Allah –
Victor for the Religion of God. With his authority enhanced, he countered the
Fatimids' naval aggression in the western Mediterranean and subsidized revolts
against their rule locally in North Africa. There had been widespread rebellions
in Spain during the preceding reign, that of the caliph's grandfather 'Abd Allah,
and it took some 20 years of campaigning before full authority was restored.
Toledo, centre of the last major Muslim resistance to the caliph, fell in 933.
León paid homage but retained its independence despite the prolonged
campaign waged against it.

*By the early sixth century the
Visigoths had spread from
southern France into Spain and
their kingdom was centred on
Toledo, once a Roman city.
The kingdom survived until
711, when Umayyad Muslim
troops advancing from the
south took the city, heralding
the Muslim conquest of the
peninsula. This is a view of
the 14th-century San Martin
Bridge spanning the River
Tagus at Toledo.*

Preoccupied by the danger of local dynasties emerging to threaten his rule, the caliph made frequent changes in the personnel of provincial governorships and an entire new city, Madinat al-Zahra', was built 3 miles (5 km) from Cordoba to house his expansive bureaucracy and royal household. This consolidated Spain prospered economically and coins of pure silver and gold were struck at the newly established national mint.

Expansion of Umayyad Spain

Externally too its successes would be remarkable. The Fatimids largely abandoned their western campaigning and concentrated on Egypt, where they gained dynastic control in 969. Umayyad Spain therefore expanded into the power vacuum which had emerged in the Maghrib of northwest Africa.

This area would be transformed into the viceroyalty of Cordoba by the prodigious Abu 'Amir al-Mansur who as the caliphate's chief minister (978–1002) was Islamic Spain's effective ruler. Commanding his own highly professional army, most of whom were Berbers fanatically attached to his person and leadership, al-Mansur enjoyed an easy predominance over the Arab aristocracy and controlled a government whose high officialdom contained many slaves personally appointed by him. His patronage of poets and scholars was in the highest traditions of Islamic and Arabic culture but this was the last great age of Moorish Spain and its territorial unity fragmented in the 11th century with the advance from the north of the Reconquista, Christian Spain's campaign of territorial recovery.

Cordoba remained intellectually distinguished and its chief *qadi* (judge), Averroes (1126–98), was Europe's supreme commentator on Plato and Aristotle. The Cordoban-born Moses Maimonides (1135–1204) was internationally renowned as an Islamic jurist and philosopher. But mid-12th-century Muslim Spain was ruled by the Almohads, a revolutionary and fanatically Islamic sect of Moroccan Berbers who were struggling to contain the Reconquista. Fleeing their anti-semitism, Maimonides was in Egypt by 1165. In 1212 the Berber tribal federation in Spain was defeated in battle by the Christian coalition of León and Navarre, Castile and Aragon. Cordoba's glory had passed and the city would fall. By 1236 the Great Mosque, which had once heard the Prophet's word, echoed to the sound of the Catholic Mass.

BASIL II, *'The Bulgar Slayer'*, Emperor of Byzantium

R. 976–1025

At the end of July 1014, a stocky and scruffy 56-year-old warrior, Basil II, heavily bearded with brilliant blue eyes, enacted a cruelly exact vengeance against the Bulgar people who had plagued his empire for over two centuries.

The Bulgars were the descendants of an originally Turkic group of central Asian invaders who had arrived in the European steppe, west of the Volga, by the late fourth century. One grouping (or 'horde') had settled on the plain between the Danube and the Balkan mountains and, by the seventh century, they were intermarrying with the local population of Vlachs as well as the recently arrived Slavs. Krum, khan of the Bulgars (802–14), had killed the Byzantine emperor, Nicephorus I, in 811 before besieging Constantinople. Conversion to Christianity under their ruler Boris I (852–89) had given the Bulgars their own Slavonic liturgy and a deep cultural unity, but had not diminished their readiness to kill Greeks and grab the Byzantine territories to their south.

Basil's Brutal Campaign
Basil II's campaigning in 1000–4 had already restored to Byzantine control most of the eastern Balkans stretching from Thessaloniki to the Iron Gate on the Danube, the gorge separating Serbia from Rumania. Now in July of 1014 he advanced to the narrow Cimbalongus Pass leading into the valley of the River Struma near the town of Seres and found that the army, led by the Bulgarian tsar Samuel, had occupied the defile and blocked entry to it by building a series of wooden palisades. A Byzantine detachment was sent up the wooded hillside to attack the Bulgars from the rear while the emperor led the successful assault through the palisades. Basil ordered that his 15,000 prisoners be divided in units of a hundred. All were blinded in both eyes with the exception of one in each unit; blinded in just one eye, he guided the shuffling survivors back to their tsar who had escaped the slaughter.

It was October by the time they arrived at Tsar Samuel's castle in Prespa. The tsar, on seeing them, collapsed in apoplexy and died after a two-day coma. After another three and a half years' campaigning Basil entered the Bulgarian capital

of Ochrid (now in modern Macedonia) in triumph. The whole of the Balkans was once again Byzantine and on his progress across the region the emperor received the homage and oaths of fealty due to one who had earned his cognomen of Bulgaroctonus – 'Bulgar Slayer'.

Early Years and the Time of Nicephorus

Basil's apprenticeship in brutality started early. His father Romanus II died in March 963 and his mother Theophano summoned the general Nicephorus Phocas to protect herself and her two young sons, Basil and Constantine. The

This frontispiece from an early 11th-century psalter shows Basil II standing triumphant over the conquered Bulgarian chiefs. The 'righteousness' of his actions is illustrated by Christ handing down a crown for an angel to place on his head.

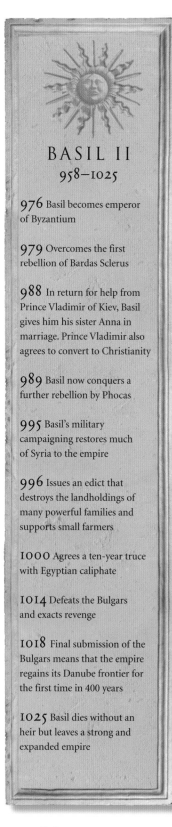

ascetic Anatolian aristocrat, who had regained Crete for the empire by destroying the occupying Saracens in 961, was encamped with his army near Caesarea in Cappadocia and already on his way back to Constantinople after his victories against the Arabian emir Saif ed-Daula during the Syrian campaign of 961–2. He carried with him, as a proof of both his piety and his prowess, the tattered tunic of St John the Baptist seized at Aleppo, where his army had captured the city in 944 and then burnt to the ground the emir's magnificent palace. Arriving in Constantinople, Nicephorus had the tunic carried before him as he made his way to the Hippodrome for his formal triumph. On rejoining his troops in Cappadocia that summer his generals raised him on their shields to proclaim him an emperor in the ancient Roman manner, and in St Sophia on 16 August the patriarch placed the imperial diadem on the head of Nicephorus II Phocas.

The new emperor was also the protector of the two child co-emperors, but the dynastic principle had been broken, and Nicephorus's marriage to Theophano further strengthened his position. As emperor however he alienated powerful factions. The church was outraged by his edict stopping it from accepting further benefactions to add to its already vast estates. By making land available to the highest bidder he had discriminated against small proprietors who had previously benefited from legislation giving first refusal to the owners of adjacent properties. Tax had soared and Nicephorus had also refused to pay the annual subsidy to the Bulgars, which, since 927, had kept them as a useful buffer state between the Byzantines and the state of Rus, centred on the region around Kiev. This new Russian power had been consolidating since its mid-ninth-century emergence and Nicephorus's decision to subsidize Prince Svyatoslav of Kiev to wage war on the Bulgars was a disaster. Heading an army of Russians, Magyars and Pechenegs, Svyatoslav had defeated the Bulgars and, in the autumn of 969, he was threatening Byzantium on its Thracian border.

John Tzimisces and Assassination

By the morning of 11 December 969 Nicephorus was dead, killed during the night by Theophano's new lover, John Tzimisces, another Anatolian general. John went to the palace's throne room, pulled on the purple imperial buskins and, with Theophano, Basil and Constantine at his side, was hailed by palace officials as the new emperor. He swiftly exiled Theophano and rescinded the anti-church measures. John's brother-in-law Bardas Sclerus joined the former emperor's nephew, Peter Phocas (a eunuch and therefore without dynastic ambitions) at the head of an army which defeated the Russian invasion force at Arcadiopolis in the spring of 970. By 972 Svyatoslav had conceded defeat and was withdrawing through Bulgaria when he was killed by his angry former Pecheneg allies, who turned his skull into a drinking cup. John forced Tsar Boris to abdicate and the Bulgarian crown was placed in triumph on the high altar of St Sophia in symbolic termination of the country's independence. He also repulsed the

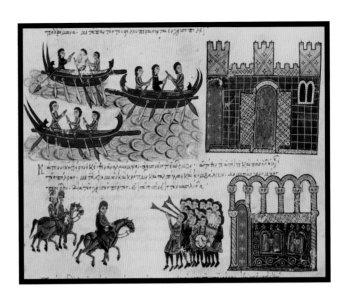

caliphate of Egypt which, under its Fatimid dynasty, had advanced across the Sinai to attack Antioch in 971. By 974 John's campaigning had restored to Byzantium its control over most of Syria, Lebanon and Palestine.

Basil Succeeds to the Throne

After John's sudden death, Basil succeeded to the throne in 976. Basil needed to reassert his family's dynastic authority and, in 985, he exiled the long-serving court chamberlain, also called Basil, a notoriously corrupt eunuch, and confiscated his vast estates. Bardas Sclerus, considering himself to be John Tzimisces's true heir, was in command of the eastern armies and initiated a three-year civil war. Bardas Phocas, another nephew of the emperor Nicephorus, had been exiled to Pontus in the Black Sea after leading a rebellion against John Tzimisces. Basil persuaded him to swear loyalty and to lead the campaign which ended in Sclerus's flight to Baghdad. But in 987 Sclerus resumed his fight for the imperial throne and formed an alliance with Phocas, who, however, betrayed and imprisoned him before leading an army through Asia Minor in order to attack Constantinople. At the same time, the Bulgarian problem returned. Western Bulgaria had been largely unaffected by the recent war and it was here that a new Tsar, Samuel, emerged to lead a national insurrection. In 986 the city of Larissa, in Byzantine Thessaly, fell to Samuel's forces and the Greeks' counter-offensive ended in humiliation.

This illustration tells the story of the triumphal entry of Nicephorus Phocas into Constantinople in 963 following his victories in Crete and Syria.

New Dynamics

An appeal for military aid to Vladimir, prince of Kiev, resulted in the arrival in Constantinople by December 988 of 6000 Varangians, the Russianized Vikings who were central to the Kievan state's military success. The emperor agreed to Vladimir's price, marriage with Basil's sister Anna, as long as the pagan prince embraced Christianity. The new Russian church became part of the patriarchate of Constantinople and Orthodox culture acquired a dynamic new element.

Vladimir's giant Varangians crossed the Hellespont in February 989 and destroyed Phocas's force at nearby Chrysopolis. Phocas himself subsequently fell dead of a massive stroke and the released Sclerus, now almost entirely blind, made his submission to Basil, counselling the emperor that the only way to deal with the Anatolian barons was to tax them and diminish their land holdings. Basil's subsequent edict of 1 January 996 restored to the previous owners, without compensation, all property acquired in the last 61 years. This destroyed the power base of great families such as the Phocas, strengthened the small landowners who formed the imperial army's backbone and ensured the return of vast estates to the emperor's own domain.

Basil's meticulously trained army travelled across Anatolia, covering 600 miles (1000 km) in just 16 days in April 995. 17,000 men were then drawn up before the city walls of Aleppo, now being besieged by Fatimid forces. Aleppo, and with it northern Syria, was saved and a ten-year truce with the Egyptian caliphate, agreed in 1000, secured Basil's eastern, Syrian, frontier. To the west Samuel's Bulgars had invaded the Byzantine province of Hellas, plundered their way to Corinth and occupied the Adriatic port of Dyrrachium (now known as Duress in Albania) before advancing through Dalmatia and into Bosnia. Basil protected his western front, again in 1000, by turning the Dalmatian coast into a protectorate ruled by the Venetians under Byzantine suzerainty.

The assassination in the same year of Prince David of Upper Tao in Georgia was similarly helpful, since David's punishment for supporting Bardas Phocas's rebellion included the reversion of his lands to the empire on his death. These included the vast areas to the north of Lake Van which had been ceded to him previously by Byzantium and which supplemented his own hereditary domains. Basil made Bagrat, king of Abasgia, governor of this new eastern frontier and advanced north towards his spectacular crushing of the Bulgars.

Byzantine Territorial Expansion

Byzantine rule over the Bulgars proved to be conciliatory and taxes were kept low. The Bulgar empire became the Byzantine regions of Bulgaria and Paristrium, while in the west, local princes ruled under imperial suzerainty in Croatia, Dioclea, Rascia and Bosnia. Basil appointed the archbishop of the Bulgarian church which, in other respects, kept its autonomy.

Elsewhere there was still campaigning to do. George of Abasgia abrogated his father's agreement and invaded Tao after Bagrat died in 1014. Basil's campaign of 1021–2 restored his authority in Georgia and then, by diplomatic agreement, extended it to the Armenian district of Aspurakan and into Azerbaijan. At his death he was getting ready to invade Sicily which, although re-conquered for the empire by Belisaurus in 535, had been Arab-occupied since the late ninth century.

Basil identified himself completely with Byzantium and the empire attained its greatest territorial expansion during his reign but, being unmarried and without an heir, he also bequeathed a problem of dynastic succession. Ahead lay Manzikert, the Seljuk Turks' victory of 1071 which deprived Byzantium of Anatolia. Profiting from the Seljuk attacks, the Bulgars reasserted themselves in the national revolt of 1185 which created a second Bulgar empire. This became the Balkans' greatest power in the first half of the 13th century after which it fell victim to Mongol and then Serb attacks before its final late 14th-century destruction by the same power which would then crush Byzantium itself: that of the Ottoman Turks.

Among the territories won by Basil II towards the end of his reign were Armenia and Georgia. This stone sculpture of the Madonna and Child stands near the 13th-century Haghartsin monastery in Armenia in the northern province of Tavush.

OTTO III, A Teenage Visionary as Holy Roman Emperor

R. 996–1002

The fact that Otto III was only three years old when he was crowned king of the Germans and still in his teenage years when he assumed government as emperor attracted contemporary attention, but it was the practical impact of his new imperial vision that astonished his subjects. This brief, but intensely focused, rule of barely six years changed the way the empire was viewed in Europe – it became less an instrument of narrowly German overlordship and more of a federal union which respected the rights of central and eastern Europe's non-German countries.

The imperial crown of the Holy Roman Emperor, first worn in c.962 by Otto I and thought to have been made in western Germany. Unlike most crowns, it is octagonal rather than circular in shape and has eight hinged gold plates lavishly studded with pearls and precious stones.

Medieval European society with its high mortality rates was well used to the sight of very young, even adolescent, kings surrounded by equally youthful courtiers and advisers. For the ruling elites high office frequently arrived early in their lives as a result of their predecessors' deaths. By the same token they themselves could not rely on a long tenure at the top. Most of the medieval Holy Roman Emperors were under 25 when elected, which was just as well since they needed physical fitness and an ability to adapt quickly to different environments. Their life was one of ceaseless travel on horseback in a period of itinerant government that tried to hold together territories extending from the North Sea coast to the Mediterranean shores.

The Ottonians

Otto was a member of Saxony's ruling dynasty, the Ottonians. His grandfather, Otto I, Duke of Saxony, was elected king of the Germans in 936 by the dukes who headed the German tribes and was crowned emperor in 962, the year which was also the starting date for the history of the Holy Roman Empire. Saxony was rich following the discovery of silver deposits in the Harz Mountains during the early tenth century. A huge flow of rents and chattels, tributes and slaves, also came to its rulers from the conquered Slavonic peoples. The new wealth enabled the Ottonians to present increasingly

sophisticated displays of kingly power as they became first a German dynasty and then an imperial European power. Travelling in state across their domains they could afford elaborate displays of solemn entries, festival coronations and crown wearings. The new money also meant that the Saxon army had the military technology, the swords, helmets and armour, which enabled it to go on the offensive. Gone were the trademark straw hats of their predecessors and Saxon soldiers were notorious for the deadly precision of their sword techniques.

Otto I's decisive victory over the Magyars at the Battle of the Lech (955) established his right to be crowned an emperor. But he had also extended his authority into southern Italy following military success in Lombardy. The arrival of Germans in southern Italy ensured conflicts with Constantinople whose emperors still claimed a title to rule in the region. In 972, a year before he died, Otto I arranged for his son and heir to marry the Greek princess Theophano, niece of the emperor, John Tzimisces. This appeased the Byzantines initially before they resumed hostilities in southern Italy during the reign of Otto II. But the son of this marriage would prove to have a powerful and practical understanding of both sides of his ancestry.

Young Otto III and His Regents

As a boy, Otto III asked his tutor, the Frenchman Gerbert of Aurillac, to kindle the 'Greek subtlety that lies like a spark hidden beneath the ashes of my Saxon greenness'. His other tutors, the Greek John Philagthos and the Saxon Bernward, form part of the same mix of Greek and Roman, of Saxon and, ultimately, Frankish, influences on the boy king. When he was just three his 28-year-old father died after a ten-year reign (973–83) and Otto was immediately crowned king of the Germans by the archbishops of Ravenna and Mainz at Aachen on Christmas Day 983. Charlemagne and the Carolingian idealism about a European and Christian empire would be continuous and powerful influences on him. Theophano governed the empire on Otto's behalf until she died in 991 and his grandmother Adelheid, Otto I's widow, did the same job until the boy was old enough to rule rather than just reign. This moment arrived early. While still in his teens Otto would seek to reconcile the eastern Roman traditions of Byzantium with those of the Catholic west and he also worked to reform the papacy which was going through a bad patch in the late tenth century. Pope John XII, who crowned Otto I emperor, was an illiterate sensualist who died in the arms of his mistress while Pope John XV was a particularly nepotistic client of the Crescentii, a local Roman aristocratic family.

Otto's Popes and Byzantine Ceremonial

In 996, on the death of Pope John XV, Otto nominated his chaplain Brun, another grandson of Otto I, to the papacy. Brun reigned as Gregory V and was succeeded by another of Otto's nominees, his tutor Gerbert, who chose the title

This illustration from a Gospel Book made for Otto III (c.1000) shows the emperor flanked by members of the clergy and noblemen bearing swords. The magnificent cloth of honour behind the central figure, the orb, the eagle-topped sceptre and the gem-encrusted crown all serve as symbols representing imperial power.

of Sylvester II. Both popes supported their patron's ambitions for a papacy in touch with the European intellectual and spiritual renewal – a process that was now well under way with the monastic-led reform movements gaining adherents in the continent's west. But Otto also thought the papacy needed a guiding imperial hand in order to achieve that goal. He himself harked back to Justinian, the sixth-century emperor of Byzantium, who had presided over a remarkable revival of the eastern Roman empire by recovering Italian provinces it had lost during the barbarian invasions.

He therefore portrayed himself on his imperial seals as a Greek *basileus* or king with a full beard; his understanding of the importance of iconography and symbols was acute. Otto's shoes were studded with symbolic eagles, dragons and lions – animals associated with imperial and kingly power. On the church's high feast days he wore a dalmatic, a liturgical vestment usually made of silk, damask or velvet. Otto's was decorated with golden eagles. His official robe was sewn with 365 bells, one for each day of the motions of the heavenly bodies since this was an emperor who ruled in the name of a cosmic harmony. These innovations show the influence on Otto of Byzantine ceremonial with its care for ritual and precisely determined rank. His example ensured that the same ceremoniousness was adopted by the papal court with its new concern for vestments and emblems.

New Titles for Otto

Understanding the importance of titles, Otto adopted in 1000 that of 'Servant of Jesus Christ' before changing it a year later to 'Servant of the Apostles'. The new form of words was crucial, recalling as it did Constantine's chosen title of '*isapostolos*' or 'equal of the apostles'. Otto was now claiming in other words that he was the representative of St Peter, and therefore the legitimate ruler of the territories associated with the papal see. Behind this action lay his exposure of the forgery known as the 'Donation of Constantine', an eighth-century document purporting to record the emperor's fourth-century bestowal of territorial, spiritual and temporal power on the popes. Crucially, it was also used to support papal claims to appoint secular rulers in western Europe. Otto did oblige the papacy by returning some north Italian territories to which it laid a claim. But he only did so as a personal favour to Gerbert and made it clear that, as emperor, he retained a superior title not just to those lands but to any territories that Constantine might have granted to St Peter's successors. The papacy, he pointed out, had governed its territories incompetently and, having lost through negligence so much of its own territorial patrimony, it had used forged deeds to grab imperial lands.

Otto was substituting his own idealized view of a Rome which was 'capital of the world' for the real and disorderly Rome of *c.*1000. He thought that it should be the city of the emperors rather than of the popes. Lordship over Italy, a revived city of Rome, and control over the papacy: these were the components of Otto's policy of imperial power in Italy. But his plans for the German core of his empire, and the church there, were equally ambitious.

The German Imperial Church

The German imperial church was very much a creation of Otto I and he had used it in order to consolidate his rule internally over an often fractious nobility. But it was also instrumental in the eastward expansion of the Ottonians. The bishoprics and archbishoprics established in Poland and Bohemia, Moravia and Hungary, were the outposts of the ecclesiastical centres at Mainz and Magdeburg, Salzburg and Passau. They were part of a policy of imposed Germanicization in cultural terms and also central to the colonial power sought by the Ottonians in the east. This imperial patronage of the missionary church had led to a brilliant renaissance in the architectural and decorative arts. It was also a resumption of Charlemagne's attempt to defeat the Slavs who had pressed hard on his empire's eastern boundary along the River Elbe.

Otto's Visit to Aachen

Otto paid a special visit to Aachen in 1000 in order to pay tribute to Charlemagne's memory. But he also knew that Charlemagne had never been able to absorb the Slav populations and that this latest push to the east was beyond the resources of his empire's German core. He also thought it was strategically stupid since the subjugated and hostile might turn to Byzantium for support. Otto therefore renounced the mission to the Slavs, and developed a federal policy for the eastern territories. He still expected those lands and their rulers to honour his imperial title, but they now enjoyed an internal autonomy within an imperial structure which was looser than Otto I's tight model of subjugation.

Otto's Magnanimity to Poland

In Poland therefore Otto created an autonomous archbishopric at Gnesen as well as its three suffragan sees at Kolberg, Cracow and Breslau. And his magnanimity extended to a remission of tribute payments previously made by Polish rulers to the emperor. These dramatic changes told the Poles that in order to join the Latin west they didn't have to become Germans and their impact on Stephen, the Hungarian prince then engaged in asserting his supremacy over other Magyar nobles, was profound. He married Gisela, sister of the duke of Bavaria, as part of a process that would orientate Hungary towards the west. Encouraged by Otto, he also opted for obedience to the see of Rome when it came to the Christianization of his recently pagan country. Accordingly, he was crowned in about December 1000 as Stephen I, the first king of Hungary, with a crown sent him by the pope.

Otto's view of himself as Peter's deputy had transformed views previously held both of the papacy and of German kingship. When he died at the age of 21 his imperial kingship had achieved a new synthesis of European cultures, one whose effects guided the religious loyalties, the dynastic allegiances and the political aspirations of millions of Europeans in the millennium that lay ahead.

The coronation of Stephen I in 1000 marked Hungary's first step towards joining the family of European Christian nations. Stephen was canonized in 1083; this equestrian statue of Stephen raising the double cross stands in the Fishermen's Bastion district of Budapest.

WILLIAM I, '*The Conqueror*', King of England

R. 1066–1087

In January 1066 William, Duke of Normandy, decided to invade England and seize that country's crown. Feudal diplomacy, quarrels and wars extending for over half a century lay behind this decision. The Norman interest in Anglo-Saxon England dated back to the alliance of 1002 when King Ethelred II of England married Emma, whose brother, Count Richard II, was William's grandfather. Two of her sons would sit on England's throne: Edward the Confessor (1042–66), son of Ethelred, and also Hardecanute (1040–2), the issue of Emma's subsequent marriage to Canute, the Danish invader and England's king (1016–35). Edward died without issue on 5 January 1066 and the English nobility acclaimed the king's brother-in-law, Harold, Earl of Wessex, as his successor. This may have been Edward's ultimate wish but it probably contradicted the king's assurances to his cousin William.

Edward had lived mostly in exile in Normandy after his father's death in 1016. Canute's marriage to Emma had been a clever ploy to stop Norman military intervention in support of her son's claim to the English throne. Edward, mindful of his mother's role in this manoeuvre, seized her English properties when he became king in 1042. But Edward's past protection in exile by his Norman relatives, as well as the ties of kinship and the king's childlessness, encouraged William's ambitions. The duke had proved helpful to Edward during a reign notable in its early years for the favour shown to Normans at the English court.

The Bayeux Tapestry illustrates the Norman Conquest of England, using a sequence of pictures with Latin captions. This detail shows William killing King Harold at the Battle of Hastings in 1066.

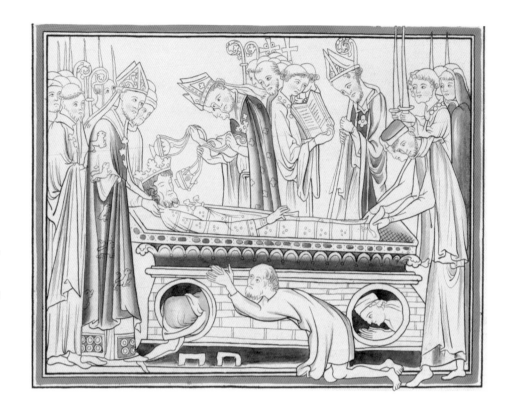

Edward the Confessor is the only English king to have been canonized. After his death on 5 January 1066 he was buried in Westminster Abbey, where William was crowned later the same year. This illustration from a 13th-century manuscript depicts the deposition of Edward's body in the tomb at Westminster.

Earl Godwine, father to Harold and England's pre-eminent noble, took a dim view of the king's Norman clique despite the fact of Edward's marriage to his daughter Edith. Edward's quarrel with Godwine led him to dismiss Edith and outlaw her entire family in 1051. This foolish policy was reversed two years later when Godwine, just before his death, ensured the restoration of his family's lands and the dismissal of Edward's Norman favourites by leading a military force against the king. Harold, succeeding his father, had demonstrated his military superiority and political skill by leading an English army against the Welsh in 1063 and negotiating with rebellious Northumbrians in 1065. Nomination to succeed to the throne would have been a recognition of Harold's dominance in England. But the accession of Harold II went against the interests of a thickset, graceless and shrewd Norman warrior keen on what he took to be his rights.

The Norman Character

Viking blood flowed in William's veins as one of the *Nortmanni* or 'men of the North'. These pagan Scandinavian pirates had been plundering and killing on their raids to the south and west from the eighth century onwards and the duke was descended from those Vikings who had established themselves in the lower Seine valley by *c.*900. The Viking Rollo was ceded lands around the mouth of the Seine by the Franks in 911 and from this base his descendants, by now known as 'Normans', had within a generation extended their rule westwards to 'Normandy'.

Conversion to Christianity and adoption of cavalry warfare did not affect the Normans' typically piratical traits: brutality, materialism, restlessness and perfidy. Readiness to learn, adapt and assimilate gave them a swift command over conquered territories and the Normans' evolution of the motte-and-bailey castle, a mound surrounded by a ditched enclosure, marked their implacable territorial penetration. Having mastered the principles of Carolingian feudalism, they turned it to their own ends and built up Europe's most centralized feudal domain in Normandy. Their championing of religious orthodoxy was typically authoritarian but their foundation of Benedictine monasteries, especially those of Bec and Caen, turned Normandy into a centre of 11th-century learning.

William's Struggle to Survive

William needed his Norman qualities in order to survive to manhood. He was the only son of Duke Robert I and succeeded when he was seven, but his mother was the concubine Arlette and William's illegitimacy was held against him. Three of his guardians died in violent circumstances and his tutor was murdered. Knighted in the Norman manner in 1042, the young duke had to confront baronial rebellions, often led by his relatives, from 1046 to 1055. Fortunately, he enjoyed the initial support of his feudal overlord, Henry I of France. Duke Robert had assisted Henry in 1031 when the king's younger brother disputed the royal succession and Henry, conscious of a debt to Normandy's dukes, helped William defeat a major rebellion in 1047. By stages the lost ducal rights and revenues were recovered. Henry at first also supported William's ambition to extend south from Normandy into Maine and his consequent campaigns against Geoffrey Martel, Count of Anjou. Further internal rebellions forced William to make peace with Geoffrey in 1052 but, by then, he was in serious negotiations with Edward.

In 1051, the year of the Confessor's decision to outlaw Godwine, William may have extracted a promise from Edward that he would succeed him. William may also have been using European diplomatic alliances to pressurize Edward. By 1053 William had married Matilda, daughter of Baldwin V of Flanders, an imperial vassal but one in open rebellion against the emperor Henry III. The fact that both Edward and William were already allied in support of Baldwin may have been used by the duke as a compelling argument for the creation of an Anglo-Norman power block.

Earl Harold Swears an Oath

By 1063 William had conquered Maine and sometime in 1064–5 Edward sent Earl Harold to Normandy on an unspecified mission to this now mighty duke. Later Norman accounts claimed that during this visit Harold swore an oath to uphold an earlier commitment by Edward to bequeath his throne to William. But in the late winter and spring of 1066 events were moving quickly: Harold's exiled brother and now sworn enemy, Tostig, Earl of Northumbria, had already offered his service to William in a possible conquest of England. Like William, marriage had made him an ally of the count of Flanders. He was now ready to invade England himself. In May he was already raiding the English coast and, by September, in alliance with King Harald III Hardraade of Norway, his forces lay off the Northumbrian coast.

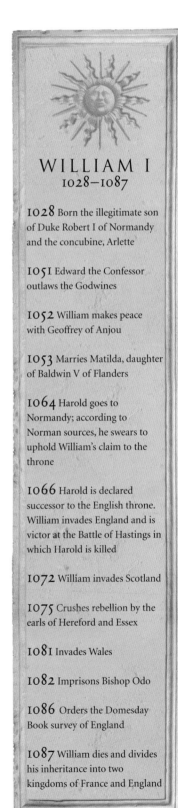

WILLIAM I
1028–1087

1028 Born the illegitimate son of Duke Robert I of Normandy and the concubine, Arlette

1051 Edward the Confessor outlaws the Godwines

1052 William makes peace with Geoffrey of Anjou

1053 Marries Matilda, daughter of Baldwin V of Flanders

1064 Harold goes to Normandy; according to Norman sources, he swears to uphold William's claim to the throne

1066 Harold is declared successor to the English throne. William invades England and is victor at the Battle of Hastings in which Harold is killed

1072 William invades Scotland

1075 Crushes rebellion by the earls of Hereford and Essex

1081 Invades Wales

1082 Imprisons Bishop Odo

1086 Orders the Domesday Book survey of England

1087 William dies and divides his inheritance into two kingdoms of France and England

Invasion and the Battle of Hastings

The Norman had to act. Strong winds detained his forces assembled by August at the mouth of the Dives river. September's westerly gales would see his fleet forced up the Channel. William regrouped at Saint-Valéry on the Somme and on 27 September, the wind having dropped to the south, he sailed for England's southeast coast, where he landed the following day and established his bridgehead at Hastings.

The victory at Hastings would orientate English kingship away from its Scandinavian associations and towards France, one version of European influence in England thereby replacing another. But the Norman victory was hardly predictable: on 25 September Harold II of England had defeated and killed both Tostig and Harald Hardraade at Stamford Bridge, near York in the north of England. William was taken by surprise when the English army emerged from the woods near Hastings on 13 October and in the next day's battle he was almost driven from the field. Displaying immense tenacity, rather than strategic flair, William regained ground lost and towards the day's end Harold fell in battle. William moved swiftly to consolidate his military position and on Christmas Day was crowned in Westminster Abbey.

Expansion, Rebellion and Consolidation

William left England quickly after his coronation, but had to return to deal with the major rebellions of 1067–71, in the course of which the native English aristocracy was destroyed. Frontier consolidation followed with the invasion of Scotland in 1072 and that of Wales in 1081, leading to the creation of 'marcher' counties along the borders. But defence of his dukedom's borders was William's major preoccupation and in the last 15 years of his life he was more often in Normandy than in England. He did not visit his kingdom at all throughout five of his years on the throne, and most of the new Anglo-Norman baronage remained with him when he was in Normandy.

England's government was left to her bishops with the extremely capable Lanfranc (the former prior of the Norman monastery at Bec), who was William's personal friend and now archbishop of Canterbury, becoming a dominant figure in English administration. This form of episcopal rule represented an English application of William's methods in Normandy where, personally presiding over synods, he had secured a church administration which was notably pliant and free of corruption. His decision to allow the English to keep their native courts and laws was also typically Norman. William, aided by his barons and bishops, would rule through the inherited structures and bend them to his will.

Within three months of his coronation William ordered the construction of a castle in the city of London. The White Tower (above) is part of the original Norman building.

The attempted rebellion of 1075 led by the earls of Hereford and of Essex, aided by a Danish fleet, was the last major outbreak of internal disorder. But in 1082, William had to arrest and imprison his half-brother Odo, another son of Arlette. As bishop of Bayeux and earl of Kent, Odo was central to the Norman regime but, wishing to travel to Italy in defence of the papacy against Emperor Henry IV, he tried to raise his own army without royal permission. This clear breach of feudal obligation had to be punished.

Domesday Book

A national assertion of William's ultimate authority took place in the same year when he took personal oaths of fealty from all of England's major landowners at Salisbury. These oaths overrode any obligations of vassalage that these magnates might have incurred to anyone other than the king. In 1085 another threatened Danish invasion was disposed of and, now convinced of the solid base to Norman rule in England, William ordered the detailed 1086 survey of his kingdom's economic resources and tenures which survives in the two volumes of the *Domesday Book*.

Normandy, though, worried him continuously, and especially since Philip I of France had joined Robert of Flanders and Canute IV of Denmark in alliance against him. William had to settle for a compromise peace with Anjou in 1081: his eldest son Robert Curthose could be count of Maine but had to be a vassal of Anjou's counts. Robert, however, was a chronic intriguer who had rebelled against his father once in 1077 and would do so again in 1083. The county of Mantes, bordering on the French royal demesne, fell to Philip's forces in 1077 and England's king died ten years later of injuries sustained while attempting to regain the towns of Chaumont, Mantes and Pontoise.

William's conquest of England was his greatest achievement but a historical irony marked its consequences. Robert Curthose's disloyalty meant that William divided his inheritance. Robert was allowed to rule in Normandy and Maine while his younger brother, William Rufus, became William II of England. Those Norman barons in England who wanted one Norman ruler to reign in both domains were frustrated. England's exceptionalism and independence had survived the 'Norman Conquest'.

ROGER II, King of Sicily

R. 1130–1154

Every year on Palm Sunday Roger II, king of Sicily, would ride Christ-like on a white donkey into church for the services that marked the start of Holy Week. If he went to the Church of Martorana in his capital of Palermo he could look at the mosaic depicting his coronation by Christ and note how the artist had given him and the Son of God much the same features.

This was appropriate enough, perhaps, since this king claimed to be God's deputy within his Sicilian kingdom which included not just the island but also the southern Italian peninsula from Calabria at its toe right up to Abruzzi just south of the papal states. The mosaics in Palermo's Palatine Chapel took up the same gratifying theme and showed him as a new David returned to rule on earth. Here the architecture and decoration showed his kingdom's cultural mix: a Latin church layout, Byzantine mosaics and a typically Arabic stalactite roof.

Roger's Sophisticated Court

On these high ecclesiastical festivals Roger was elaborately dressed as both king and priest: his tunic and dalmatic were of Sicilian silk while the king's mantle, just like his silk shoes and stockings, was deep red, a colour evoking the purple worn by the emperors of ancient Rome and Byzantium. The royal tombs that he commissioned made the same insistent point since they were made of porphyry, the purple marble used by Roman emperors. But this king also had a harem, a Saracen bodyguard and an Arab chef. Muslim poets, benefiting from his patronage, sang Roger's praises at court while to the south of Palermo, again in the Arab style, there were parks, lakes and summer houses built for a ruler's delight. This was the Mediterranean's most sophisticated courtly milieu. But behind all the refinement lay the victories won by the Norman aggression and ambition dominant in Roger's genes.

The Martorana church – formally known as Santa Maria dell'Ammiraglio – in Palermo has a sumptuous Byzantine-style interior. While the church is best known for its gold mosaics, notably one depicting Roger II being crowned by Christ, the ceiling contains a number of spectacular fresco paintings, as seen here.

The Norman Conquest of Sicily

From the beginning of the 11th century Norman adventurers moved into southern Italy and organized a series of local insurrections, which overthrew Byzantium's precarious presence in the region. Roger was the son of Count Roger I of Sicily who, with his brother Robert Guiscard, had led the last phase of conquest. Bari on the mainland fell in 1071 and Palermo, the most significant emirate on the mostly Arab-populated island of Sicily, was taken in 1072. In 1105 Roger succeeded in boyhood to his father's title, with his mother as regent; he assumed the reins of government in 1112. He then sidelined his Guiscard cousins who were facing baronial rebellions in their south Italian domains. Having given them military support he received in return control of their Sicilian territories. Calabria, a mostly Greek area on Italy's toe, had already been taken by his father from the Byzantines in the 1060s. In 1127 Roger invaded neighbouring Apulia in a dramatic move following the death of its Norman duke. Both areas were now incorporated in his kingdom.

Seeds of Conflict with the Papacy

But what Roger wanted was a crown and the authority unique to a king. In 1130 there was a disputed papal election and Roger supported the rebel Pope Anacletus II whose emissary duly crowned him that year in Palermo. After Anacletus died in 1138 Roger captured the rival Pope Innocent II who then obliged him by confirming the kingly title in 1139. Sicily's relationship to the papacy was unusually close ever since Roger I had been made an apostolic legate in 1098 by Urban II. This gave the count the right to appoint bishops and collect church revenues in Sicily but, far from being a concession of its authority, the papacy saw it as a mere expedient. Sicily had been Muslim for centuries and had no Latin church administration. What Christians there were followed the Greek rite and there was also a large Jewish population. Even under Roger II western Sicily remained mostly Arab. The church could not achieve the island's mass Christianization on its own and Roger I was the only effective agent available for this particular aspect of the papacy's general crusading policy. The popes therefore continued to regard kings of Sicily as vassals whose authority was derived from the see of Peter.

Towering over the coastal town of Cefalù in Sicily, this cathedral was built on the orders of Roger II and intended as his personal mausoleum. A three-aisled columned basilica with an enormous transept and choir, it demonstrates Norman influences and incorporates elements of the Byzantine and Islamic styles that were already present in Sicily.

Here, however, lay the seeds of conflict. Roger II claimed to be an apostolic legate just like his father but the papacy insisted that the honour was not an inheritable office. The wording of his title as king mattered enormously and the one he settled on, ' King of Sicily, of the duchy of Apulia and the principality of Capua', reflected papal concern. As papal vassal states these lands had to be acknowledged as having a separate existence. Still, Roger now had his crown and popes agreed that there was only one king who ruled in these territories.

Roger's Assembly

Roger could draw on other sources to assert his authority. Sicilian history supplied him with a precedent since there had been dynastic rulers here in classical antiquity when the island contained Greek colonies. The fact that the technical Greek term for them was *tyrannos* was a problem given the word's new associations – as papal apologists pointed out. But Constantine's notion of a supreme ruler uniting spiritual and temporal power in his own person could be put to Norman use and was dutifully illustrated in the mosaics of Greek craftsmen. Justinian's heritage was a major intellectual resource since his jurists showed how rebellion against a divinely instituted ruler was a form of sacrilege. The emperor's law codes, the basis of Roman law, circulated widely in 11th-century south Italy, and heavily influenced Roger's own code promulgated at the Assizes of Ariano in 1140. Feudal notions, by now common in western Europe, could also be pressed into service. In 1129 Roger assembled his barons at Melfi in central southern Italy and at this *parliamentum*, or gathering of nobles, he proclaimed a land-peace. This was a very Norman baronial endorsement of a feudal overlord. And the mixture of influences deployed to confirm Roger's rule did not end there. If he seemed like a Greek *basileus* to his Greek subjects, his Arab ones looked on him as the latest *emir* set over them.

The one theme common to all these strategies was Roger's determination to rule his kingdom as a single territorial unit forming no part of a wider empire. He might delegate some powers to feudal lords but expected military service in return, and because he controlled the rights of inheritance to

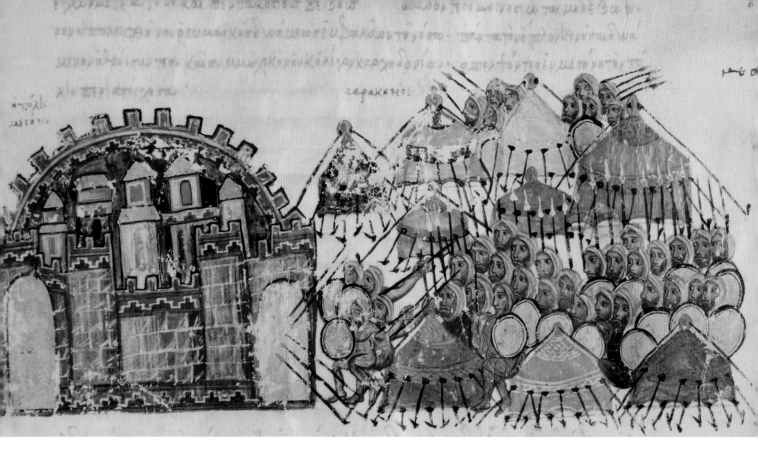

Arabs, or Saracens, ruled Sicily for almost two centuries. This 14th-century manuscript illumination depicts the Saracen assault on Messina in the northeast of the island in 843. The Saracens' stronghold in Sicily came to an end in 1091 but their contribution to the island's science, agriculture, commerce and the arts was long-lasting.

fiefs he could bar vassals he deemed unsuitable. Only the king's courts, rather than those of abbots and counts, could try capital cases and justiciars, judges appointed by the crown, travelled deep into the remote southern Italian countryside to dispense Roger's justice. Baronial power remained a significant fact on most of the mainland but things were different on the island of Sicily and in Calabria. Since most of the island consisted of royal demesne land under direct government control, the king was also its landlord. A Norman bureaucracy controlled the towns' administration, the activities of their merchants and the organization of supplies. The monarchy also had extensive rights over salt production, while iron and steel manufacture was an exclusive regalian right. This gave Roger an unusually concentrated degree of economic power regulated by a civil service built on Norman foundations and supplemented by Greek and Arab influences.

Sicilian Wealth and Trade

The agricultural wealth was based on Sicily's fabled, well-watered fertility. In Roger's reign Sicilian wheat and grain exports were feeding a European world whose population levels were rising quickly. Trade was booming too with buoyant demand for the Sicilian luxury goods which travelled along the trade routes to Genoa and Pisa, Venice and Provence. Sicily's navy protected those routes and, since it was so central to state affairs, its head, or *emir*, was also the king's chief minister. Naval power attacked the Saracens whose raids had plagued the western Mediterranean and it also enabled Roger to establish a foothold in North Africa where he intervened in the disputes between local Arab rulers.

The revenue riches were spent on waging war. A long insurrection on the mainland, supported by Emperor Lothair II, threatened Roger's rule there until the late 1130s. But war and conquest could produce good returns in the form of booty, tribute and tax receipts. One of many raids on the Greek coastline led to the seizure of Thebes's silk workers who were taken and then established in Palermo's royal workshop. Roger's monarchy also bribed on a grand scale – especially in Lombardy where Sicily needed the local towns to maintain their resistance to the encroaching German emperors. If Lombardy fell, he reasoned, Sicily would be next.

The Book of Roger

The money was also spent on cultural display, court life and patronage of learning. Roger's chief intellectual interest was science and he commissioned the North African Muslim al-Idrisi to produce the *Kitab Rujar* (Book of Roger) which aimed to describe the known world's natural resources. Sicily was also an important centre for the translation of ancient Greek texts into Latin, and Roger's patronage in this area contributed to a major cultural renaissance in 12th-century Europe.

Roger's kingdom was intended to be a Latin one and this proved to be the main trend in 12th-century Sicily at the expense of its Greek component. His government issued its documents in Greek, Latin and Arabic, but that was a pragmatic need and the only way to ensure that the king's will was understood by his subjects. Showing favours to Muslims at court was Roger's political way of keeping his Greek and Norman nobles in their place by demonstrating that he had another reliable clientage system. His smattering of Arabic and personal cultivation certainly came in useful when he succeeded in getting trade agreements out of the Fatimid rulers of Egypt. Domestically, though, Roger's aims were hardly multicultural and Muslims promoted to the highest levels in his service were expected to convert.

Roger's Legacy of Kingship

The marriage in 1184 of Roger's posthumous daughter, Constance, to Henry VI, son and heir to the German emperor, Frederick I Barbarossa, changed the political and military landscape of the central Mediterranean. Sicily and the empire were reconciled by a personal union between the dynasty of Sicilian Normans and that of the Hohenstaufen, although Sicily's crown retained its independence within the empire. The marriage produced the emperor, Frederick II, who inherited the abilities of both his grandfathers as well as their defining ambitions: Barbarossa's southward thrust into Italy and Roger's exalted notion of a supreme kingship. In 1204 the forces of the Fourth Crusade captured and sacked Constantinople. From now on Greek emperors were unconvincing representatives of the ancient idea of a universal empire whose rulers enjoyed both spiritual and temporal power. Frederick's empire would now perform that role and as a result the papacy's greatest fear had been realized: the hostility of a united force threatening it simultaneously from both north and south.

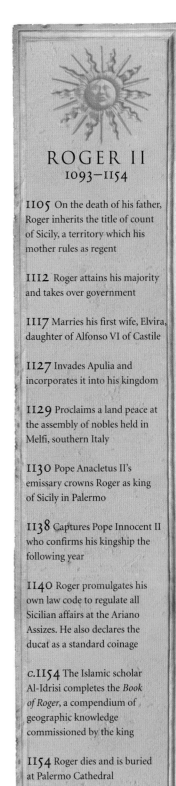

ROGER II
1093–1154

1105 On the death of his father, Roger inherits the title of count of Sicily, a territory which his mother rules as regent

1112 Roger attains his majority and takes over government

1117 Marries his first wife, Elvira, daughter of Alfonso VI of Castile

1127 Invades Apulia and incorporates it into his kingdom

1129 Proclaims a land peace at the assembly of nobles held in Melfi, southern Italy

1130 Pope Anacletus II's emissary crowns Roger as king of Sicily in Palermo

1138 Captures Pope Innocent II who confirms his kingship the following year

1140 Roger promulgates his own law code to regulate all Sicilian affairs at the Ariano Assizes. He also declares the ducat as a standard coinage

*c.***1154** The Islamic scholar Al-Idrisi completes the *Book of Roger*, a compendium of geographic knowledge commissioned by the king

1154 Roger dies and is buried at Palermo Cathedral

SURYAVARMAN II, King of Cambodia
R. 1113–1150

The shrine raised by Cambodia's ruler in celebration of Vishnu, the four-armed deity that protected the universe and all the other Hindu gods, was Angkor's largest and most significant temple, or *Wat*. Precise astronomical calculations determined the symmetrical details of the building's location at this Khmer royal capital and Hindu cosmology permeated its architectural evocation of India's mythical Mount Meru, home of the gods. The series of rectangular walls encasing Angkor Wat's central shrine represented Meru's mountain chain, while the stone-lined moat that enclosed the entire temple symbolized the encircling cosmic oceans.

Suryavarman II's major building project marked his identification with Vishnu's divine glory as source of all existence, but it also portrayed his own earthly successes. The sinuous sculptures of *apsarases*, or nymphs, represented the erotic joys awaiting victorious kings, conquering generals and devout saints in the hereafter, while bas-relief carvings decorated with gold leaf on the walls illustrated the triumphant progress of the king's mounted warriors. Yet more bas-reliefs recorded episodes from the *Mahabharata* and *Ramayana*, the Indian Hindu epics which had entered deep into the Cambodian folk consciousness. Sacral kingship had invariably affirmed its unique ability to ensure the realm's prosperity and safety. But Angkor Wat also showed the institution's capacity to delight.

The Great City – Angkor Thom

The tradition which maintained that the mountains were especially sacred as the dwelling places of the gods was already well established among the peoples of Southeast Asia in the first millennium AD. Cambodia's Khmer population had

One of five towers on the great temple at Angkor Wat, which are thought to represent the peaks of Mount Meru, home to the Hindu gods. From their capital at Angkor the Khmer kings ruled over a vast domain reaching from China to Vietnam and to the Bay of Bengal.

good reason therefore to regard their entire capital as an especially sacred place since it had been built around just such a mountain located in the country's northwest. During the initial period following its late ninth-century foundation, the city had been known as Yasodharapura, named after Yasovarman I, the Khmer ruler (*c*.890–*c*.910) who based his royal administration here. Only in the early 13th century did the entire site and complex of associated buildings acquire its definitive title of Angkor Thom – 'the Great City'.

Angkor was by then the capital of an empire extending from the tip of the Indo-Chinese peninsula in its south to the Chinese border lying to its north, and from Vietnam in the east across to the Bay of Bengal in the west. Buddhism, still an elite religion in 13th-century Cambodia, would become a religion of the people during the mass conversions of the next two centuries. But the very word Angkor, derived from the ancient Sanskrit word for city, showed the profound influence of India's Hindu religion and culture on the peoples of the region since the beginning of the first millennium AD.

The apsarases, or dancers, that decorate the walls and pillars of many Cambodian temples were a Khmer innovation. Typically carved in bas-relief, the figures were inspired by stories from Hindu mythology that told of heavenly female nymphs who were born to dance for the gods.

Jayavarman II's Reign

Numerous small kingdoms had flourished in the Cambodian region during the sixth to the eighth centuries and one of the regional princes in eastern Cambodia had taken the title of Jayavarman II in 790. Having asserted control over the Mekong river valley, Jayavarman was re-consecrated in northwestern Cambodia as *chakravartin*. This was a decisive enhancement of his authority for the ancient Sanskrit word not only signified status as a world ruler, it also denoted that the ruler was one especially favoured by the gods on account of his moral virtue.

In 802 Jayavarman rejected vassalage to a power on the island of Sumatra, asserted the independence of what was then called Kambuja-desa and was installed as *devaraja* or god-king and, as such, a manifestation of the Hindu god Siva. Elaborate Hindu ritual marked the ceremony in which sacred kingship was communicated to the new ruler through the agency of the phallic idol, which represented Siva's power. The religious rituals of Cambodian kings evolved from the divine status that had been ascribed to them: they maintained the land's fertility through their intercession with the gods and their subjects owed them military service in return.

Khmer Temples

Cambodia's overwhelmingly Khmer population gave it an unusual degree of ethnic homogeneity compared to its Southeast Asian neighbours, but the history of its throne following Jayavarman's death in 850 was one of rebellion and usurpation. The reign of Indravarman I (r. –*c*.890), though himself probably a usurper, anticipated two ways in which royal authority might be restored and elevated. The king's decision to build Bakong, the first Cambodian temple made

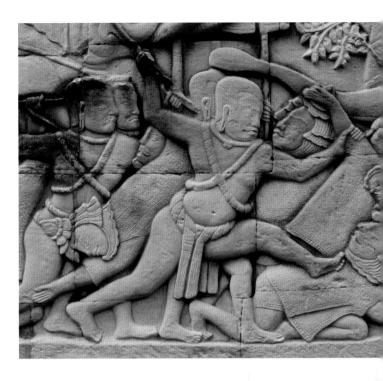

of stone rather than brick, was a major influence on the later architectural development at Angkor and its associated revival of sacral power. Indravarman also showed how reservoirs, canals and lakes could form an irrigation scheme controlling the flow of Cambodia's rivers, thereby allowing rice to be grown in previously unproductive areas. This agricultural revolution extended the areas under royal control and enabled Cambodia's kings to feed the vast labour force required to build the country's steadily expanding number of elaborate temples.

Yasovarman I (r. 890–c.910), son of Indravarman, established his new capital on the Angkor site, building city walls to defend it on either side. Imitating his father, in 893 he ordered work to begin on his own 'temple mountain' of the Bakheng ('mighty ancestor'). Raised on the city's mountain, the building with its 108 tower shrines arranged on terraces surrounding a central pyramid dominated the city below. Just like the later Angkor Wat, the Bakheng was designed to illustrate a parallel with Mount Meru, and a power at once both sacred and secular was meant to emanate from the mountain and from the great building erected on its slopes. The entire city was therefore a microcosm of the world and it was pervaded by an insistent symbolic system which served the purposes of Cambodian kingship.

In the 13th-century Bayon Temple built by Jayavarman VII at Angkor Thom, two series of bas-reliefs depict both historical and mythological events. The detail above shows Khmer warriors fighting the Cham army.

Angkor's other temples represented those mountains supposed to mark the edge of the known world, while its water system was interpreted as signifying the patterns of the world's major rivers. Nonetheless, the canals and reservoirs were now also ensuring a more pragmatic function as a huge acreage of rice fields resulted from the very effective irrigation of the central Cambodian plain.

A New Dynasty – Suryavarman I and II

These technological successes and architectural glories had been achieved by a workforce drawn widely from the territories under Khmer dynastic control. But Cambodian internal turbulence nonetheless continued into the beginning of the tenth century, and Angkor had been abandoned for some 30 years preceding the restoration of central authority from the mid-tenth century onwards. Although he was yet another usurper, Suryavarman I (r. c.1004–c.1050) was a commanding figure during this renaissance and he restored to the crown those territories that had become semi-autonomous. The empire of the Khmer now expanded westwards into Thailand and, with commercial prosperity spreading across the imperial lands, the number of Cambodian cities increased from some 20 to almost 50. Renewed fragility within the power structures typified the late 11th century but the arrival of a new dynasty, whose most significant ruler was

The Bayon Temple stands at the centre of Angkor Thom, Jayavarman VII's 13th-century capital. The construction of a temple primarily designed for Buddhist worship marked a turning point for the previously Hindu population.

Suryavarman II, meant that Cambodia survived and then advanced. The new king followed through his predecessors' advances into Thailand but his most significant military initiative was the campaign against the kingdom of Champa, based in central and south Vietnam, following its earlier attacks on Angkor.

The Angkor of Suryavarman II was a city in which technology, religion and politics combined to illustrate and enforce royal power. Angkor had always been popularly venerated as a sacred city. Its command of the river-controlling technology which brought agricultural fertility and therefore the means of life to the Cambodian plain was yet another reason for popular worship. Royal ceremonies maintained the city's status and cultivated the dynasty's reputation, with the king performing the role of an intercessor on behalf of his people in the religious rituals which sought to ensure that the rains would fall and so continue to produce the source of life from an irrigated land.

Cambodia Becomes Vulnerable to Invasion

Court personnel combined the duties of imperial administrators with those of religious officialdom, since they served the needs and wishes of a king who would be united in death with the god he had claimed as his patron. Construction of the irrigation structures had produced mounds of earth on the Cambodian plain, and these were turned into artificially constructed mountains which supported the shrines containing images both of the gods and of Cambodian royalty. But the temple, which was Angkor's glory and the king's pride, may also have imposed such immense strain on the country's economic resources and manpower capacity that Cambodia became vulnerable to invasion.

In 1177 Champa forces again advanced into the country from Vietnam and sacked Angkor, the first time this had happened in Cambodia's history. This constituted a major military challenge to the Khmer kings, as well as an immense religious one. Royal intercessions with the deities, intended to protect Cambodian territories, had evidently failed. But the campaign of recovery launched by Jayavarman VII (r. 1181–1220) was remarkable. By 1181 he had driven the Cham out of his own country, invaded theirs and then made all of Champa an imperial province. He celebrated his achievement by building his own city of Angkor Thom close to the original settlement. This civic extension contained 16 kilometres (10 miles) of moats, yet more vast irrigation schemes and architectural complexes including the Bayon Temple.

A Change to Buddhism

The king's decision to attach himself to one of the Buddhist *boddhisatvas* or saints rather than embrace a Hindu god as his personal deity, along with his adherence to the Mahayana branch of Buddhism, broke 400 years of Khmer royal tradition. Buddhism had spread into Cambodia from India centuries previously and Hindu–Buddhist relations had been remarkably amicable. But this was the first time Buddhism had acquired a Khmer ruler as its patron, and the shift may reflect the royal disenchantment with Hinduism following the Cham invasion. The subsequent spread of Theravada Buddhism, the religion's older and simpler version, would have a profound influence on the Cambodian people.

Jayavarman VII presided over the last great age of Khmer kingship and territorial expansion ceased on his death. Kingdoms of Thais in what is now northern Thailand were able to assert independence of Khmer Cambodia during the 14th century and in 1351 a major Thai presence was established in the area, which became known as Siam. It became a dominant regional power and was able to push the Khmer people down towards the Mekong Delta. Theravada Buddhism had now become the religion of the mass of the Cambodian population and it replaced sacral kingship as the focus of popular belief and loyalty. By the early 15th century the kingdom had dwindled to a region surrounding Phnom Penh. Angkor had been abandoned, its very existence an object of speculation and subject of rumour in the outside world as the jungle advanced across the courtyards and temples where Khmer kings had once strode.

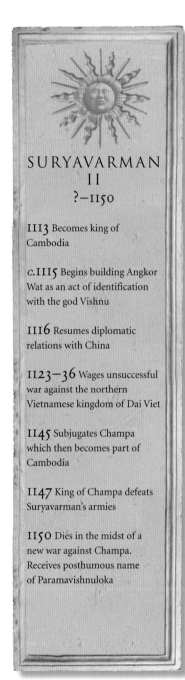

SURYAVARMAN II
?–1150

1113 Becomes king of Cambodia

*c.***1115** Begins building Angkor Wat as an act of identification with the god Vishnu

1116 Resumes diplomatic relations with China

1123–36 Wages unsuccessful war against the northern Vietnamese kingdom of Dai Viet

1145 Subjugates Champa which then becomes part of Cambodia

1147 King of Champa defeats Suryavarman's armies

1150 Dies in the midst of a new war against Champa. Receives posthumous name of Paramavishnuloka

ELEANOR OF AQUITAINE, Queen of France and of England

R. 1137–1152, 1154–1204

In her youth Eleanor was high-spirited and strong-willed, and even in old age she continued to play an important part in affairs of state. Her tomb effigy shows the queen in pious contemplation.

While they were travelling together on crusade in the Holy Land during 1147–9 Louis VII, king of France, fell out of love with his queen. This daughter of William X, duke of Aquitaine and count of Poitiers, was heiress to domains greater than those of France's kings, and on William's death in 1137 she had inherited the duchy.

The following month Eleanor married Louis in a dynastic alliance first conceived of by his father Louis VI and by Abbé Suger, the royal adviser, as a way of extending the authority of France's Capetian dynasty. But the young king also fell in love with his beautiful and well-read wife who exercised political as well as personal influence on him.

Crusading

Crusading activity to liberate Palestine's sacred Christian sites from Islamic rule had been a particular cause of French monarchs ever since their compatriot Pope Urban II had proclaimed the First Crusade in 1095. The Latin kingdom of Jerusalem, extending from the borders of modern Turkey to those of Egypt, was founded as a result of the success of that crusade. But by the 1140s the kingdom, a French feudal outpost ruled by expatriate nobles, was exposed to the formidable campaigning of the Syrian emir Nur al-Din and a Second Crusade became necessary.

The jealous king, conscious of Eleanor's flirtatiousness, did not wish to leave her in Paris and insisted that she join him on crusade. This proved a foolish and provoking act. Not only was the journey long, it was also plagued by hunger and

A miniature painting from a manuscript entitled 'History of the Emperors' portrays the battle which culminated in the conquest of Antioch in 1098 by western European armies during the First Crusade. Almost 50 years later Louis VII would embark on the Second Crusade, which would end in failure.

Middle Eastern heat. Eleanor, with her strong will, was irritated by signs of her husband's weakness and she took refuge in the arms of her young uncle, Raymond of Aquitaine, prince of Antioch. In 1148 the crusaders were attempting, unsuccessfully, to take Damascus – by which time it was rumoured the queen was having an affair with a Moorish slave.

Eleanor's Divorce and Marriage

Defeats inflicted on him by Nur al-Din compounded Louis's personal misery while at home his younger brother, the comte de Drieux, threatened rebellion. Writing from Paris, Suger told the king that he had to return immediately and assert himself instead of being '… like a prisoner in exile. As for the Queen … we counsel you … to conceal your resentment until, having come home by God's grace, you can settle that matter with all others …'.

When the royal couple did return Suger was adamant that Louis should not divorce Eleanor. Both her inheritance and her flair for administration had made her central to the kingdom's interests, but Suger's death shortly afterwards enabled a humiliated king to follow his instincts. Using the pretext that he and Eleanor had been too closely related, he obtained an annulment of marriage from the pope in 1152.

Within two months of that decree being finalized, Eleanor had married Henry Plantagenet, England's future king – Henry II. The lands of Aquitaine had, in feudal style, reverted to her on her divorce and control of this rich domain was therefore transferred across the Channel on her marriage to a ruthless English warlord who would eventually inflict defeat and further ignominy on the French king.

Eleanor's Influence on Europe

Eleanor's long life and the influence of her progeny, as well as her own influence on them, make her a figure central to the history of 12th-century Europe. The eight children she bore Henry Plantagenet included Geoffrey, duke of Brittany as well as Richard the Lionheart, the knightly hero of the Third Crusade and king of England from 1189 to 1199. He was succeeded by another of her sons, John, nicknamed Lackland or 'Sans Terre'. Her daughters were Matilda who married Henry the Lion, duke of Saxony and Bavaria; Eleanor, the wife of Castile's ruler Alfonso VIII; and Joan who married first William II, king of Sicily and then Raymond VI, count of Toulouse.

Eleanor's love of music and poetry may have been inherited from her grandfather, William IX, an early troubadour poet. This scene portraying a troubadour comes from a late 13th-century manuscript, 'Cantigas de Santa Maria' (Songs to the Virgin Mary).

Her personal involvement in their careers placed her at the centre of European military and diplomatic policy. But she also adorned the culture of the age as the greatest single patron of the tradition of courtly love whose troubadour poets were among the brightest stars of the Aquitainian court at Poitiers.

Hildegard of Bingen, the German abbess, poet, mystic and composer, and Heloise, the wife of the Parisian theologian and philosopher Peter Abelard, are two other women whose intellects show the expansiveness of the 12th-century intellectual milieu. But Eleanor's position also enabled her to extend artistic patronage and to display her aesthetic taste as an aspect of regal power. *Amour courtois* and its idealization of physical passion in a neo-religious cult of love was an international phenomenon which extended from Aquitaine and Provence to the courts of northern Italy and then into Germany.

Artistic Patronage

Eleanor's patronage was fundamental in establishing the movement's aristocratic appeal and explains the presence in England of the Provençal troubadour poet Bernard de Ventadour during 1152–5. She also supported another major literary movement, the *matière de Bretagne* or legends of Brittany, a collection of prose tales concerning the legendary early British king, Arthur. These originally Welsh legends had been compiled by Geoffrey of Monmouth in his *Historia Regum Britanniae* of 1135–8, and Eleanor's patronage of their further evolution forms part of a Franco-British culture which developed rapidly during the short-lived 'Angevin empire' presided over by her new husband.

Henry II's Angevin Empire

Henry, 11 years Eleanor's junior, had succeeded his father as duke of Normandy in 1150 and then as count of Anjou in 1151. Through his mother Matilda, the daughter of Henry I who was William the Conqueror's youngest and ablest son, he was related to the English royal house. Following Henry's 1153 invasion of England, King Stephen accepted him as a co-ruler on the English throne. Stephen's death in the following year gave Henry an extensive domain which, including Eleanor's Aquitaine, spread from Scotland through England and then along the whole of western France to the Pyrenees. He received homage among the Welsh nobility having invaded, but not conquered, their country in 1157. A subsequent expedition of southern Welsh barons established an Anglo-Norman ascendancy in the Irish province of Leinster in 1169 and Henry also received homage from Scotland's king, Malcolm III, in 1174.

Although Henry's campaigning meant that he only spent some 14 years in England during a 34-year reign, his renewal of the kingdom's Anglo-Norman institutions makes him one of the great administrative geniuses of English history. His Constitution of Clarendon (1164) asserted the rights of the crown

ELEANOR OF AQUITAINE
1122–1204

1137 Eleanor's father, William X, duke of Aquitaine and count of Poitiers, dies. Eleanor inherits his territories. Eleanor is married to Louis VII of France

1152 Louis VII has his marriage to Eleanor annulled. Within two months she marries Henry Plantagenet – the future Henry II of England

1173–4 Eleanor and the king are estranged and he detains her in custody

1189 Henry II dies and Eleanor is released. Her son, Richard the Lionheart, becomes king and Eleanor acts as regent when he is on crusade

1192 Richard is imprisoned by the emperor Henry VI

1194 Richard returns to England after Eleanor personally negotiates his freedom

1199 Richard dies and John succeeds to the throne

1202 John frees Eleanor at Mirebeau-en-Poitou

1204 Eleanor dies and is buried at Fontevrault alongside Henry II and Richard I

over the church in questions such as episcopal appointments, clerical immunity and appeals to Rome. He was intimately involved in the work of the inner council of ministers which sat as the Exchequer, and his Assize of Clarendon (1166) formulated many of the practices of the English common law as well as the criminal justice system. Trial by jury replaced ordeal by battle, and a national network of courts emerged presided over by the king's judges.

Eleanor's governmental role was especially important during her husband's absence abroad. But although this was initially a good partnership she grew intolerant of his affairs and played a role in the reign's two disasters: Henry's conflict with his former chancellor Thomas Becket, now archbishop of Canterbury, and the king's series of quarrels with his sons.

Louis VII's hostility to his former wife extended also to her husband, and he was active in supporting Becket's defence of church autonomy. The archbishop's murder by a group of Henry's knights in 1170 caused a European sensation and, although not instigated by the king, he was regarded as ultimately responsible.

Henry's alienation of his four sons who survived infancy resulted from his habit of dividing dominions among them while reserving full authority to himself. In 1170 he crowned his son Henry as co-regent but, discovering himself to be without real power, the young king turned against him and in 1173 he opposed his father's proposal to find territories for John at Geoffrey's expense. Richard joined the protest and was supported by Eleanor. Louis VII aided the resulting general revolt of the barons which spread through England and Normandy until Henry contained it in 1174.

Captured in France
Eleanor was captured while seeking refuge in France and kept in custody until her husband's death. A second filial rebellion broke out in 1181 when the two brothers, Henry and Richard, quarrelled over the government of Aquitaine. Young Henry's death in 1183 eased matters but Aquitaine flared up as an issue in the following year since Richard resented John being asked to run the domain. The king's further attempts at finding John an inheritance resulted in Richard joining a coalition against Henry led by France's new king, Philip II Augustus, a greater warrior than his father Louis VII. Henry had to concede defeat just before dying near Tours in 1189.

Eleanor Resumes Active Politics
Her husband's death revived Eleanor's career as a dynast. She was released from custody and resumed active politics while preparing for her son Richard's coronation. Running the English administration while Richard was on crusade, she successfully thwarted the intrigues of John and Philip II Augustus against the

king. While on his return journey to England in 1192 Richard was captured by Leopold, duke of Austria, whom he had insulted, and he was subsequently held prisoner by the German emperor, Henry VI, who demanded the colossal ransom of 150,000 marks for his release. Eleanor arranged for the payment of most of this sum and went in person to collect her son from his captivity in 1294.

Eleanor Protects the English Crown

Eleanor feared that John's accession to the throne in 1199 would imperil the entire Plantagenet structure. Now nearly 80, she crossed the Pyrenees in 1200 to fetch her granddaughter Blanche from the Castilian court and married her to the French king's son, hoping to establish peace between the Capetians and the Plantagenets. She also secured John's French possessions by organizing the defence of Anjou and Aquitaine against the aggression of her grandson Arthur of Brittany. At Mirebeau-en-Poitou in August 1202 her forces held out until John was able to relieve them and defeat Arthur.

Henry II, whose tomb effigy is seen here, was buried at Fontevrault Abbey in Anjou, western France. It was to the convent at Fontevrault that Eleanor retired a few years before her death. Eleanor's tomb lies next to her husband's and that of her son, Richard I.

End of Empire

She died two years later in the same year that Philip II Augustus entered Rennes and then captured Rouen, the Angevin capital in France, followed by all of Normandy. This was the end of Henry II's Angevin empire. Aquitaine however had reverted to Eleanor on Richard's death, and when she died its title was united with the English crown. The struggle for Aquitaine formed part of the Anglo-French 100 Years' War until French forces asserted control over the last remnants of English authority there in 1453 during the conflict's latter stages. But if Eleanor's territorial inheritance was lost to the English crown, her half a century as England's queen left a more enduring legacy: the profound impact of France's culture on the English imagination.

KUBLAI KHAN, Great Khan of the Mongols and Emperor of the Chinese

R. 1260–1294

In 1271 Kublai Khan issued a declaration which both distanced him from his Mongolian past and whose terms signalled his ambition to be a true emperor of the Chinese. Kublai had already, in 1260, instituted a reign period, a Chinese practice whose dating system was a feature of bureaucratic order alien to nomadic warriors. But this later imperial decision was an even more significant step since it involved adopting a Chinese phrase, Ta Yuan, or 'Great Origin', as his dynasty's name.

Kublai Khan, the founder and first emperor of the Yuan dynasty. He was the grandson of Genghis Khan, who led the Mongol invasion into China in the early 13th century.

Kublai retained his overlordship of the other Mongol khanates established in central Asia and Iran but this title was increasingly nominal. Besides which, he had long since surrounded himself with Chinese scholar-officials whom he found personally congenial, although he showed no sign of trusting them with real power. Kublai's proclamation of a new dynasty was intended to ally his personal power with the traditions bequeathed by past Chinese emperors. Yet the phrase he had adopted was an innovation so far as his new subjects were concerned. Previous Chinese dynastic names had referred to the rulers' original territorial base, as in the case of the Han, Chou and Ch'in. Kublai Khan's adoption of a non-geographic term showed that he was still a new kind of ruler in Chinese history.

Birth and Death of the Ch'in Dynasty

The northern Chinese regions conquered by Genghis Khan (c.1162–1227), Kublai's grandfather, in the 1210s had long experience of 'barbarian' rule by the Juchen from Manchuria, who had formed an empire that covered much of inner Asia and the whole of northern China. A Sung alliance had helped them

This detail from a 12th-century painting, 'The Qing Ming Festival by the Riverside', provides a vivid representation of everyday life in China during the period before Mongol rule.

to overthrow their overlords, the Khitan tribe who, as the Liao
dynasty, governed Manchuria, Mongolia and northeastern
China. However the Sung emperors – who were also contesting
Liao dominance – soon discovered that their enemy's enemy
was no friend as the Juchen proceeded to attack the Sung. Once
in control the Juchen adopted the Chinese name of Ch'in to
mark their dynastic rule (1115–1234), and their regime evolved
its own version of indigenous bureaucratic traditions in order
to rule northern China.

In Xanadu did Kubla Khan
A stately pleasure-dome decree:
Where Alph, the sacred river, ran
Through caverns measureless to man
Down to a sunless sea.
So twice five miles of fertile ground
With walls and towers were girdled round ...

Kubla Khan BY Samuel Taylor Coleridge

The Ch'in maintained a rigorous cultural and ethnic separation from the local
population, banned Chinese clothing and customs from its armies and remained
true to its own tribal traditions of government for the purposes of controlling
its inner Asian territories. The Ch'in state in northern China however became
increasingly vulnerable to the Mongol advance. Chung-tu (modern Beijing), the
Ch'in capital, was taken in 1215 and, in its much reduced territorial form, the
state survived as a precarious buffer zone between Sung China and the Mongols.
Genghis Khan's death in 1227 led to a brief suspension of campaigning, but by
1230 the Mongol cavalry was once again on the offensive. Sung China, hoping to
regain some of its northern territories, formed an alliance with the Mongols who
by 1234 had established complete control over Ch'in territories. Sung's northern
boundary therefore became the Mongol state's southern one.

The Cultural Achievements of the Sung Dynasty

Sung cultural achievements marked a high point in Chinese artistic history. The
pioneering use of movable type in the 11th century led to a mass printing of the
Confucian classics and accompanied the high literacy rates achieved in private
academies and state schools alike. The system of competitive examination for
civil service entry was at its most rigorous under the Sung and the period's
artistic refinement produced landscape painting of the highest quality, as well
as pottery characterized by purity of colour and a technically advanced glaze.

Sung musicians may have adopted the two-string fiddle from the Mongols but
their artistry was part of a high musical culture far removed from Mongol wailing
especially in the evolution of a new genre, that of the *tz'u*, or sung poems. This
refinement was entirely alien to steppe barbarism and in 1126 the Sung northern
capital of Pien-ching, a city celebrated for the beauty of its tall pagodas, was
burnt to the ground by the Juchen.

Conquest of the Sung

The Mongols who prepared to resume their southern campaign in 1250 were
equally indifferent to Sung culture, and with the extinction of the dynasty in 1279
foreign invaders were in occupation of the whole of China for the first time in its

history. Yet the country was also united under a single ruler for the first time since the T'ang dynasty (618–907), a fact that explains Kublai's ambition for his reign.

Kublai Khan's Xanadu

Kublai's distancing from his origins was first evident in 1260 when he moved the Mongolian capital from Karakorum to Shang-tu (or Upper Capital) in inner Mongolia, the site of his summer palace and subject of western speculation as 'Xanadu'. On 5 May of that year he was elected 'great khan' in succession to his brother, Emperor Mongke, at a *kuriltai,* or general assembly, held in Shang-tu. But another brother, Arigboge, announced his own succession to the khanate in a rival *kuriltai* held at Karakorum shortly afterwards. Arigboge eventually submitted to Kublai's rule in 1264 and died two years afterwards but other forms of this family rivalry persisted.

Family Rivalries

In 1269 the tribes in Mongolia recognized Kaidu, great-grandson of Genghis Khan, as their legitimate khan. Kaidu's power base extended to Turkestan and included Karakorum inside Mongolia: he maintained an unremitting campaign against Kublai's authority within these areas and utterly rejected any Mongol assimilation into Chinese culture. Kublai kept his summer residence at Shang-tu but in 1267 he transferred the centre of his government to Chung-tu. It was here that he ordered the construction of a new walled city, later to be renamed Ta-tu ('Great Capital') complete with palaces and administrative offices.

The Polo Family

He had turned his back on the Mongol warrior aristocracy of the steppe but retained a life-long suspicion of his Chinese subjects. Kublai therefore appointed a large number of foreigners to official posts, including the Polo family of Venice, Niccolo and his brother Maffeo along with Marco, Niccolo's son. Having first

Stones from the ruins of Karakorum were used to build the 16th-century Erdene Zuu monastery which stands outside the town of Kharkhorin near the ancient capital.

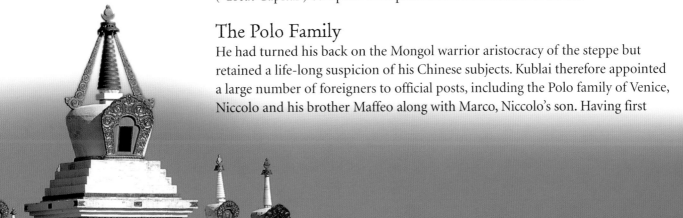

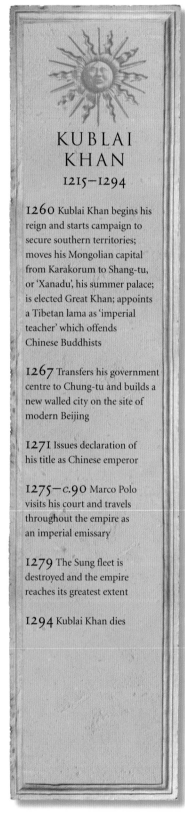

KUBLAI
KHAN
1215–1294

1260 Kublai Khan begins his reign and starts campaign to secure southern territories; moves his Mongolian capital from Karakorum to Shang-tu, or 'Xanadu', his summer palace; is elected Great Khan; appoints a Tibetan lama as 'imperial teacher' which offends Chinese Buddhists

1267 Transfers his government centre to Chung-tu and builds a new walled city on the site of modern Beijing

1271 Issues declaration of his title as Chinese emperor

1275–c.90 Marco Polo visits his court and travels throughout the empire as an imperial emissary

1279 The Sung fleet is destroyed and the empire reaches its greatest extent

1294 Kublai Khan dies

arrived in China as merchants the two brothers were received at the Shang-tu court in 1265 and served as Kublai's ambassadors to the pope on their return to Europe. During the family's subsequent extended stay in China from the mid-1270s to *c.*1290, Marco represented the emperor on a number of fact-finding missions to the Chinese provinces.

The Mongol ruling class in China divided their subjects into four categories whose divisions broadly corresponded to Ch'in practice. They themselves comprised a small, privileged and dominant minority who worked closely with the *se-mu jen* (people of special status) who consisted of other foreigners such as Turks, Central Asians and Muslim immigrants from the Middle East. Both groups were tax-exempt. The Chinese population of the north was categorized as the *han-jen;* that of the south was referred to abusively as *man-tzu,* or 'southern barbarian', and barred from holding any posts in the higher officialdom.

Kublai's Administration

The Central Secretariat, an innovation of the first years of Mongol rule in China, had established a degree of unity in the civil administration but its authority had been attacked by the Mongols' own group of chosen comrades (*nökör*), those defecting Chinese, Juchen and Khitan nobles who had rallied to their cause and were determined to preserve their own local power. In the 1260s the Secretariat, along with its various provincial offices, was revived but the Chinese were still only allowed to serve in its lower echelons. Non-Chinese continued to dominate higher officialdom but Kublai's suspicion of his fellow Mongol aristocrats meant that few of them were employed at the administration's highest levels.

The army's high command however was Mongol-dominated. China's greatest bureaucratic resource, its Confucian scholar-officials, were largely excluded from government and restricted to the lower administrative ranks. Confucian scholars enjoyed a greater entrée to court life under Kublai compared to his Mongol predecessors who had discontinued the bureaucracy's recruitment system through examination. But it was only in 1313 that the system was re-introduced – and even then very ineffectively.

Ch'in legislation and more ancient Chinese laws remained in place but were supplemented by the Mongols' own legal traditions (especially so, unsurprisingly, when it came to penal law). Both the legal system and the bureaucracy required an army of Mongolian–Chinese translators and interpreters, since hardly any of the conquerors and native population understood each others' languages. This ignorance may explain why so much anti-Mongol satire and criticism was able to circulate in Chinese literature. It was against the odds that this system should acquire deep roots in China's total population of 80 million and it was only the exercise of Kublai Khan's remarkable personality which enabled it to work at all.

The Italian explorer Marco Polo recorded his travels in 'The Book of Wonders' – this miniature painting from his book depicts a hunting scene and one of his meetings with Kublai Khan. Polo earned the emperor's trust and completed a number of confidential missions for him across large areas of China.

Cultural Decline; Economic Advance

Chinese culture, faced by so alien a governing force and one without any artistic tradition of its own, withdrew into itself. Lacking the confidence to develop experimentally, it lapsed into conservative sterility. Calligraphy and painting became mere imitations of the past. Porcelain manufacture replaced originality with bulk reproductions. No foreign literary works were translated into Chinese during the entire Yuan dynastic period and there are few Mongolian translations of the great Chinese literary, philosophical and historical works. The one exception to the cultural wasteland was the emergence of novels and tales written in the Chinese vernacular and whose natural readership was the newly prosperous class of urban merchants and traders.

China's Material Prosperity under the Mongols

China's political reunification had integrated the Chinese economy and the 'Great Canal', a structure linking the river systems of the Yangtze, Huai and Huang rivers since the seventh century, was repaired and extended in 1292–3. The canal now reached Ta-tu and transported grains as well as textiles on a new scale from the south to the north where Mongol garrisons were eager consumers. The Mongols, unlike the traditional Chinese governing class, approved of private businesses and Kublai's regime allowed Chinese businessmen to export grain to foreign markets from the southeastern coast. These private fleet operators made huge fortunes and their consequent public unpopularity led Kublai's successors to withdraw the concession in the early 14th century. Currency unification facilitated trading transactions and was part of the new general prosperity: in 1260 paper money (first introduced under the Sung) became the empire's sole legal currency, entirely displacing the use of bronze and copper coins.

Chinese Taoism's occult elements and toleration of magic appealed to the Mongols but it was Tibetan Buddhism that really seized their imagination. In 1260 Kublai appointed a Tibetan lama, 'Phags-pa, to be the 'imperial teacher', and two special government agencies were established for Buddhist affairs in the south and in the north (including Tibet which remained independent at this stage). But the missionary arrogance of Tibetan lamas was offensive to Chinese Buddhists and represented yet another intrusion of an unsympathetic and alien force into Chinese culture. One Mongol lesson however was learnt very thoroughly by the native Chinese – the use of military force in order to get rid of political opponents. In 1386 Chinese rebels took their country back, expelled the Yuan dynasty to the steppe and established the Ming dynasty.

BAYBARS I, Mamluk Sultan of Egypt and Syria

R. 1260–1277

In 1382 Islamic civilization's greatest historian left his native Tunis and travelled to Cairo. It was his first visit to Egypt, a country run for over a century by Mamluk slave soldiers, and Ibn Khaldun was overwhelmed on seeing their capital. This self-perpetuating military elite was based in what he considered a true metropolis: 'garden of the world, meeting-place of the nations, palace of Islam, the seat of dominion'.

High up on the city's Muqattam hill was the Citadel, the sultan's palace built by Salah al-Din, founder of the Ayyubid dynasty, Egypt's previous rulers. Within its precincts Mamluk sultans held a weekly council to adjudicate on major cases, a subject of special interest to Khaldun since he himself was a *qadi* (judge). Cairo, like other cities in Egypt and Syria, was filled with *madrasahs* training students in theology and in Islamic law's four major schools. Cairo's mosques were by now mostly domed and many were also tombs where saints were venerated, an architectural feature which recalled Egypt's pharaohs.

Sunni Muslim Power

The typically Islamic link between ruler and city was especially intense in Mamluk Cairo and affirmed in great ceremonies such as the cutting of the dyke during the flood season as the Nile's waters flowed into the city's canal. These rulers stood in the tradition of Salah al-Din's Islamic jihad and his unique concentration of a Sunni Muslim power extending from Egypt to Syria, the Yemen and upper Mesopotamia. But they also saw themselves as heirs to the dynastic grandeur of a more ancient Egyptian civilization.

Egypt in the 1380s was a peaceful and secure state whose trade routes were benefiting from the decline of Mongol power in Iran, Iraq and Asia Minor. Traders alarmed by the consequent disruption in those areas now concentrated on the routes which led from the Indian Ocean and the Red Sea through Egypt to Alexandria's port. Here the western merchants waited for spices and pepper, precious cloths and luxury goods such as porcelain which, being subject to import and export duties, were major Mamluk revenue earners. Both Syria and Upper Egypt were being protected from Bedouin attacks and the Mamluks had persuaded these tribesmen to expand into Nubia.

'On the Way Between Old and New Cairo, Citadel Mosque of Muhammad Ali
and the Tombs of the Mamelukes', an oil painting from c.1872 by American artist
Louis Comfort Tiffany.

This previously Christian region had therefore been Islamicized and the southern conquest meant that black slaves from central and east Africa joined the cargo route to the north. Khaldun spent the rest of his life in Cairo but there was more than comfort, legal work and visual delight to keep him here. Years of service in the Andalusian and north African courts of Islamic rulers had led him to an interest in a central question. All ruling elites, he thought, were characterized by a certain solidarity and it was this common spirit (*'asabiyya*) which drove their will to power. Loss of it undid them. It was the key to the rise and fall of states, dynasties and civilizations. The theme was outlined in his celebrated introduction to the world history (*Kitab al'ibar*) he had been working on since 1375. But what was the source of this elite awareness and how was it maintained? A closer investigation of these Mamluks would illustrate one possible answer.

Origin of the Mamluks

The Kipchak were a Turkic people and by the early 13th century their homeland was on the steppe north of the Black Sea and around the lower Volga. By the early 1240s they had been defeated by the Mongols and absorbed into the khanate of the Golden Horde. But the new rulers also sold the Kipchak as slaves, and some became known as Bahri Mamluks, their nomadic background making them especially valuable as soldiers. Slave soldiers had been used in Muslim armies since the ninth century and these Mamluks became the military backbone of most Islamic states. In Andalus and North Africa they were generally of Slavic origin but the Islamic states to the east found their supply mostly among Turks. Saladin had a slave military corps and the Kipchak provided his Ayyubid successors with Mamluks useful both in the fight against the crusaders and as a defence against internal rivals.

Baybars was one such Kipchak, bought at a Black Sea port and then trained as an elite soldier in Ayyubid service. Once freed, he became commander of the sultan's bodyguard and distinguished himself in the campaign of 1250, which captured Louis IX of France (St Louis) as the army of the Seventh Crusade retreated to Damietta in the Nile Delta. Mamluk prestige was greatly enhanced by this major propaganda victory and shortly afterwards Baybars led the rebellion which murdered the last Ayyubid sultan and installed the first Mamluk one, Aybak.

During the years of discord that followed, Baybars left for Syria with his own force but was invited back to Egypt in 1260 by the third Mamluk sultan. In September of that year he defeated a Mongol force in Palestine and expected to be given Aleppo as a reward. Sultan Qutuz's (r. 1259–60) failure to do so sealed his fate. During the army's march back to Egypt Baybars approached Qutuz and asked to be given a captive Mongol woman. His kiss of the sultan's hand on being granted this wish was the pre-arranged signal for Mamluk troops to seize the sultan, who was then stabbed in the neck and killed by Baybars.

Saladin, or Salah al-Din, founder of the Ayyubid dynasty, was born in Tikrit in modern Iraq. He is renowned in Christian and Muslim worlds alike as a great military leader. Supported by Mamluk slave soldiers, he recaptured Jerusalem for the Muslims during the Third Crusade in 1187.

Baybars Rules as Fourth Mamluk Sultan

As fourth Mamluk sultan, Baybars rebuilt the Syrian fortresses and citadels destroyed by the Mongols, and ended the area's rule by federated Ayyubid princes. Jaffa and Antioch were taken in 1268 and the crusading offensive in Palestine never recovered. The Assassins, an Islamic Shi'ite sect who considered terrorist murder a religious duty, had been attacking Egyptian rulers since the early 12th century. Having seized their Syrian mountain strongholds (1271–3) Baybars wiped them out while further north he attacked the Christian Armenian kingdom located in Cilicia, southeast Anatolia. But he realized how his power, in order to be secured, had to be legitimized and diplomatically recognized.

Constantinople, occupied for 57 years by the crusaders, had been retaken for Byzantium in 1261 by Emperor Michael VIII Palaeologus who received Baybars's envoys and allowed Egyptian merchants to sail through the Bosphorus. Representatives were also sent to the Italian states and in 1264 Charles of Anjou, later king of Naples and Sicily, sent an embassy of recognition to Cairo. Mongol divisions were exploited: Baybars kept up his offensive against the khanate in Iran but cultivated that of the Golden Horde. A member of Baghdad's 'Abbasid dynasty, destroyed by the Mongols in 1258, was persuaded to move to Cairo and established as caliph. This figurehead presence showed the city's status as an Islamic religious centre and Baybars was sedulous in his patronage of Mecca and Medina's Arab rulers.

Baybars's 17 Years of Energetic Rule

Baybars's 17 years of power set the pattern for a unique governmental system. The Mamluk sultans and the emirs through whom they ruled were members of a caste whose power could only be maintained by regular replenishment of its membership through slaves who were bought and then trained. This cadre was the basis of the state and its members were immensely loyal to those they had been brought up with in the various Mamluk households.

Successive sultans and emirs were a minority within this caste and, because the system excluded any hereditary element, they could only be replaced voluntarily or by force. Freed former slaves led the slave corps and arranged the succession. Coups, though frequent, were mere rearrangements within an overall structure of Mamluk power. The sultan drew half the state revenues and leased the remainder in the form of land revenues (*iqtas*), also non-hereditary, to his emirs who in return raised soldiers for the sultan's campaigns. The core of the Mamluk army was the royal Mamluks enlisted by the ruler or taken over from his predecessor and trained in the palace schools.

High-ranking officers trained their own body of military retainers within their household. Sons of Mamluks could only serve in non-slave regiments and were

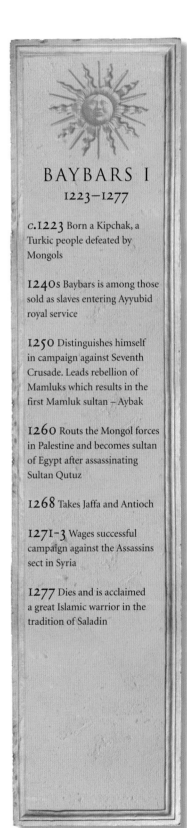

BAYBARS I
1223–1277

*c.*1223 Born a Kipchak, a Turkic people defeated by Mongols

1240s Baybars is among those sold as slaves entering Ayyubid royal service

1250 Distinguishes himself in campaign against Seventh Crusade. Leads rebellion of Mamluks which results in the first Mamluk sultan – Aybak

1260 Routs the Mongol forces in Palestine and becomes sultan of Egypt after assassinating Sultan Qutuz

1268 Takes Jaffa and Antioch

1271-3 Wages successful campaign against the Assassins sect in Syria

1277 Dies and is acclaimed a great Islamic warrior in the tradition of Saladin

An engraving from c.1860 depicting the 1811 massacre of Mamluks in Cairo. This event brought Mamluk power in Egypt to an end and established Albanian-born Muhammad Ali Pasha as the new and undisputed ruler.

excluded from holding the administrative offices reserved to Mamluks. The sole hereditary element was provided by the Jews and Copts who served within the bureaucracy, divided into *diwans* or departments of state each headed by a *nasir*. Shared experience and a common Turkic language explained the Mamluk elite solidarity, while the absence of hereditary rule gave each new generation a keen competitive edge on arrival from the Black Sea ports.

Egypt Weakens Through Plague and War

Ibn Khaldun saw this system operating at its height but from the late 14th century onwards Circassian slaves from the Caucasus replaced the dwindling supply of Turkish ones. The first Mamluks to rule Egypt had made military effectiveness the sole criterion for advancement but their successors diluted that principle, and a common Circassian ethnicity became the main qualification for high office. A militarily weakened state became vulnerable to Bedouin attacks which disrupted both the trade routes and the agrarian base whose surpluses were the basis of state revenues. Timur's sack of Aleppo in 1400 was a major dislocation and the plague hit Egypt especially hard, with Cairo's population declining to some 150,000 by the mid-15th century compared to 250,000 in the previous century. The Ottomans' greater manpower reserves, reliable agricultural surpluses and advanced technology, including artillery and firearms powered by gunpowder, enabled them to conquer Egypt and Syria in 1517. Although progressively Arabized in culture, the Mamluks had remained an alien governing class and their Egyptian subjects did little to save them from defeat.

The Mamluk System Degenerates

The Mamluks served the Ottomans as a provincial governing class in Egypt and Syria with slaves still being imported into their ranks. Mamluk sons however could now serve in their fathers' regiments and hold offices previously restricted to Mamluks. This major dilution of established principle led to the emergence of lineage loyalties which destabilized the entire system. Dynastic families rivalled each other for predominance and the Ottomans exploited these divisions to their advantage. The Mamluks' oligarchy nonetheless endured and during the Ottomans' 17th-century decline its members re-emerged to assert control over the local Egyptian army and administration, including revenue collection.

The weakened Ottomans were reduced to recognizing the effective autonomy of whichever Mamluk group was most effective at delivering annual payments to Istanbul. When Napoleon invaded Egypt in 1798 he discovered a country which was still being run by the Mamluks and they were only finally disposed of in the 1811 massacre of their numbers organized by Muhammad Ali Pasha, founder of a new Egyptian dynasty. *'Asabiyya* had served them well.

HAYAM WURUK,
Rajasanagara, King of the
Majapahit State of Java
R. 1350–1389

In 1365 the kingdom of Majapahit on the island of Java –
now in modern Indonesia – was at the height of its power
and in that year the court poet Prapanca wrote a narrative
poem in order to glorify his patron, the king. Hayam
Wuruk, who took the title Rajasanagara, had inherited the
throne 15 years earlier and, guided by his chief minister
Gajah Mada, his kingdom gained an imperial authority
across territories within the Indonesian archipelago.

*By the eighth century central
Java was ruled by the
Sailendra kings who espoused
Buddhism and built many
temples and monuments. Some
of the finest early examples of
Buddhist art are carved stone
panels and sculptures made
to adorn the monument of
Borobudur, where this carved
relief of dancing girls can
be seen.*

Political power was centred on the *kraton* of Majapahit city, a palace and sacred
centre surrounded by a thick, high wall of red brick with watchtowers and huge
ornamental iron gates. Prapanca's poem, the *Nagarakertagama*, describes a ruler
carried in state on his jewel-studded palanquin with peacock feathers protecting
him from the sun's rays. The sound of drums, trumpets and conches fill the air
and herald the imminent arrival of Rajasanagara, whose clothes glitter with gold.
On other occasions the poem describes the king's procession in an open wagon
decorated with gold and jewels: in his retinue there are elephants, horses and 400
carts. Clouds of incense surround him when seated in courtly state and Brahmin
Hindu priests sit respectfully in front of the king. 'Harmonizing pairs of maidens'
carry the yellow state sunshade, the sacred *kris*, or sword of state, and a golden
box containing betel nuts which will be used to delight the regal taste buds.

The Golden Age of Indonesia

This was the Indonesian 'golden age' and literature accordingly mingles myth
with fact as it evokes a time when a distinctive and unifying culture spread across
the archipelago. But the belief that Rajasanagara possessed *kesaktian*, the divine
power claimed by Indonesian rulers, is an undoubted part of his kingly story and
was the source of his legitimacy. Gajah Mada, borne aloft on his red palanquin,
was allowed to use the yellow sunshade usually reserved for royalty. But the
pusaka, or emblems of sovereignty, which were kept in the inner sanctuary of
the *kraton* attested to the king's unique authority as preserver of hierarchical
order and focus of his society.

Majapahit was the last and greatest power to flourish in the Southeast Asian archipelago before the arrival of European traders and colonizers transformed the region in the 16th century.

The Kingdom of Srivijaya

Kingship was an institution with ancient roots right across this maritime region, and its islands had been exposed for centuries to powerful commercial and cultural influences from India to the west and China to the north. By the seventh century the kingdom of Srivijaya in southeastern Sumatra had emerged as the greatest single power within the archipelago whose numerous independent ports and polities had been competing with each other for centuries.

Kingly power in maritime Southeast Asia had to perform duties determined by geography and climate. The region's fertile mountains could also be destructive volcanoes, just as the seaborne trading routes could produce fatal storms, and the rituals of kingship were designed to appease these natural forces. The Srivijayan king was therefore 'Lord of the Mountain' as well as 'Lord of the Isles' and, in order to propitiate the 'Spirit of the Waters of the Sea', he would throw gold bricks daily into the estuary at Palembang, centre of his realm.

Borobudur, built by the Sailendra dynasty and probably completed by the early ninth century, consists of a series of terraces topped by bell-shaped structures known as 'stupas'. The massive stone monument was intended to represent the path to spiritual enlightenment: pilgrims were expected to walk clockwise around the terraces to the summit, studying on their way carved panels based on important Buddhist texts.

The early Southeast Asian maritime kingdoms tended to emerge in the river basins since it was here that the mountainous and maritime forces were brought together as rainwater which had fallen on the mountain tops flowed into the sea. Rivers and water were closely associated with the kingly magic whose rituals were designed to encourage fertility. The connection was so strong that it was feared a king might cause a flood if he stepped into bath water which had not been made safe beforehand by treating it with flower petals.

The Power of Water

In the Srivijayan kingdom myths about water's power reflected a political and economic fact since the Musi river connected the hinterland with the coast. The river valley's agricultural produce (including rice), forest products such as resin intended for overseas exports, reserves of manpower: all travelled down river to Palembang. The Musi then flowed on to connect the capital with the coast 50 miles (80 km) away. The Srivijayan kingdom had often used military force to

subjugate its neighbours, but the river network was also the basis of an alliance system that distributed and exchanged goods in return for recognition of overlordship.

Buddhist priests were also sent along the river route to establish contact with the hinterland's leaders who were then encouraged to hold religious ceremonies which honoured both the Buddhist faith and the Srivijayan king. Royal cults and oath-taking ceremonies held at the kingdom's geographic centre enforced loyalty. I Ching, a Chinese traveller of the seventh century, describes a ceremonial centre near Palembang which housed 1000 priests and where he saw golden bowls in the form of lotus flowers being offered to gold and silver statues of the Buddha.

Srivijaya's prosperity was based on its control of the region's international trade routes and it incorporated a number of ports on Java's northern and western coast. But central Java, an area ruled by the royal house of the Sailendras from *c.*760–*c.*860, remained independent and was a major exporter of rice to Srivijaya, its closest ally. In return, central Java gained goods imported along the maritime routes and it also opened up to the influence of Indian religion, arts and architecture.

The Influence of India

A Hindu temple complex was built on the Dieng Plateau in the central Javan mountains and also at Prambanan, while the great Buddhist monument known as Borobudur was built by the Sailendras and probably completed in the early ninth century. Indian religion enabled some kings to assert primacy over their neighbours with elaborate rituals and state ceremonies demonstrating the intimate relationship between these superior rulers and the divine. The Sanskrit literacy of those priests based at court also helped rulers to assert administrative order and the Sailendras of the eighth century – the first to proclaim themselves rulers of a Javanese state – were also the first to adopt the title *Maharaja*, the Sanskrit word for 'Great King'. Srivijaya enjoyed an equally close commercial alliance with the Hindu royal houses, who succeeded the Sailendras as rulers of central Java, and this dual ascendancy lasted until the early 11th century.

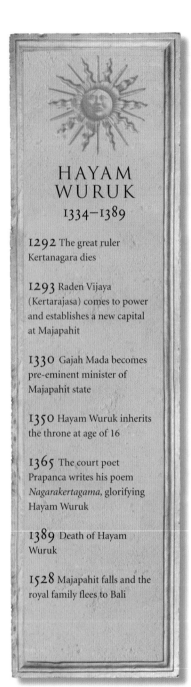

Trade with China

Trading patterns however were now shifting eastwards as more Chinese sailors penetrated the region and established direct relationships with producers. Srivijaya therefore lost its dominance as an *entrepôt* and it was eastern Java that was best placed to exploit the new trading patterns which exported rice in return for spices (especially cloves and nutmeg) produced by the tropical rain forests in the further eastern areas of the archipelago. Porcelain exports from China had also now become a major element in the region's trade.

King Airlangga (*c.*991–1049) exploited these economic advantages and developed a new power based on the delta of the Brantas river in eastern Java. His authority was such that he was able to build a series of dams to control the river's flow and he also asserted his hegemony over central Java. During the next two centuries eastern Java became a world economic power with imports of gold and silver, Chinese silk and porcelain, lacquerware and metalwork providing the material basis of an advanced civilization.

The Kingdom of Singharasi

The kingdom of Singharasi grew to dominate eastern Java in the first half of the 13th century. Its greatest ruler, Kertanagara (r. 1268–92), had been inducted into secret Tantric rituals involving alcoholic drink and sexual activity, and the king attributed his success in defeating his opponents 'demonic' forces to the ecstasy induced in him by such rituals. Prapanca's poem however also describes him as a religious ascetic whose patronage of both Hinduism and Buddhism reasserted Javanese unity, and the easy co-existence of the two religions was an important feature of the island's culture.

Kertanagara's military forces expanded into Sumatra and, by 1286, he had established hegemony over the straits separating the island from the Malay peninsula. This brought him into direct conflict with the southern expansion of China's new Mongol rulers and in 1289 Kublai Khan sent envoys to Kertanagara demanding homage. The king responded by tattooing the emissaries' faces and this insult led to the despatch of 1000 Chinese-Mongol warships to enforce Javanese submission. Before this fleet could arrive however Kertanagara died during a local rebellion led by the previously subordinated state of Kadiri.

The State and City of Majapahit

Kertanagara's son-in-law and successor, Kertarajasa (r. 1293–1309), cleared a forest site which he named Majapahit, and this royal city became the new centre of the dynasty's power. When the Mongols arrived in 1292–3, Kertarajasa persuaded them to join him in attacking Kadiri's ruler. After he had destroyed local rivals, the new king then turned on his Mongol allies and proceeded to expel them from Java.

In the following decades the Majapahit state asserted its authority over most of the islands that comprise contemporary Indonesia: it made peace with the Mongols, had strong commercial links with China and developed, through Venice's trading network, a new European market for the spice exports shipped from the port town of Surabaya. The city of Majapahit lay inland along the Brantas river and nearby Bubat was its commercial twin, a city where traders from India, China, Cambodia, Vietnam and Thailand met to do business and pay homage to the king.

Kingly Rituals

Rajasanagara, just like his successors and predecessors on the throne, would arrive at Bubat in the early spring for the first seven days of the annual *Caira* festival involving music, dancing and drama, as well as games and trials of combat such as tugs-of-war. The king here received cash and goods from his subjects and the international traders, before returning to Majapahit city for a further seven days of festivities. During this second stage the festival ceremonies were explicitly designed to demonstrate the inter-dependence of each element within the kingdom: the rice-producing interior and the trade of the high seas, the court personnel, farmers and military. Formal speeches delivered to the audience by royal princes regularly insisted on the need to maintain public works such as dams, bridges, marketplaces and roads in order to ensure the kingdom's survival and prosperity.

The Decline of Majapahit

The expansion of the spice trade beyond a point at which it could be controlled by any single kingdom undermined Majapahit both economically and politically. By the early 15th century the Chinese had their own trading links with the pepper-exporting Sumatran ports, and Melaka on the Malay peninsula became a major spice distribution centre. This loss of economic supremacy meant that ports previously subordinated to Majapahit regained their independence and the new self-confidence of the coastal trading areas' population was reflected in their mass conversion to Islam. In 1513 a coalition of such communities in northern Java launched a sustained campaign against the centre of Majapahit, which fell in 1528: the royal family was forced to flee to Bali.

Islamic faith had established a powerful new bond between rulers and subjects in these northern areas, and it was this new community of interest which demolished the aristocratic society of the Majapahit kingdom, its rights, privileges and rituals.

The Tenggerese people of eastern Java are thought to be descended from refugees who fled from Majapahit in the 16th century. Unlike the majority of Indonesians, the Tenggerese do not subscribe to Islam, and most practise a blend of Hinduism and animism. This is reflected in the annual ceremony of Yadnya Kasada, when rice, fruit, livestock and other produce are thrown into the Mount Bromo crater as offerings to the god of the mountain.

COSIMO DE' MEDICI, First Medici 'Ruler' of Florence

R. 1434–1463

He had always been cautious, and a night-time return from exile suited him well. It was through a small gateway near the Palazzo del Bargello that Cosimo de' Medici slipped back into his city in 1432. A year previously his enemies, the Albizzi family, had persuaded the *Signoria*, Florence's supreme executive, to arrest him because he had 'sought to elevate himself higher than others', a capital crime in a supposedly democratic city.

Trumped-up treason charges were brought against him but the Medici clientage system proved resilient. This was Europe's richest financier and his family bank was Europe's biggest business with branches in London, Bruges and Geneva, as well as all the major Italian cities. Foreign governments, needing Medici loans, had protested against Cosimo's imprisonment. Business interests and prudent marriages intertwined his fortunes with those of the Florentine elite and his sardonic jibes had made him popular among the city's masses.

Cosimo's Populist Touch

He could rely on the power of cultural protest too, since Florence's humanist scholars and artists relied on Medici patronage. Cosimo bribed the *gonfaloniere*, the official who headed the *Signoria* and, instead of being executed as the Albizzi and their co-conspirators had planned, he was exiled. In Venice, Florence's ally, he waited for the tide to turn. It didn't take long. Bribed electors ensured that Medici supporters once again ran the *Signoria*. A *balia*, or popular committee, was elected 'to reform the city for the good of the people', and this institutional relic of Florence's republicanism revoked his sentence. On his return Cosimo was told that the city was now deprived of some of its greatest names. Banishment had been inflicted not just on the Albizzi but also on many of the Peruzzi and Guasconi, the Strozzi, Guadagni and Guicciardini. 'Two yards of rose-coloured cloth', he replied, 'will make a new gentleman'. Money and subtlety gave this man his power but a politician's populist touch was useful too.

*Jacopo Pontormo's portrait of Cosimo de' Medici was painted
in about 1520 and was based on previous portraits of the
pre-eminent Florentine citizen.*

Giovanni de' Medici was an important patron of Florentine art and donated funds for the commissioning of the North Doors of the Florence baptistery. That commission was won in 1402 by Lorenzo Ghiberti, who took 21 years to complete the work and then almost immediately received a request to design a set of doors for the east portal. The 'Gates of Paradise', shown above, were finally completed in 1452 and are considered to be Ghiberti's masterpiece.

Giovanni de' Medici

Giovanni de' Medici (1360–1429) had established the family bank in 1397 and quickly grasped the importance of political connections when it came to making money in Florence. Cultural patronage also mattered since it showed a businessman's solidarity with the city's cause and thereby gained him public approval. Giovanni was therefore one of the donors of the Florence baptistery's bronze North Doors which were the sculptor Lorenzo Ghiberti's first important commission. He was also among the seven parishioners who persuaded the *commune* to restore San Lorenzo and it was his own money that paid for the church's sacristy and its Medici family chapel. As redesigned by Filippo Brunelleschi from 1425–46 San Lorenzo's cool elegance became the epitome of early Renaissance classicism and a symbol of Medici munificence.

From youth onwards Giovanni's son, Cosimo, was steeped in the city's literary culture and he had wanted to travel to Palestine in search of Greek manuscripts before his father, alarmed at this precocious ambition, set him to work in the bank. Links with the papal curia accounted for some half of the Medici's profits and by the early 15th century they were running the most successful of Florence's 70 or so banking and bill-brokering businesses. Their representatives in the great European centres were not only bankers, but also importers and exporters of spices, dyes, furs and jewels. Those who wanted to get hold of a sacred relic or wild animal, a valuable slave or talented choirboy, would go to the Medici agents who were also in effect the republic's diplomats, and their despatches on foreign affairs were read carefully by both Giovanni and Cosimo.

The Government of Florence

Florence's republican government was defined in the Ordinances of Justice (1293), which vested sovereignty in the *popolo* – a body restricted to the bankers and doctors, merchants and tradesmen enrolled in the seven major guilds. Every two months lesser guildsmen, such as butchers, stonemasons and shoemakers, joined the *popolo* to elect six priors who ran the city as its chief magistrates. This was the politics of the *commune* and the arrangements, adopted by the many north Italian city-states influenced by Florence, guaranteed endemic conflict. Although the subject of much republican posturing, Florence's constitutional forms were nonetheless controlled by oligarchic groups. These, in turn, were bitterly disputatious and the pages of Dante (1265–1321) record the Florentine struggles between the pro-imperial Ghibelline party and the pro-papal Guelphs who were themselves internally divided. Medici bribery and patronage brought stability to the system, and since the family were careful to keep up republican appearances, they also preserved Florentine self-respect.

On his deathbed Giovanni counselled Cosimo on the ways of power: 'Do not appear to give advice, but put your views forward discreetly in conversation. ...

Always keep out of the public eye.' In theory Cosimo remained a mere private citizen and official correspondence went through the *Signoria*. But despite his disingenuous claims to the contrary, supreme power rested with him. When Pius II asked Cosimo to supply two galleys for an anti-Turkish crusade he reminded the pope, 'how limited is the power of a private citizen in a free state under democratic government'. But it was Florence's excellent trading relations with the Turks that explained its leader's refusal.

Cosimo Supports Francesco Sforza

Cosimo silenced his critics by subjecting them to selective taxation and established the *cento*, a council of 100 with tax and security responsibilities. But it was his *accoppiatori*, or commissioners, who controlled the selection of candidates standing for election to the Florentine executive. His support for the *condottiere* Francesco Sforza's claim to the duchy of Milan encountered a rare degree of Florentine opposition. The Milanese had proclaimed themselves a republic on the previous duke's death in 1447 but Cosimo had lent Sforza huge sums drawn from his bank, subsidized him with Florentine tax receipts, and wanted him to win. Venice and Naples, both of which had claims to Milan, declared war after Florence and Milan signed an alliance in 1450. But Venice was now preoccupied with the Turkish threat. The Holy League of 1454 formed between Florence and Milan, Venice and the papal states, guaranteed the new Italian status quo and secured Cosimo's plan for Milan.

Medici power however still required Medicean circumspection. Brunelleschi's design for a Palazzo Medici was rejected as ostentatious, and Cosimo's architect for the building would be Michelozzo di Bartolommeo, a friend who had shared his Venetian exile. Michelozzo's use of rusticated blocks of stone on all three floors still made for an imposing structure whose rooms would accommodate the painter Fra Filippo Lippi and the sculptor Donatello.

The Medici Library

Lorenzo, Cosimo's grandson, extended the same hospitality to the young Michelangelo, and the intimacy of such patronage elevated the social status of Renaissance artists. The fine book collection which forms the core of the Medici Library was acquired by Cosimo and housed in a vast hall designed by Michelozzo at the monastery of San Marco, but care for public opinion meant that Cosimo's friends were allowed to consult it. In 1439 he was elected *gonfaloniere* to mark the general council of the Orthodox and Catholic churches which was held in Florence that year as a result of his papal connections. The visiting Greek scholars and clergy inspired the city's intellectuals and their already burgeoning interest in classical civilization: Cosimo commissioned his adopted son Marsilio Ficino to provide a Latin translation of Plato's works and Ficino would head the Platonic Academy established at the Medici villa in Careggi.

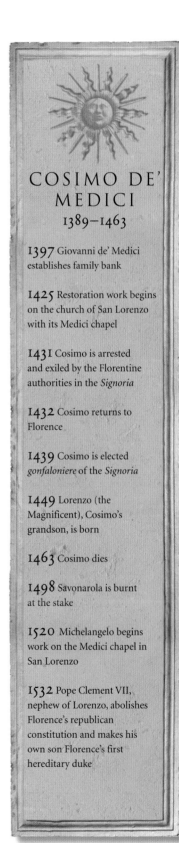

COSIMO DE' MEDICI
1389–1463

1397 Giovanni de' Medici establishes family bank

1425 Restoration work begins on the church of San Lorenzo with its Medici chapel

1431 Cosimo is arrested and exiled by the Florentine authorities in the *Signoria*

1432 Cosimo returns to Florence

1439 Cosimo is elected *gonfaloniere* of the *Signoria*

1449 Lorenzo (the Magnificent), Cosimo's grandson, is born

1463 Cosimo dies

1498 Savonarola is burnt at the stake

1520 Michelangelo begins work on the Medici chapel in San Lorenzo

1532 Pope Clement VII, nephew of Lorenzo, abolishes Florence's republican constitution and makes his own son Florence's first hereditary duke

With peace and oligarchic stability came lower taxes, increased riches and a greater readiness to flaunt wealth. The Florentine rich had often served as committee members overseeing the restoration and building of churches and hospitals. This experience gave them the architectural experience and educated taste which informed their ambition to build *palazzi* worthy of their status. Local quarries produced both the lime sandstone of the *pietra forte* and the softer grey sandstone of the *pietra serena*.

Florence's Palazzi

Florence's large population of highly skilled stoneworkers therefore set to work on the grandiose Palazzo Pitti, as well as the palaces commissioned by the Strozzi, Gondi and Pazzi-Quaratesi. Leon Battista Alberti, that embodiment of Renaissance diversity as poet, painter, philosopher, mathematician, musician and athlete, designed the Palazzo Rucellai. Such buildings were now marked with family emblems. Dolphins for the Pazzi and roses for the Ricasoli, sails of fortune for the Rucellai, crossed chains for the Alberti and poppies for the Bartolini: these competitive forms of self-assertion were new in Florence's history. Even Cosimo displayed his own personal emblem of the three peacock feathers.

Lorenzo de' Medici

'*Il Magnifico*' was a conventionally obsequious form of address in the Florence of Lorenzo de' Medici (1449–92). But his political energy and cultural enterprise were in the high Medici tradition. He expanded the Medici Library, encouraged the first printing of books in Florence from 1471 onwards and advocated the literary use of the Italian language in its Tuscan dialect form. As Ficino's faithful pupil Lorenzo encouraged the study of Greek at the university of Florence, and his patronage of an expanded law faculty at Pisa's university secured the emigration of many Florentine lawyers who queried his political methods. He averted war with Naples and, following his suppression of the conspiracy against him led by the Pazzi family in 1478, oligarchic control was strengthened with a *balia* approving the reduction of the *cento* to 70 elected on five-year terms.

Princely expenditure financed the spectacular tournament of 1469 which marked Lorenzo's betrothal, and late 15th-century Florence was celebrated for its festivals and firework displays, for the mock battles on the Piazza Santa Croce and their aquatic equivalents, the *naumachia* on the Arno. But although a major connoisseur and collector of antique vases, medals and coins, bronzes and carved gems, Lorenzo could not afford to commission his friends Sandro Botticelli, Antonio Pollaiuolo and Domenico Ghirlandaio. He took little interest in the Medici bank, a business whose political involvements exposed it to an unusual degree of financial risk. The London branch had to close after Edward IV failed to repay his loans, and the bank's entire international structure collapsed under Lorenzo. Charles VIII of France, campaigning to secure his claim to Naples,

Among Michelangelo's most famous marble sculptures is the tomb of Lorenzo II de' Medici, grandson of Lorenzo 'Il Magnifico', in the Medici chapel (c.1520–34). Beneath the central form of Lorenzo himself lie figures representing Dusk (on the left) and Dawn (right).

overwhelmed Florence in 1494. A shamed city sent the Medici into an 18-year exile and Savonarola's impassioned campaigning for a Christian republic consumed the city until the *Signoria* restored order and burnt the Dominican friar at the stake in 1498.

Europe's Most Intelligent Patrons

Michelangelo's marble monuments within San Lorenzo's Medici chapel were executed between 1520 and 1534. They are his tribute to European history's most intelligent patrons and to a family proud of being *popolani*. That identification with the populace allowed them to achieve by subtle means a form of dynastic greatness that needed no hereditary title. But in 1532 Pope Clement VII, Lorenzo's nephew, abolished the old constitution and installed Alessandro, reputedly his illegitimate son, as Florence's first hereditary Medici duke. Cosimo's direct lineage had dwindled into insignificance and so would Florence.

MONTEZUMA II, Ninth and Last Aztec Emperor of Mexico

R. 1502–1520

The idea that empires could be gained and ruled by exploiting their divisions was well established in Renaissance Europe. Explorers and writers alike could refer back to Roman imperial techniques, and history was generally regarded as a useful source of lessons that could be applied in contemporary circumstances. Niccolò Machiavelli's *Il Principe* used Livy's histories of Rome to provide analogies, and his handbook on the pursuit of power became the genre's most celebrated example.

Hernán Cortés (1485–1547), had been educated at the university of Salamanca, Spain, one of the great centres of humanistic learning, and would have been very familiar with such attitudes towards the past. He had been noted in his university days for being not only clever but also ruthless and haughty, as well as eager to find out more about the 'Indies' that were being explored by his Spanish compatriots. He was, in other words, an ideal candidate for conquistador glory and it was in that role that he set out at the age of 19 for Hispaniola, the modern Santo Domingo, in 1504.

Montezuma Succeeds as Aztec Emperor
Montezuma had also been trained for a role but in an austere tradition of hierarchy and religious sacrifice which rivalled anything that even Castilian Spain, that land of notoriously ceremonious *hidalgo* nobility, could offer by comparison. In 1502 he had succeeded his uncle Ahuitzotl as emperor at a time when the Aztecs' power was at its height. Their territory had now spread

The subject of this painting is the Battle of Otumba of 1520, which resulted in a resounding victory for Cortés's forces against the far more numerous Aztecs and ultimately led to the fall of the Aztec empire. Some historians put the number of slain at over 20,000.

From the Codex Magliabecchi, created c.1600–50, this illustration shows an Aztec sacrifice. A priest offers the beating heart of a human victim to the war god Huitzilopochtli.

south to present-day Honduras and Nicaragua. Originally a farming people, the Aztecs had migrated from the west and into the Mexico Valley in *c.*1200 and taken advantage of the power vacuum in the region following the dissolution of the Toltec empire. Tenochtitlán, founded in *c.*1325, was their first major settlement and by the early 15th century a distinctive Aztec monarchy had emerged, able to impose tributary status on other states in the Mexico Valley.

Aztec Wars of Conquest

The Aztecs' rise to dominance had been swift but this race of comparative *parvenus* had alienated many of their subject peoples. Foremost among the local grievances was the Aztecs' insatiable demand for victims who might be used in the ritual sacrifices that affirmed their power and appeased their gods. Wars of conquest were justified as a means of obtaining the human victims used in these sacrifices: hearts, freshly extracted, would be offered to images of the gods, some of which were made out of a paste formed by kneading human blood with seeds and vegetable matter. Montezuma had led many such campaigns of conquest in order to appease Huitzilopochtli, god of war and of the sun in the Aztec pantheon.

The Myth of Quetzalcoatl

In the early 16th century it was another god, Quetzalcoatl, supposedly white of skin and bearded, who had become most feared among the Aztec governing class. Aztec mythology portrayed how this originally Toltec deity had been overthrown by rival gods on account of his opposition to human sacrifice. He had gone east but had vowed to return to reclaim the Aztec kingdom. Quetzalcoatl's arrival was now expected imminently and the anticipated consequences were both incalculable and terrifying.

By 1511 Cortés was in Cuba and had established himself as a landowner and colonial official but his restless spirit was not easily contained, and he therefore joined an expedition to establish a colony on the mainland. He arrived in Yucatán, southeastern Mexico, in February 1519 with some 500 soldiers and

100 sailors, the core army of the conquest that was to follow. His genius partly lay in his ability to transplant European ideas of overlordship and allegiance and make them relevant in a new environment.

Cortés's Campaigns

He therefore established the Mexican coastal town of Veracruz specifically so that his soldiers, in their capacity as newly enrolled citizens, could elect him as their captain general and chief justice. His force therefore, though so small, was marked by an extreme solidarity – all the more so since their leader had deliberately burnt the ships that might have taken them back to Spain. Cortés discovered that the peoples of Tlaxcala, in central Mexico, had never accepted Aztec control and were maintaining a vigorous campaign of opposition. They opposed Cortés as well to begin with but, having been defeated by him, they became keen allies in his next stage of campaigning. As he advanced towards Tenochtitlán, the Aztec capital, Cortés's small force was supplemented by some 1000 Tlaxcaltecs.

The huge metropolis that Cortés entered on 8 November 1519 covered 5 square miles (13 sq km) and had a population of some 400,000. Located on two islands in the middle of Lake Texcoco, the capital was connected to the settlements along the lake shores by several causeways which also functioned as dykes. Within the city lay Montezuma's main palace, a building described in the first Spanish colonial records as having 300 rooms centred around three courts. As with the other palace-dominated societies of early civilizations the building was much more than just a home for the monarch. Covering an area of 4 hectares (10 acres), the palace's libraries, storehouses, workshops, courts of justice and financial bureaux made it the heart of the state. The presence of hundreds of temples, mostly grouped in complexes, signified that Tenochtitlán was also a sacred city – as did the sacrificed victims' skulls placed in great wooden racks near the temple sites.

An Incarnation of Quetzalcoatl

Since Cortés was white and bearded, Montezuma supposed him to be an incarnation of Quetzalcoatl and was therefore keen to appease him. The emperor was, in effect, detained by Cortés who may also have hoped to govern the Aztec empire through him. He had every reason to resort to diplomacy. He had a small military force and it was only the exercise of his remarkable personality which had enabled him to establish his power in the capital. But his success in persuading the imperial court and Montezuma himself to set aside their ancient religion was remarkable.

Cortés had entered Tenochtitlán's main temple, a huge building with 40 towers in which the Aztec nobility were buried, and washed its chapels of the human blood

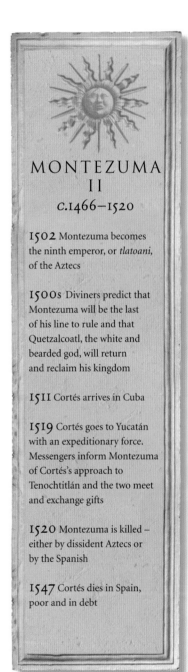

MONTEZUMA II
c.1466–1520

1502 Montezuma becomes the ninth emperor, or *tlatoani*, of the Aztecs

1500s Diviners predict that Montezuma will be the last of his line to rule and that Quetzalcoatl, the white and bearded god, will return and reclaim his kingdom

1511 Cortés arrives in Cuba

1519 Cortés goes to Yucatán with an expeditionary force. Messengers inform Montezuma of Cortés's approach to Tenochtitlán and the two meet and exchange gifts

1520 Montezuma is killed – either by dissident Aztecs or by the Spanish

1547 Cortés dies in Spain, poor and in debt

used in sacrificial rituals. Montezuma had remonstrated mildly when Cortés replaced Aztec religious statues with images of the Virgin and of various saints, but he capitulated quickly on being given a swift sermon by Cortés on Christian monotheism and the barbarism of Aztec idolatry. Revealingly, Montezuma told Cortés that the Aztecs' ancestors had emigrated to their present territory and conceded that after so long a time away from their original lands the Aztecs might have fallen into error. Cortés, being a more recent arrival, he admitted, knew better what the Aztecs should now believe. He was clearly insecure and saw Cortés as the fulfilment of earlier premonitions that Aztec rule was doomed to extinction.

Montezuma's Ceremonial Display

Montezuma might be a barbarian but his style of kingship impressed Cortés. 'No Sultan or other infidel lord', he wrote to Charles V, 'ever had so much ceremonial in his court'. Six hundred nobles were in attendance at the palace from dawn each day, and 300 or 400 youths served the various meals with Montezuma sitting on a small cushion 'curiously wrought of leather'. Montezuma's ceremoniousness involved being dressed every day in four different suits which were never worn again and 'those for whom he sends ... incline their heads and look down, bending their bodies; and when they address him, they do not look him in the face …'. He was rarely seen in public but when he did leave his palaces Aztec ritual was observed: 'all those who accompanied him, or whom he accidentally met in the streets, turned away without looking towards him, and others prostrated themselves until he had passed'.

Cortés's account emphasizes the affinities between Aztec imperialism and European kingship while also revealing a scale of magnificence inconceivable even to Renaissance princes. In a palace separate from Montezuma's main palace there were cages 'nine feet in height and six paces square' containing birds of prey 'of all the species found in Spain, from the kestrel to the eagle, and many unknown there'. Several large halls were filled with immense cages containing 'lions, tigers, wolves, foxes, and a variety of animals of the cat kind'. Yet another palace 'contained a number of men and women of monstrous size, and also dwarves, and crooked and ill-formed persons, each of which had their separate apartments as well as their respective keepers'.

Montezuma's figures of gold and silver were 'wrought so naturally as not to be surpassed by any smith in the world; the stone work executed with such perfection that it is difficult to conceive what instruments could have been used; and the feather work superior to the finest productions in wax and embroidery'. But the city's technology also impressed him with fresh water for the city's domestic use being conveyed through two pipes made of masonry laid along one of the city's causeways.

Aztec religion was based on a pantheon of deities, each of which received tribute every day. This statue represents Xochipilli, god of flowers, love and song and one of the gods responsible for fertility and agriculture.

Spanish Massacre of Aztec Chiefs

Cortés ruled the city until the middle of 1520 when he had to leave to defend his position against a Spanish force sent by the governor of Cuba, who wanted to relieve him of his command. His soldiers defeated this expeditionary force but, on his return to Tenochtitlán, Cortés found that the small garrison he had left behind was being besieged following the Spanish soldiers' massacre of Aztec chiefs during a festival. He retreated and regrouped with his Tlaxcaltec allies and in the winter of 1520–2 laid siege to the city which was then retaken by August 1521. The Aztec empire was now his and Montezuma was dead.

Whether the emperor was killed by Aztecs who blamed him for the loss of their empire (as the Spaniards claimed) or by the Spanish army is uncertain. Cortés had to return to Spain in 1528 to defend himself against charges of maladministration. His arrival laden with Aztec treasure mollified the Spanish court at Toledo, although litigation pursued him to the end of his days. After returning to 'New Spain' in 1530, Cortés built his own palace 30 miles (48 km) south of Tenochtitlán, which had now become Mexico City, but by 1540 he was back in Spain, where he later died poor and in debt.

A Clash of Cultures

The encounter between the Aztec emperor and the Spanish general personified a clash of cultures which was also a conflict between monarchies. Montezuma was the embodiment of the Aztec state and he therefore reflected its inner insecurities. The fear that their time of earthly dominion was coming to an end had gripped the emperor and his warrior aristocracy long before the arrival of Cortés and his conquistadors. Cortés died a disillusioned warrior, but the European overlordship that he exercised on behalf of a Christian emperor represented a style of dominion destined to shape the politics, religion and culture of 'Latin America' in the half-millennium that lay ahead.

HENRY VIII, King of England

R. 1509–1547

In about 1431 Owain ap Maredudd, a Welsh mercenary soldier, secretly married Catherine de Valois, widow of the English king, Henry V (r. 1413–22), and decided to adopt his grandfather's Christian name of Tudur as his own surname. Owain's ambitions had led him to enrol in the service of Henry V and then of Henry VI (1422–61, 1470–71), who were both members of the House of Lancaster. He was an active Lancastrian supporter in the Wars of the Roses (1455–85) during which the House of York became initially predominant and established Edward IV on the English throne (r. 1461–70, 1471–83).

Owain was beheaded after the Yorkist victory of 1461 but his sons Edmund and Jasper, half-brothers to the feeble Henry VI, maintained a vigorous pro-Lancastrian campaign. Edmund had been made earl of Richmond in 1452 and continued the family policy of dynastic ambition by marrying Margaret of Beaufort, great-granddaughter of John of Gaunt, duke of Lancaster and son of Edward III. By now the family had anglicized its surname and Henry Tudor, Edmund's son, was posthumously born in January 1457 at his uncle's castle in Pembroke, southwest Wales. It was from here that Jasper, accompanied by his young nephew, sailed for France in 1471 and during their subsequent exile the two sought alliances in support of the Lancastrian cause.

Henry VII
Internal divisions within the Yorkist camp formed the background to Richard III's accession in 1483 and this split was exploited by Henry, who was now the sole surviving Lancastrian claimant. In the summer of 1485 he returned to Pembrokeshire and landed with an army of some 4000 men, consisting mainly of French mercenaries and Lancastrian exiles. On 22 August, Henry's forces defeated Richard's army at Bosworth Field in the English Midlands and the earl of Richmond became England's king. Henry's swift marriage in January 1486 to Elizabeth, the Yorkist heiress and daughter of Edward IV, completed this takeover with the dynasty's emblem superimposing Lancaster's red rose on York's white one.

*Portrait of Henry VIII by Hans Holbein the Younger, c.1534–6. The
king's authority is conveyed by the magnificence of his gold and silver
clothing, enhanced by the artist's use of powdered gold in his paint and the
application of the expensive ultramarine pigment to the background colour.*

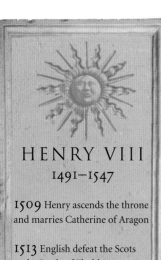

HENRY VIII
1491–1547

1509 Henry ascends the throne and marries Catherine of Aragon

1513 English defeat the Scots at the Battle of Flodden

1520 Anglo-French alliance celebrated at the Field of the Cloth of Gold

1529 Cardinal Thomas Wolsey falls from power (executed 1530)

1533 Thomas Cranmer, the archbishop of Canterbury, annuls Henry's first marriage. Henry and Anne Boleyn are married and she gives birth to a daughter

1534 The Act of Supremacy is passed

1536 Anne Boleyn is executed, Henry marries Jane Seymour

1537 Edward VI is born but Jane dies 12 days later

1540 Henry marries and then divorces Anne of Cleves. Marries Catherine Howard

1542 Catherine Howard is executed

1543 Marries Catherine Parr

1547 Henry dies leaving his son Edward to rule under a regency

Henry's avoidance of war, control of expenditure, and assertion of royal fiscal rights built up the English crown's international reputation to a point at which, in 1501, he was able to arrange the marriage of his heir, Arthur, to Catherine, daughter of Ferdinand II of Aragon and Isabella I of Castile. When Arthur died the following year Catherine became engaged to the surviving prince, Henry – although a subsequent Anglo-Spanish dispute meant that the marriage did not take place until Henry became king in 1509.

Henry VIII – a Renaissance Prince

Henry VII was a ruler formed by the insecurity, exile and penury of his youth but his son, nurtured in comparative security, showed all the traits of confident kingship. Physically imposing at six feet tall and powerfully built, Henry VIII was a natural athlete, excellent dancer and skilful hunter. He was also undoubtedly clever and enjoyed showing off his theological learning in conversations with scholars and men of letters. These abilities in combination encouraged the view, common at least among Henry's own courtiers, that England was now ruled by a Renaissance prince, one formed by the humanist movement's revival of classical learning and a figure who could bear comparison with his dazzling contemporaries, Francis I of France and the emperor Maximilian.

Princely style, however, demanded princely levels of expenditure. Henry's marriage to Catherine was celebrated with conspicuous consumption and such early displays of magnificence ate into the royal surplus bequeathed to Henry by his notoriously prudent father. The English exchequer also had to pay war expenses because, in 1512, Henry entered the Franco-Spanish disputes over control of Italy and supported his father-in-law Ferdinand of Aragon in the conflict. The continental involvement was also an opportunity for this assertively Catholic monarch to demonstrate England's loyalty to the papacy, an institution then under threat from French arms. Anti-French positioning however exposed England to the threat of invasion by Scotland, France's ally, and in August 1513 James IV's army crossed the border. The Battle of Flodden, which was fought on 9 September, ended in the annihilation of the Scottish aristocracy, an act that gained Henry substantial popularity in England.

Thomas Wolsey, Chancellor, Cardinal and Archbishop

Henry's court conformed to the European norm: position and favour came to those who cultivated the king's good opinion and in the mid-1510s Thomas Wolsey had established his predominance among Henry's courtiers. Wolsey had commanded the first campaign in France and by 1515 he was lord chancellor, archbishop of York, and a cardinal. Wolsey's ascendancy in English politics lasted until 1527 but its power base, personal friendship with a monarch whose character was at once domineering, inconstant and self-righteous, was precarious.

As European diplomat Wolsey entertained the hope that he might become pope and he also encouraged Henry's ambition to succeed to the imperial throne when the emperor Maximilian died in 1519. But the election of Charles V created an European power block to which England was at best marginal.

Wolsey stuck to the French alliance, which was celebrated in an ostentatious display of wealth and power extending over three weeks in June 1520 near Calais. This took place in specially erected pavilions and great tents decorated with gems and 'cloth of gold'– a special fabric of interwoven silk and gold strands. The pointlessness of this display became very evident after Charles V smashed the French forces at Pavia in 1525. England's own, rather more relevant, cloth consisted of fabrics exported to the Netherlands and Charles, as duke of Burgundy, was able to impose restrictions on this major English trade. England's domestic financial problems, however, were already considerable. Wolsey disliked parliaments but the need to raise taxation forced one to be called in 1523. The tax levels approved, however, were below what was necessary and next year's attempt at raising another tax provoked such violent resistance that the measure had to be rescinded. But in the late 1520s the English crown was overwhelmed by an even graver problem, that of 'the King's great matter'.

Anne Boleyn, whom Thomas Cromwell described as having 'intelligence, spirit and courage', was a strong-willed woman who exerted great influence over Henry even before their marriage in 1533. At her urging, Thomas Wolsey was dismissed and exiled. Yet her failure to bear Henry a male heir sealed her fate; her only surviving child later became Queen Elizabeth I.

'The King's Great Matter'

English diplomatic policy from 1527 onwards was driven by Henry's desire to divorce his queen. The king was not just infatuated with Anne Boleyn, one of the ladies of the court. He had also convinced himself that by marrying his brother's widow he had contravened divine law and that the failure to produce a male heir was a result of this transgression. But the earlier papal injunction allowing his marriage to take place had overridden the biblical text in Leviticus which forbade such unions. In asking Pope Clement VII for an annulment, Henry was therefore demanding that the papacy should accept that it, too, had erred. But England's queen was also aunt to Charles V, a ruler whose high view of family honour led him to oppose Henry's scheme. Besides which, Clement was in awe of Charles V's power – especially since the emperor had kept him prisoner in 1527–8.

Wolsey paid the price and fell from power in late 1529, but the crisis caused by Henry's need for a male heir continued for another three years. The eventual

solution involved a major boost in the powers of English kingship and a profound change in the country's relationship to a European continent, now wracked by religious conflict as a result of the religious revolution started by Martin Luther.

The Church of England Emerges

Henry's Latin pamphlet of 1521 had asserted the necessity of the church's seven sacraments and attacked Luther personally. But by the spring of 1532 Thomas Cromwell was pre-eminent within the council of state and this energetic lawyer with Protestant sympathies convinced Henry that England's church should be separated from allegiance to Rome. The 'Church of England' thereby created would be a spiritual department of the state's central government. King Henry, being God's deputy on English soil, would be its head and could keep the title *Defensor Fidei* ('defender of the faith') originally given him by the papacy in recognition of his pamphleteering in its defence.

The confident swagger of the pose Henry adopted in the famous portrait of him painted in *c.*1538/9 (previously attributed to Hans Holbein the Younger) reflects this new regal authority and the king could also now set Catherine aside. In 1533 the new archbishop of Canterbury, the protestant Thomas Cranmer, therefore declared the king's marriage invalid. Henry fiddled endlessly with the theological details of his new position. He remained a believer in clerical celibacy and in transubstantiation, by which the elements of bread and wine became Christ's body and blood at the priestly consecration. But Henry also became increasingly convinced that humanity did not need priestly intercession in order to gain salvation. This quasi-Protestantism rationalized the king's self-interest, but the process of an 'English Reformation' that Henry inaugurated so inadvertently led to an increasingly profound Protestantization of the English people.

Parliament's Importance Grows

Parliament became more central to English kingship from the 1530s onwards since it was carefully drafted legislation that asserted the new powers – especially in the Act of Supremacy (1534). It was now the combined institutional power of 'King in Parliament' which passed laws and expressed sovereignty in the king's name. The Act of Parliament therefore became a more powerful legislative instrument and carried the full weight of religious authority behind it. Parliamentary acts overrode the status of royal edicts but Henry worked well with his parliaments, especially since the new process allowed for the imposition of clerical taxation, and enabled the transfer to the crown of the substantial wealth of the monasteries which were dissolved in 1536–40.

Refusal to accept the king's title as 'Supreme Governor' of the Church of England had become tantamount to treason and it was on this charge that Thomas More,

Hans Holbein the Younger's 1527 portrait of Sir Thomas More captures the intellectual intensity of Tudor England's most eminent humanist thinker. More's principled refusal to accept that the king could be 'Supreme Governor' of the English church led to his trial and execution in 1535.

England's leading humanist scholar and its chancellor (1529–32), gained a martyr's crown. More's beheading in July 1535 blackened Henry's reputation among the learned and some 50 other 'traitors' were convicted under the new treason laws.

Five More Marriages for Henry

Successive marriages made Henry look foolish as well as tyrannical: Boleyn was executed in 1536 on the grounds of possible adultery as well as treason; Jane Seymour died shortly after giving birth in 1537 to a male heir, Edward; Anne, sister of the duke of Cleves, was swiftly divorced by Henry. She had become England's queen because Cromwell wanted a north European alliance directed against both France and the empire. The marriage failure undermined Cromwell's position and, in 1540, he too was executed. Queen Anne's successor was Catherine Howard whose adultery despatched her to the block in 1542. Catherine Parr found herself married to a fat paranoid.

In 1542 Henry resumed an anti-Habsburg foreign policy by forming a French alliance, which in turn meant a financially ruinous war against the Scots. The crown therefore had to sell off the monastic lands it had gained, and this together with coinage debasement led to calamitous inflation.

Henry's aura of magnificence existed to serve his ruthlessness, which was the sole constant element within an otherwise capricious ego. Nonetheless by speech, act and gesture he had personalized English monarchy to a degree unique in its history and thereby made it central to England's national identity.

CHARLES V, Holy Roman Emperor

R. 1519–1556

In 1519 a Spanish king (reigning as Charles I) who was also a ruler in the Netherlands was elected 'King of the Romans', the German title which made him Holy Roman Emperor-elect and thereby gave him authority in central and eastern Europe. It cost Charles the huge sum of 852,000 Rhenish gulden (the equivalent of two tons of pure gold) to secure his election and it was the Fugger banking dynasty in Augsburg, as well as financiers in Florence and Genoa, who advanced him the credits necessary to buy the votes of the other electoral princes.

As archduke of Austria, this young lantern-jawed prince was already the dynastic ruler of a substantial collection of territories within the empire, but in other imperial lands he would be constrained by his electoral vows and could exercise few direct powers. Nonetheless, the election was a major Habsburg coup especially since Charles had beaten his dynasty's greatest rival, Francis I of France.

Charles's Early Life and Dynastic Connections
Born in Ghent in 1500, the son of Philip who was heir to the Habsburg ruler and Holy Roman Emperor Maximilian I, Charles was raised there by his paternal aunt, Margaret of Austria; she ruled the Netherlands as regent during the period of his minority after his father died in 1506. The prosperous, cloth-producing county of Flanders was a key component of the Habsburgs' trans-European ambitions and had become attached to the dukedom of Burgundy in 1384, when Philip the Bold inherited it through his wife Margaret, the Flanders heiress. Maximilian's marriage to Mary, heiress to the last independent duke of Burgundy, had made Flanders a Habsburg possession.

Emperor Maximilian had also engineered the marriage of his son Philip to Joanna, heiress to the united crowns of Aragon and Castile through her parents Ferdinand and Isabella. This monarchical domain would eventually include most of the rest of Spain, and it also extended from Naples and Sicily (the two kingdoms attained by Aragonese conquest) to the New World of largely

A study in triumphalism: the Venetian painter Titian's equestrian portrait of Charles V after his major victory over a confederation of German Lutheran princes – the Schmalkaldic League – at the Battle of Mühlberg in 1547.

Castilian conquest. Charles's mother, Joanna, died in 1555 but her insanity had already taken her out of the dynastic game and Charles therefore entered into his Spanish inheritance on the death of his grandfather Ferdinand in 1516. His younger brother, also called Ferdinand, succeeded to the throne of Hungary after the catastrophic slaughter inflicted by the Turks on the Hungarians, including the death of their king, Louis II, Ferdinand's brother-in-law, at the Battle of Mohács (1526). Consequently, the Habsburgs' eastern frontier was exposed to the Turks.

A European Empire

Maximilian had been a supreme exemplar of Renaissance kingship, an ideology that was determined to strengthen princely power by all means available.

Commissioning cheap and easily produced woodcuts, he had used the new print technology which was especially advanced in south Germany to produce propaganda on behalf of himself and his dynasty. In the late 1510s, his successor Charles had seemed to be on the point of realizing the Habsburgs' long held ambition of creating a European empire. The new emperor was a sincere believer in the ideal of a united Christendom and therefore worked hard, despite papal opposition, to secure an internal reformation of the Catholic Church – a policy that eventually bore fruit in the work of the Council of Trent.

Adrian of Utrecht, the eminent humanist scholar (and, briefly, a pope), had been his tutor in youth and an important member of the *devotio moderna* movement which, from the 15th century onwards, had spread new standards of learning and piety among the laity of the Netherlands. But Lutheranism, a force whose appeal Charles never really understood, divided Europe sharply between equally convinced Protestant rulers and Catholic ones. With his chivalric code and attachment to an obsolete conception of European imperial unity, Charles came to be seen as the last of the medieval rulers.

The Irrelevance of Chivalry

Charles's predecessor as Holy Roman Emperor, his grandfather Maximilian I (r. 1493–1519) extended the influence of the Habsburg dynasty through a series of military conquests and prudent marriages.

Typically, he thought his quarrels with Francis I could be sorted out in the personal and knightly manner by challenging the French king to a duel. Charles's sister, Eleanor, was married to Francis and the fact that Francis had infected her with syphilis affronted Charles. On a less personal level, the French kingdom's involvement in a series of wars in northern Italy was the result of a consistent hostility to Habsburg power and it would countenance a Turkish alliance for the same reason. Charles issued his challenge three times and each time Francis refused to duel. The ambitions of dynastic forces in a new Europe dominated by sharply defined national rivalries had turned chivalric gesture into an irrelevance.

Charles's Finances

Charles was always broke. His floating debt rose from 20,000 livres in 1516 to 7,000,000 in 1556; the real impact of New World bullion imports on the Spanish economy only started after his reign. But he did have an expert knowledge of financial instruments having been raised in the southern Netherlands which was Europe's most commercially sophisticated region. Antwerp's credit market and banking centre was especially advanced having been developed to deal with the profitable exchanges of the English textile trade. Charles pioneered the sale of government-backed bonds which paid interest: bonds such as the *renten* and *juros* kept his empire afloat.

The Flemish Art Market

Flemish prosperity was also basic to the area's vigorously local artistic tradition, which was especially concentrated in Antwerp, Ghent and Bruges. Ever since the time of Jan van Eyck these towns' apprenticeship schemes had been training their painters and craftsmen in styles for which there was a reliable local market and the resilience of that business kept the region immune from Italianate influences. Hieronymus Bosch's portrayals of a chaotic world resulted from that energetic localism and made him a firm Habsburg favourite. Charles's father commissioned a Last Judgement from Bosch in 1504 and his son Philip II would become a major collector of the Flemish painter's canvases.

Charles himself was an expert connoisseur with a fine eye for *objets d'art* as well as paintings. But the need to travel almost continuously among his extensive territories meant that there was no one central palace which could provide a focus for his work as a patron. The greatest portraitist of Charles is Titian who hated leaving his native Venice but had to travel, usually to Augsburg or Milan, to fulfil the imperial commissions. His study of Charles after his defeat of the German Lutheran princes at the Battle of Mühlberg shows him astride a horse in the manner of a conquering Roman emperor, while that painted just before the end of his reign, captures both Charles's nobility and his melancholia. Neither reflects the physical slightness of an emperor who, plagued by gout in later years, had to tie himself to the saddle with one leg in a sling.

Charles V in Spain

Charles was fluent in French, Italian and German, but when he arrived among his Spanish subjects he knew hardly a word of their language. However, after an unusually long sojourn in the country in 1522–9 he identified himself closely with the Spanish people and their culture. During this period he started, but left uncompleted, his Renaissance palace at the Alhambra in Granada and, at about the same time, the Castilian nobility displaced the Burgundian-Flemish aristocracy's predominance at his court. This Hispanicisation made him unpopular in papal Rome, since Spain had been notorious for its varieties of

CHARLES V
1500–1558

1500 Born in Ghent

1506 Becomes ruler of the Netherlands with his aunt initially acting as regent

1516 Becomes king of Spain as Charles I

1519 Becomes Holy Roman Emperor elect

1522–9 Resides in Spain

1525 Defeats the French at the Battle of Pavia

1527 Rome is sacked by Charles's mutinous troops

1530 Formally crowned Holy Roman Emperor by the pope

1535 Victory at Tunis over the Turks

1555 Charles abdicates as ruler of the Netherlands; the Peace of Augsburg formalizes the division of Europe into Catholic and Protestant realms

1556 Charles renounces his claim to the imperial crown, but does not formally abdicate until 1558

1558 Charles dies at a house in San Geronimo de Yuste near the Hieronymite Monastery

Christian heresy in the Middle Ages. The jibes of papal circles about Jewish and Moorish blood running in the veins of Spanish kings survived Ferdinand and Isabella's final expulsion of the Jews in 1492. Matters were not helped when the emperor's mutinous Spanish troops (aided by some German Lutheran mercenaries) sacked Rome on 6 May 1527 after Pope Clement VII had intrigued with Francis I and against Charles.

New Ways at Court

There were, however, limits to Charles's adopted Spanishness and in the formal political testament written to counsel his son and heir Philip in 1543, he stressed the need to keep a certain distance from the Spanish nobility. In particular he noted the need to keep faith with Burgundy and its traditions since this was *nuestra patria* ('our fatherland'). This loyalty and care explains why he decided in 1548 to reorganize Philip's court in Castile and impose on it the famously ceremonial etiquette of the Burgundian princes. Philip, a very Spanish prince, had to be educated in his wider role. Similar innovations in ritual had been introduced to Charles's court early in his reign, such as the arrangement of table knives in a Burgundian cross when the king dined in public on state occasions. But the reforms of 1548 were on a different scale involving a large number of new aristocratic jobs. Philip's household of major officials doubled to some 200 and the aim was to bind the aristocracy to the dynasty's service.

It was now, for example, the lord high steward's unique right to hand the royal napkin to the prince at dinner. The great chamberlain drew back the curtains from the royal bed in the morning and the office of *sumiller de corps*, a figure regularly in attendance at the royal close-stool, would be keenly contended for among ambitious courtier-politicians. Charles was therefore now appointing the nobility to new household offices as a reward for personal service to the king rather than as a formal recognition of their hereditary status. The Spain of Charles V was no more than a federation of lands each with its own separate court. What unity there was came from the politics of those courts and that of Castile enjoyed predominance among them. The implications of the Burgundian ritual's introduction therefore amounted to a major political innovation and excited protests in the Castilian *cortes*.

Charles enjoyed a number of major successes. The victories in Tunis (1535) against Turkish-backed pirates are celebrated in a series of fine tapestries. On 22 February 1530 he was crowned with the iron crown of Lombardy after concluding a peace deal with the northern Italian towns. The *trionfo* accorded him in Bologna two days later, when he was formally crowned emperor by the pope, is one of the great set pieces in the history of European imperial kingship with the attendant heralds bearing the arms of England, France, Hungary, Savoy and Lorraine.

Abdication and Retreat

But at Brussels on 25 October 1555 Charles signed his abdication as ruler of the Netherlands and in the same year he relinquished the imperial crown: the subsequent division of his titles between the Spanish and the Austrian branches of the Habsburgs was a recognition of personal failure. In Germany he had supported various territorial leagues as constitutional solutions to the empire's now chronic chaos. These all failed. By the terms of the peace of Augsburg (1555) he allowed Germany's Catholic and Lutheran states to coexist with their populations being forced to follow the rulers' confessional allegiances; this principle is enshrined in the phrase *cuius regio, eius religio* ('the ruler's religion is also that of his realm'). The ideal of a universal Catholic and imperial order had been abandoned.

Titian had painted Charles holding the imperial and holy lance. Yet no such triumphalism marked the disillusioned emperor's journey from Brussels to his adopted Spain in September 1556 where he spent his few remaining years in the house built for him at San Geronimo de Yuste, near the monastery of the Hieronymite order among whose members he now prepared to make his final account to God.

After his accession to the Spanish throne in 1516, Charles set about rebuilding the magnificent Alhambra at Granada, the former seat of the Moorish rulers of Spain. His unfinished Renaissance palace can be seen on the right of this view of the fortress.

SULEYMAN I, the Magnificent Sultan

R. 1520–1566

Suleyman the Magnificent, shown in a portrait from the workshop of Titian. His reign brought major expansion of the Ottoman empire, in Iraq, North Africa and Europe. Suleyman's fleet dominated the Mediterranean for many decades and he also presided over a great flowering in art, literature and Islamic law.

A new palace had arisen on the heights of the Byzantine acropolis in what had been Constantinople but was now Istanbul. Sultan Mehmed II, whose forces took the city in 1453, had ensured that the Topkapi Palace, his government's nerve-centre, commanded both a western and an eastern view. Those expansive horizons on either side of the Bosphorus suited the scale of Ottoman ambition, and artistic patronage illustrated the same theme of universal rule

Three pavilions, built in Iranian, Ottoman and Italian style, surrounded a courtyard inside the palace precincts and Gentile Bellini had arrived from Venice to produce portraits and medals of Mehmed based on Renaissance models.

Suleyman's Patronage of the Arts

The workshop of another Venetian, Titian, would later produce a portrait of Suleyman which evoked the balance of fear, admiration and curiosity in the western appreciation of a ruler termed 'the Magnificent' by Europeans – but known to his subjects as 'the lawgiver' or *Kanuni*.

Books in Greek, Arabic, Latin, Persian and Ottoman Turkish on history, geography and literature were being written in the palace scriptorium. Suleyman had appointed Arifi (d.1561/2), the first official Ottoman chronicler, to write in Persian the first *History of the House of Osman*. These dynastic histories which anchored the Ottomans in world history were themselves works of art in the beauty of their calligraphy, illuminations, miniature illustrations and bindings. The imperial architect Sinan (1489–1588), recruited from an Anatolian Christian family, had provided Suleyman with the greatest architectural statement of his imperial dignity – the Suleymaniye mosque.

The Rise of the Ottoman Dynasty

The Turkic peoples, originally based on the central Asiatic steppe, had been moving westwards ever since the impact on them of the Huns in the first and second centuries AD. Those Turks who were ruled by the house of Seljuk became a major 11th-century power and, having consolidated their position in Iran and Transcaucasia, they established their power in the old Arabic-Islamic heartlands.

Their victory at Manzikert (1071) deprived the Byzantines of Anatolia, an area which, after the collapse of the greater Seljuk empire, was ruled by the Seljuks of Rum. By the late 13th century the Mongols had defeated the Seljuks, occupied eastern Anatolia, and established their suzerainty elsewhere in the region.

The house of Osman, founder of the Ottoman dynasty, ruled one of the surviving independent Turkmen principalities in the northwest of Anatolia. This principality attracted great masses of nomads and of the urban unemployed who now roamed the Middle East searching both for a livelihood and a way to fulfill their vocation as *ghazi* warriors for Islam. Absorbing other Turkmen principalities, the 14th-century Ottomans first concentrated on seizing Byzantine lands in southeastern Europe; from 1354 Gallipoli became their key military base. Victory at Kosovo in 1389 gave them control of large areas of the southern Balkans. By the 1390s the Ottomans had assimilated the Turkmen principalities of eastern Anatolia and their rulers had been granted the title of sultan by the 'Abbasid caliphate of Cairo despite that institution's subjection to Egypt's Mamluk rulers.

The campaigns of Timur who, although a Turk, wished to restore a Mongol empire, destabilized the first Ottoman empire. Having defeated the Ottomans at

The imposing interior of the Suleymaniye mosque in Istanbul, the masterpiece of Suleyman's chief architect Sinan. Its minarets and semi-domes were surmounted by a magnificent main dome, and from the 1550s onwards, the Suleymaniye mosque dominated the skyline of Istanbul, centre of the world's largest political entity west of China.

Ankara in 1402 Timur restored power to the local Turkmen principalities. But he made no attempt to consolidate his rule in the area, having only aimed to protect his west flank in Anatolia before resuming his conquest of India. The Ottomans were thus able to regain imperial control but remained suspicious of the traditional Turkish nobility who had abandoned them during Timur's assault. Accordingly, they built up the power of non-Turkish converts to Islam who entered the sultans' personal service. The Janissary infantry was this group's military arm and the *devsirme* system drafted Christian youths from the Balkans into it.

The sultan favoured this circle by granting it conquered European territories, and its members therefore became the foremost advocates of a continued policy of western expansion while the nobility, seeing its influence thereby reduced, opposed such campaigns. The decision to launch a final push against Constantinople, bitterly opposed by the nobility, was a victory for the *devsirme* and, after 1453, many of the nobility were either executed or exiled to Anatolia and their European estates were confiscated.

Selim I and his Conquests

Suleyman was the son of Selim I, the beneficiary of a Janissary coup which had dethroned Bayezid II. Wishing to secure his own position against a repetition of such familial intrigue Selim killed his brothers and their seven sons as well as four of his own five sons. Suleyman's evident ability singled him out and saved his life. His inheritance from Selim included a new emphasis on total subjection to the sultan as the defining characteristic of the ruler's immediate circle. Selim's campaigns against the Safavid dynasty of Iran and the Mamluks of Egypt also bequeathed to him immense military, cultural and ideological advantages.

The Safavids were a Turkic group who had rebelled against the Ottoman authoritarianism and invaded Iran where, being drawn to a mystical interpretation of Islam, they established Shi'ite teaching as the state religion. The dynasty (1502–1736) spread a message of religious heresy and political rebellion in eastern Anatolia before Selim's campaigns, massacring thousands, reasserted Ottoman control and Sunni Islam authority in the area. This gave Selim the base from which he went on to conquer the Mamluks, rulers of Syria as well as of Egypt, in 1516–17. Ottoman territories doubled and revenues soared making the dynasty one of the world's richest. As the new rulers of Mecca and Medina, the Ottoman sultans became undisputed leaders of the Islamic world and, because the heartlands of the ancient caliphate were also now within their new empire, they gained access to the riches of Islamic civilization, whose intellectuals and artists now flocked to Istanbul. Mamluk defeat also gave the Ottomans control over the Middle Eastern parts of the overland, east–west trade routes which, however, were dwindling in significance after the Portuguese pioneered a maritime route round the Cape.

A print showing a leader of the Janissary corps, the bodyguard and household troops of the Ottoman sultan. This elite military unit grew steadily in influence in Istanbul after its inception in the 14th century.

Suleyman's European campaign following his capture of Belgrade (1521) concentrated on gaining control of Hungary. This brought him into direct conflict with the Habsburgs but also created a common interest with the anti-Habsburg French who became his allies. French subjects were granted extensive rights of travel and trade in Ottoman territories under the Capitulations Treaty (1536) whose provisions led to a long-lasting French cultural and commercial presence in the Levant. The Ottoman–Habsburg struggle took Suleyman's army to the gates of Vienna which he besieged in 1529, but was unable to take. In 1531 he occupied Hungary but sporadic border conflicts with Habsburg forces continued for the rest of his reign and set the westernmost limits to his expansion.

The struggle for Mediterranean naval supremacy was equally vigorous, with Charles V seeking to exploit Venice's naval decline. Suleyman expelled the Knights of Rhodes from their base in 1522 and Charles then established them in Malta in 1530 where they organised piratical raids on Ottoman shipping and lands. Suleyman enrolled in his service the great Turkish pirate Khayr ad-Din – popularly known as Barbarossa – whose fleet had already captured Algiers in 1529 and the town was therefore annexed to the empire. Barbarossa defeated the Habsburg fleet off Albania in 1538 following which Venice surrendered Morea and Dalmatia, its last Aegean possessions. Ottoman naval supremacy in the eastern Mediterranean lasted until the allied Christian victory at Lepanto (1571).

Suleyman's capture of Iraq from the Safavids, confirmed at the Peace of Amasya (1555), enabled him to build up Basra as a naval base from which to attack the Portuguese fleet, which was attempting to enforce use of the Cape maritime trade route. But he was never able to defeat the Iranian Safavid army and, at the 1555 Peace, was forced to renounce Ottoman claims to the Caucasus and Azerbaijan.

Power of the Harem

Ottoman power had reached its furthest possible limits and an exhausted Suleyman abandoned himself to the harem's delights. As a result the office of grand vizier assumed a new importance during the later years of his reign and this chief minister could himself command an absolute obedience to his will. Suleyman's patronage of the *devsirme* had raised them to a degree of influence, which undermined the authority of his successors. These factions now struggled to gain control of the state by allying themselves with different elements within an increasingly faction-ridden palace society, a development anticipated in the career of Roxelana, Suleyman's chief concubine.

Known as Rossa to the Ottomans, she had been seized by Crimean Tatars raiding Russian and Ukrainian territory and, after being sold as a slave, she joined the imperial harem. She advanced swiftly to become one of the four chief concubines. Ottoman tradition required that the sultan's successor should be the son of one

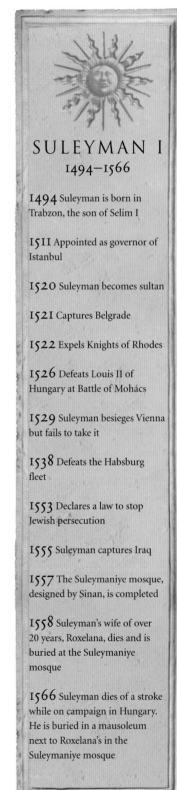

SULEYMAN I
1494–1566

1494 Suleyman is born in Trabzon, the son of Selim I

1511 Appointed as governor of Istanbul

1520 Suleyman becomes sultan

1521 Captures Belgrade

1522 Expels Knights of Rhodes

1526 Defeats Louis II of Hungary at Battle of Mohács

1529 Suleyman besieges Vienna but fails to take it

1538 Defeats the Habsburg fleet

1553 Declares a law to stop Jewish persecution

1555 Suleyman captures Iraq

1557 The Suleymaniye mosque, designed by Sinan, is completed

1558 Suleyman's wife of over 20 years, Roxelana, dies and is buried at the Suleymaniye mosque

1566 Suleyman dies of a stroke while on campaign in Hungary. He is buried in a mausoleum next to Roxelana's in the Suleymaniye mosque

The harem in the Topkapi Palace in Istanbul was home to some 300 concubines of the sultan. These women were slaves of mostly Christian origin. In this hidden and closely guarded part of the palace, the women were attended by servant girls and eunuchs; the only man granted access was the sultan himself.

of these chief concubines and Roxana intrigued against Mustafa, Suleyman's first born son, who was first banished from court in 1534 and then murdered. She then worked to ensure the succession of Selim, her son by Suleyman, and undermined the authority of her opponent, the very capable grand vizier, Ibrahim, who was dismissed and subsequently assassinated in 1536. Suleyman's devotion to Roxana saw him become the first sultan in Ottoman history to be married and his wife became his chief policy adviser, exerting a special influence in foreign affairs.

The harem became dominant during the 'Sultanate of Women' (1570–8) and the chief Janissary officers effectively ran the state for half a century after that period. It suited such factions to keep the princes isolated within the palace rather than being trained on the field of battle as Suleyman had been. He was therefore the last sultan to receive an appropriate preparation for the complexity of government run according to 'the Ottoman Way' – that immense variety of customs and beliefs which had given cohesion to the state and empire.

Ottoman Decline

Almost all the 14th and 15th century conquests in Europe had now been distributed to military officers as *timars* or fiefdoms in lieu of paying them a state salary. But this meant that the *devsirme* were in charge of huge private estates which were beyond the state's control and therefore failed to produce revenue. The tax-farm (*iltizam*) system had been introduced to pay Janissaries' salaries and meet the soaring costs of running the palace. Tax-farmers were allowed to keep a proportion of whatever they could collect, and so had the incentive of profit. But corrupt tax-farmers could deny the state its dues as central authority dwindled. Transit duties made goods carried across Ottoman lands hopelessly uncompetitive compared to the exports transported via the Cape route, which was now being run and vigorously protected by the Dutch and English.

Ottoman decline was protracted, and punctuated by schemes for imperial revival. As the sultans became increasingly remote so their subjects came to rely on the institutions which really influenced their lives: the guilds which regulated economic activity and the *millets*, self-governing administrative units that regulated social provision. Reformers at the top and the masses alike looked back to the reign of Suleyman as a golden age in which the Ottoman state had attained its classical expression. But the sultan's magnificence had been created by the same forces that would unravel his prodigious legacy.

AKBAR, Mughal Emperor of India
R. 1556–1605

A Mughal miniature of 1590 depicts Akbar receiving tribute from Abdullah Khan, governor of Malwa province. Akbar's reforms divided India into 15 provinces ('subahs').

Its seclusion had made the emperor's discussion group a subject of speculation, some of it critical. Akbar's courtship of public opinion was a feature of his reign and each morning at dawn he would stand by his window so that his subjects might see and celebrate the imperial presence in their midst.

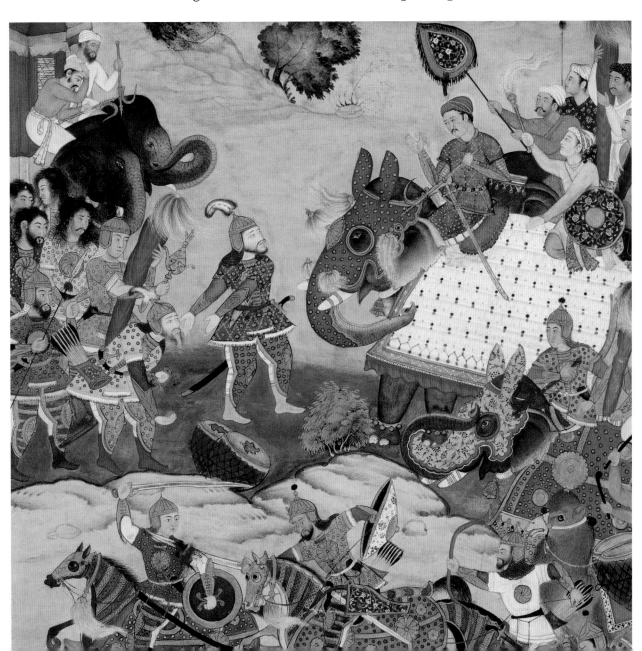

But the courtiers who belonged to the *Din e-Ilahi* ('divine faith' in Persian) met in secret, were few in number and discussed religious doctrines without either sharing sacred scriptures or obeying a priestly hierarchy. Akbar, it was known, had enlightened views seeing aspects of truth in most religions without completely subscribing to any one of them. These 19 or so chosen courtiers shared his interest in mysticism and invented their own religious rituals drawn from different traditions. Light was worshiped, animal slaughter forbidden, and the 1000 Sanskrit names for the sun recited in the Hindu manner. Earnest conversation followed on how the soul might best be purified. But for many – and especially Muslims – the *Din e-Ilahi* was dangerously near the point where courtier flattery might turn into blasphemy. *Allahu akbar*, one of the circle's formulaic prayers, certainly meant 'God is great' but critics pointed out that it could also be interpreted as 'God is Akbar.'

Akbar's Line of Descent

Akbar's grandfather Babur was a Chagatai Turk, so called because his tribe's ancestral homeland north of the Oxus river in central Asia was the heritage of Genghis Khan's son, Chagatai. Babur claimed to be 13th in the line of descent, on his mother's side, from Genghis Khan but his Mongol tribe had long since become Turkicized as a result of living in Turkish regions. He was fifth in the line of direct male descent from Timur and it was that lineage which was both the source of his power and the origin of his inspiration.

Babur's principality of Fergana lay to the Hindu Kush's north and was one of the many states run by the princes of the Timurid dynasty descended from the great conqueror. Each competed against the other to restore Timur's empire and in 1497, then again in 1501, Babur had both occupied and ruled Samarkand, Timur's capital. He did so though as a vassal of Iran's Safavid dynasty, a power assailed by Ottomans to their west and by Uzbeks (Turkic-Iranians of Mongolian origin) in their northeast. Uzbek forces dispossessed Babur not just of Samarkand but also of Fergana and he was forced to retreat to Kabul which he occupied in 1504 and then made his base. By the 1510s he had abandoned his 20-year campaign to gain Samarkand. Never again would he see that city's domes glittering in the sun with their decorations of majolica (glazed tilework) and mosaics, marble and gold. He would have to turn south to realize the Timurid ambition of world dominion.

Northern India had been invaded briefly by Timur in 1398 and in a historic resumption of his ancestor's campaign, Babur started his first raids into the region in 1519. On 21 April 1526 at Panipat, 50 miles north of Delhi, helped by the loan of Ottoman artillery, Babur's army defeated the forces of the Lodi sultanate, a confederation of Afghan and Turkish chiefs which ruled northern India (including the Punjab) from its Delhi base. The sultan Ibrahim Lodi, an

Babur, founder of the Mughal dynasty, flanked on his left by his Mongol ancestor Timur and on his right by his son and successor Humayun. The Mughal empire was to rule the subcontinent until the growth of British control over India in the late 18th century.

Afghan, was killed in battle and within days Babur was in Delhi establishing control over the former Lodi territories. Resistance continued among the Rajputs, India's traditional Hindu class of warrior-landowners whose territories and states were spread across central and north India.

Akbar Succeeds to his Inheritance

The Rajput state of Mewar was conquered by Babur's forces in 1527 and in 1535 his son, and successor, Humayun conquered the northwest state of Gujarat. Sher Shah, an Afghan mercenary, however, drove Humayun out of India in 1540 and established a new dynasty which ruled northern India for the next 15 years. With Iranian military aid Humayun took first Lahore, and then Delhi and Agra, in 1555 and his 13-year-old son Akbar became Punjab's governor. The following year, Humayun having died of injuries sustained while falling down his library staircase, Akbar succeeded to a precarious inheritance.

Afghan forces led by Hemu, a Hindu general who claimed the throne for himself, took Delhi but the battle of November 1556, once again fought on Panipat's level plain, ended in a decisive Mughal victory. The defeat of the Afghan army opened the way to Delhi where Akbar was proclaimed emperor. Initially he commanded only Punjab and the Delhi area but in 1561 the Mughal army conquered the central western state of Malwa, a power which commanded the routes to the Deccan plateau. The emperor's territorial base had been consolidated.

Military Successes and Élite Control

Akbar's military campaigns extended Mughal power to the west with the conquest of Gujarat in 1573 and then to the east by gaining control of Bengal three years later. In 1562 he married a Rajput princess, the daughter of the raja of Jaipur, who then acknowledged his suzerainty, and alliances with other Rajput rulers followed. In 1568 Akbar's army massacred the inhabitants of Chitor, capital of the Rajput confederacy of Mewar in the northwest. Mewar's resistance continued for the rest of his reign but the atrocity encouraged further submissions by Rajput rajas. Rajasthan, an area of northwest India mostly ruled by Rajputs, had largely accepted Akbar's rule by 1569.

North India's previous Muslim rulers had a long tradition of governing through the local Hindu elites but Akbar made it into a central feature of his regime, one that gave stability and élan to his empire. The hundreds of thousands of Rajput warriors and landholders were allowed to keep their strips of land and maintain their Hindu traditions as long as they gave military service in return and paid tribute to Akbar's overlordship. Rajputs were encouraged to join the army and the bureaucracy. Many became generals and provincial governors, and the imperial service mingled Persians, Central Asians and Turks with Indian Muslims and Hindus although Afghans, Akbar's unremitting foes, were mostly excluded.

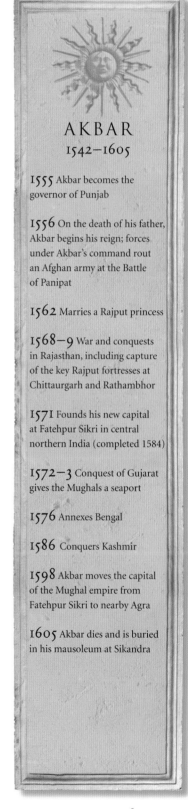

AKBAR
1542–1605

1555 Akbar becomes the governor of Punjab

1556 On the death of his father, Akbar begins his reign; forces under Akbar's command rout an Afghan army at the Battle of Panipat

1562 Marries a Rajput princess

1568–9 War and conquests in Rajasthan, including capture of the key Rajput fortresses at Chittaurgarh and Rathambhor

1571 Founds his new capital at Fatehpur Sikri in central northern India (completed 1584)

1572–3 Conquest of Gujarat gives the Mughals a seaport

1576 Annexes Bengal

1586 Conquers Kashmir

1598 Akbar moves the capital of the Mughal empire from Fatehpur Sikri to nearby Agra

1605 Akbar dies and is buried in his mausoleum at Sikandra

Akbar's arrangements with the rulers of Rapjput states were neo-feudal but the areas under direct imperial control were run by a new class of officials, the *mansabdars*, graded in 33 levels according to the numbers at their command, which ranged from 10 to 5000. These imperial bureaucrats were mostly foreigners and provided the personnel both for the army's officers and for the civil administration whose members were also given military ranking. All owed loyalty therefore to their commander-in-chief, the emperor. Like Egypt's Mamluks and the Ottomans' janissaries the *mansabdars* could not inherit their offices and they could be moved from one area to another at the emperor's will. The *mansabdars* therefore had little opportunity to build up local connections and they also lacked the money to finance any dissident private armies.

The 15 Provinces of India

The officers, both military and civilian, were either paid in cash from the central treasury or retained their salary equivalent from the revenues collected on the lands assigned to them before the remaining sums were remitted to the treasury. Akbar used this structure to divide India into 15 provinces each with its governor, revenue officer, religious administrator and judge. Government agents kept an eye on the local situation and their letters were sent directly to the central Delhi administration, which was itself divided into four main branches: the offices of prime minister, finance minister, paymaster general and chief justice whose duties also covered religious affairs. This system's effectiveness enabled Akbar to gather reliable and detailed economic statistics. By 1580 he had averaged differential crop productivity and prices over a ten-year period and related those statistics to the variability in soil quality: this data then became the basis of revenue demands.

The Necessity of Religious Toleration

Muslims were only a tiny minority in Akbar's India and a campaign for mass Islamicization a practical impossibility. The new policy of religious toleration therefore recognized India's cultural diversity while also acknowledging its potential to tear the whole empire apart. Toleration reflected Akbar's personal views. But the policy also served his imperial interests. Accordingly, the special poll tax or *jizya* paid by non-Muslims was abolished, the forcible conversion of prisoners of war to Islam was banned, and the tax paid on non-Muslim pilgrimages rescinded. Islamic legal courts continued but the judicial decisions of Hindu village elders were respected.

The imperial edict of 1579 made Akbar himself the supreme arbiter on Islamic religious issues, and he encouraged the view that religious wisdom was concentrated in his own person as an emperor who accepted all his subjects regardless of creed. This dramatic innovation made Akbar's personality a source of divine enlightenment which bypassed traditional Islamic jurists and scholars. Turko-Mongolian and central Asian traditions maintained that the prince's

The Diwan-i Khas, where Akbar held private audiences, in Fatehpur Sikri ('city of victory'). Inaugurated in 1571 and completed in 1584, this city served as the capital of the Mughal empire only until 1598, when its unreliable water supply forced relocation of the capital to Agra.

power should be shared with his immediate circle of nobles but Akbar, by contrast, made himself the very centre of government and a cult of his own attractive personality developed as a result.

His views however were integral to his character and both were used to turn the very loose federation of Muslim nobles he had inherited into an ethnically diverse ruling group loyal to himself. His central Asian retinue, fearing the loss of their exclusive powers, turned to widespread rebellion in the period 1564–74 and used as a pretext the resentments of orthodox Muslims alarmed by Akbar's religious toleration. The imperial army crushed such rebellions ruthlessly.

Akbar Founds his New Town of Fatehpur Sikri

Akbar's policy of ethnic and religious fusion achieved its best architectural expression in Fatehpur Sikri, the town he founded in 1569 west of his fortress of Agra in north central India. Until 1598 this was his capital and its buildings, especially the great mosque or *Jami'Masjid* whose massive Victory Gate commemorates the 1573 victory over Gujarat, mingles Hindu decoration with a monumental Islamic architectural form.

Conquests continued right to the reign's end as Akbar strengthened his power on the northwest frontier, an area that was a crucial source of supply for his cavalry's horses. Kashmir was conquered in 1586 followed by Sind five years later, and the seizure of Qandahar from the Iranian Safavids in 1595 was the culmination of his campaign in the region.

The Death of Akbar

At the time of his death ten years later Akbar's army was advancing into the Deccan plateau and towards southern India. He had been India's first unifier and Mughal power lasted at its most effective in northern India for almost a century after his death. His legacy was undermined by the religious intolerance of the emperor Aurangzeb (r.1658–1707) whose exclusion of Hindus from public office and persecution of Sikhs resulted in an ultimately fateful subversion of Mughal authority. The enlightened conversations of Akbar's circle had, it turned out, been more than idle chatter. The attitudes they engendered had been the very basis of the Mughal empire.

ELIZABETH I, Queen of England

R. 1558–1603

Of all English monarchs, it was this daughter of Henry VIII's disastrous marriage to Anne Boleyn who paid most attention to her image. As a result, the iconography of Elizabeth, the 'Virgin Queen', became identified with the success story of 'Elizabethan England'. This was the period when the country attained its European status as a major, and independent, power while also becoming part of the fabric of Renaissance achievement in arts and letters. Mental energy, linguistic versatility and innovative characterization typified the productions presented in the playhouses of late Elizabethan London. Christopher Marlowe's *Tamburlaine the Great* (1587) recreated the central Asian conqueror for the London stage and William Shakespeare's *Hamlet, Prince of Denmark* (1599-1601) is a profound exploration of the sanctity of kingship.

'We all loved her for she said she loved us' wrote one of Elizabeth's courtiers, Sir John Harington, scholar, wit and godson to the queen. The judgement is affectionately ironic. Elizabeth was a sophisticated figure, educated in the humanist scholarship of her time, and versed in the stylized rhetoric that typified Renaissance literature's expression of emotion. But her graceful way with words wasn't just a question of a clever person demonstrating her wit. This dexterity was used to manipulate and control her courtiers. These qualities and achievements were basic to a central political fact of her reign: the development of a personality cult built around the queen's cautious, calculating and evasive

The image of the 'Virgin Queen' became a powerful symbol of English nationhood in the late 16th century. In a speech to her troops on the eve of the attack by the Spanish Armada, Elizabeth reputedly stated: '... I have the body but of a weak and feeble woman but I have the heart and stomach of a king, and of a king of England too ...'.

ELIZABETH I
1533–1603

1533 Born the daughter of Henry VIII and Anne Boleyn

1536 Anne Boleyn beheaded

1547 Henry VIII dies and Edward VI accedes to throne

1553 Mary Tudor begins her reign

1558 Elizabeth becomes queen

1559 The Act of Supremacy is passed, declaring Elizabeth the Supreme Governor of the Church of England

1562 Contracts smallpox but then recovers

1570 Elizabeth is excommunicated by Pope Pius V

1587 Mary, queen of Scots is executed after numerous plots against Elizabeth

1588 Defeat of the Spanish Armada

1598 Revolt in Ireland

1601 The Earl of Essex's rebellion and subsequent execution

1603 Elizabeth dies and is succeeded by James I

character as she steered a course through the religious, political and military dangers which threatened both her own survival and that of her realm.

Elizabeth's Court

The cultural brilliance revolved around the court since it was here that artists sought the patronage of the queen and her noble retinue. This centre of artistic display was also the heart of government, a place where worldly ambitions were pursued, exhibitionism was indulged and flattery expected. The English and Welsh gentry had the automatic right of admission to the court, while peers of the realm enjoyed the further privilege of personal access to the sovereign. Whether any of these were in fact admitted to the royal presence depended on how busy Elizabeth was at the time, and also on how well disposed she was towards the supplicant. Regal flirtatiousness was a method of regal control.

Naturally enough, the queen surrounded herself with fewer men in close attendance on her than her father had done. Both in her public life at court and within her own private apartments Elizabeth's daily companions were her maids-of-honour, many of whom were her relatives on her mother's side and to whom she was correspondingly close as a kind of foster-mother. Almost to the end of her life Elizabeth shared in their amusements such as dances and music-playing. She might perform on the virginals while they played the lute. But it was important not to outshine the queen. When the young Lady Mary Howard appeared splendidly dressed in a velvet gown decorated with gold and pearls she was upbraided by Elizabeth for wearing something that was 'too fine'.

Male Favourites

For all the flirtatiousness of Elizabeth's milieu, and her encouragement of it, she stuck to the conventions that kept the heart in its place. The memory of what had happened to her mother, Anne Boleyn, and to Catherine Howard hung over the court and the disastrous dalliances of Mary Stuart, queen of Scots, reinforced the point. Involvement with one of the queen's own male favourites always spelt disaster for a female courtier. Lettice Knollys, the queen's cousin once removed on her mother's side, married the earl of Leicester in 1578 after an affair which began while her husband, the earl of Essex, was still alive. Elizabeth called her 'that She-Wolf', banished Lady Leicester from court and maintained that exclusion for the remainder of the reign despite the fact that her son, Robert Devereux, earl of Essex, became in turn the queen's favourite.

Elizabeth's Suspicion of Marriage

Elizabeth's avoidance of marriage was part of a policy that kept England free of inhibiting continental alliances with foreign princes. But she was also suspicious of the very institution itself despite the matchmaking that surrounded her and made her court something of a marriage market. She was constantly advising her maids-of-honour that virginity was a reasonable alternative and was notoriously averse to married clergy. John Whitgift's bachelor status helped him become archbishop of Canterbury and Elizabeth also appreciated the single status of lay courtiers such as the long-lived Blanche Parry to whom she was devoted. Sir Walter Ralegh (also spelled Raleigh) enjoyed his greatest popularity at court while he was a bachelor and never really regained it after his marriage.

Emphasis on Elizabeth's femininity also produced an English court that was more decorous than any of its European counterparts. Elizabeth's own fastidiousness extended to smell, for she had a sensitive nose. This made for difficulties with a French ambassador, M. de Reaulx, whose halitosis, complained the queen, meant that, 'I smell him an hour after he is gone from me'. Ceremoniousness at the English court was not new. Another French ambassador had been astonished to see the young Princess Elizabeth kneel three times before her father in the course of one audience. But Elizabeth took this stress on dignity to new heights. Anyone whom she saw as she passed along in procession would be expected to kneel and, on being spoken to by Elizabeth, would then be raised up by her.

Sir Walter Ralegh (1552–1618) was given handsome rewards by Elizabeth I for his military exploits and his feats of exploration in the New World on behalf of the English crown. He fell from grace when he made pregnant and secretly married one of the queen's ladies-in-waiting, an inexcusable transgression by a royal favourite.

The Virgin Queen

This was a new development in courtly ritual and the gallantry was further accentuated by the emphasis on the queen's virginity. Invocations of the Virgin Mary had disappeared from the reformed English church, but folk memories of Marian devotion survived and were incorporated into the more secular, but equally feminine and virginal, cult of Elizabeth. The numerous portraits of Elizabeth with her white pallor (the result of layers of paste used as make-up) displayed her as a new icon for England, tinged with divinity as an anointed queen and extending protection to her people. Secular mythologies were also exploited in the extravagant literary descriptions of Elizabeth. For Walter Ralegh she was the chaste goddess Cynthia, an object of always frustrated adoration. Edmund Spenser's *Faerie Queene* presents her as Astraea, the virgin goddess of classical antiquity who returned to a ruined world in order to restore the golden age of correct order, justice and prosperity.

The real Elizabeth of flesh and blood was at the centre of court entertainments, the music and dancing, plays and tournaments, feasts and card games, which diverted both her and her circle. This contrasted sharply with her father's court dominated as it was by Henry's temperamental cruelty and often suffused with an atmosphere of fear. Elizabeth's was also an intellectual court. Promotion and honour came to those who were as well read as the queen herself, to men such as her chief minister, William Burghley, as well as to the more glittering stars of Leicester and Oxford, Sidney and Southampton.

Elizabeth's Courtiers and Subjects

Baldassare Castiglione's *Il Cortegiano* was the great 16th-century manual for those who wished to be ideal courtiers with over a hundred editions of the book being published in its various translations by 1600. The paragon portrayed in its pages had to bear himself well both as warrior and sportsman, especially so in the hunt. A graceful manner and a linguistic ability qualified the courtier for social success. French and Italian were useful languages to have at Elizabeth's court, an institution that reflected European courtly sophistication. Castiglione's pages also advised on how the courtier might buy his way into princely favour by entertaining the sovereign. Many of Elizabeth's courtiers impoverished themselves because of the cost of accommodating the queen and her retinue as she went on her official 'progress' around England's great houses. But, by these means, standards of behaviour also spread beyond the court to influence the English gentry in general and so formed that ideal of gentlemanly conduct which would influence the national character.

In this picture dating from the reign's last years, Elizabeth is shown being carried as she and her courtiers process to the Chapel Royal. The personality cult of Elizabeth was deliberately fostered during her reign and has proved enduring. But her defence of the realm also entailed persecution of anyone suspected of treason and witnessed the growth of an effective state surveillance network under her chief spymaster, Sir Francis Walsingham.

Elizabeth became an object of adulation to her subjects, rather than just her courtiers, in the 1570s. It was then that her accession day, 17 November, evolved into a national day of celebration with local celebrations involving bonfires, bell-ringing, feasts and special sermons. This popular and spontaneous development helped to fill the gap created by the abolition of the pre-Reformation feast and saints' days. At court the anniversary was marked by the famous Accession Day Tilts: courtiers on horseback would, in neo-chivalric style, mount their horses and play at being jousting knights in the tilt-yard at Whitehall. Tickets were sold for this public spectacle and the different tilts with their enactment of various mythological themes demonstrate how the arts under Elizabeth served the purpose of government propaganda.

At the Tilt for 1590 there was a musical accompaniment which, according to one attendant, was 'so sweet and secret as everyone thereat greatly marvelled. And

hearkening to that excellent melody, the earth as it were opening, there appeared a pavilion made of white taffeta … like unto the sacred temple of the Virgins Vestal.' The pavilion was lit up from within and contained a pillar on which were inscribed Latin verses extolling Elizabeth's achievement in extending her empire beyond the Pillars of Hercules to the newly explored Americas.

Years of Crisis

The period 1569–72 was one of profound danger for England. Excommunicated by the pope as a heretic, Elizabeth now reigned over a country isolated on account of its Protestantism and facing the hostility of both Valois France and Habsburg Spain. But, along with the isolation, there was also a growing awareness of the queen's uniqueness as the last of the Tudor dynasty, especially so after her recovery from smallpox. The prospect of her succession by James Stuart, a charmlessly dogmatic Scottish prince, helps to explain the intensity of Elizabeth's personal appeal in her middle and old age. The 1588 defeat of a Spanish armada, the buccaneering exploits of pirates, the skill of explorers who laid the basis of England's maritime supremacy and overseas empire: these achievements helped to define the reign and national nostalgia for Elizabethan England set in early after the queen's death.

A Monarch's Legacy

However even in Elizabeth's own time, and then especially under James I, the court attracted critics who identified it with slipperiness, hypocrisy and flattery. Walter Ralegh was the archetypal Elizabethan hero but as his star at court waned he turned against it, recommending that his readers should: 'Say to the Court it glows/ and shines like rotten wood…' Such criticism became part of a political and religious divide between the culture of the court and that of the country at large, between royal loyalties and the disaffected Puritanism of those who wanted to reform the Church of England in a more Protestant direction. Elizabeth, an intuitive pragmatist, had worked with the aristocracy and gentry in a partnership which took some of the sting out of dogmatic religious disputes. In the early 17th century this close relationship of the governing elites to the monarchy broke down and Elizabeth's reign was seen in retrospect as a period of creative consensus, a time when the monarch had reigned with the love of her subjects and thereby established the unity of England.

GUSTAV II ADOLPH (Gustavus Adolphus), King of Sweden

R. 1611–1632

A century before Sweden's sudden rise to greatness, the German doctor and alchemist, Paracelsus, had prophesied the arrival from the north of a 'Golden Lion' destined to defeat another symbolic figure, the 'Eagle', associated with the Habsburg empire. An aura of prophecy had surrounded the golden-haired Gustavus from birth, and the king's father was supposed to have said of him as a child, *'ille faciet'* (*he will do it*). Gustavus was the most professionally disciplined of all early 17th-century European kings and Sweden's transition to world power status was the direct result of his intelligence and flair. Happy to share in the digging when battlefield fortifications had to be prepared, he was a leader at once approachable and an object of awe.

Protestantism, nationalism and militarism were the forces that dominated the dynastic history of the Vasa. In 1521 the dynasty's founder, Gustavus Vasa, had led a rebellion against the union with Denmark which, formed in 1397, had relegated Sweden to a subordinate status. First as lord protector (1521–3) and then as a long-lived king (1523–60), Gustavus Vasa established a dynasty whose Lutheranism anchored it in the loyalties of a Protestant-based national identity.

But the inheritance bequeathed to Gustavus Adolphus, just 17 in the year of his accession, by his father Charles IX was grim. Charles had seized the throne from

The Battle of Lützen in November 1632 was one of the most crucial battles of the Thirty Years' War. The Swedes claimed a victory, but the casualty toll was high and Gustavus lost his life. This pre-battle scene was painted by the Flemish artist Peeter Snayers in about 1642.

In translation the original French caption on this engraving of Gustav II reads: 'Gustav Adolphus II, king of Sweden, known as "the Great", came to the throne in 1611. He was killed at the Battle of Lützen, aged 39. From the icy north to the banks of the Rhine his glory is eternal. In the midst of battle he encountered death, which snatched his life but not the victory'.

his nephew Sigismund, who had tried to rule both Sweden and Poland as king. Married to an Austrian archduchess and raised as a Catholic by his Polish mother, Sigismund had been elected king of Poland in 1587. When he was crowned king of Sweden in 1594, Sigismund had sworn to uphold Lutheranism as the state religion, but his attempt at a permanent Swedish–Polish union represented a doomed deflection from the traditions of the royal house.

Charles's Disastrous Legacy

Charles's rebellion instigated a civil war, in the course of which he defeated a largely hostile aristocracy, and he became first of all the country's effective ruler from 1599 onwards and then its king in 1604. His aim was essentially that of a Protestant variant of absolute rule seeking to build up the Swedish economy by a vigorous system of administration. He therefore imported foreign craftsmen and merchants, suppressed the aristocratic-dominated council of state, executed five leading aristocratic opponents and dominated the Swedish diet by the exercise of his own coarse and intolerant personality.

Although presenting himself as a saviour of Lutheranism, he soon quarrelled with the Swedish Lutheran church and may well have been a secret Calvinist. Charles's disastrous legacy also included an intermittent military conflict with Poland and a failed intervention in Russia, where he tried to put Gustavus on the then vacant throne. At his death Sweden was losing the war (1611–13) against the country's traditional enemy Denmark, a conflict which Charles had himself provoked. Gustavus was allowed to succeed only after promising to uphold Sweden's aristocratic constitutionalism and he had to make major concessions to the Riksdag, the representative diet.

Gustavus's First Major Success

Gustavus sued for peace with Denmark and had to yield Älvsborg, which was Sweden's only Baltic seaport. The price of defeat also included crushing levels of taxation in order to pay the indemnity demanded by Denmark. Nonetheless, the king could now concentrate his forces against Russia, whose emergence as a great European power he greatly feared – especially since the election of the Romanov dynasty in 1613 had given the country some internal stability. The Peace of Stolbova (1617) was Gustavus's first major success, and the annexation of Russian territory linked up Sweden through Finland with the Swedish province of Estonia. By cutting Russia off from the Baltic the young king had pushed the country back towards its Asian base – a fact that postponed Russia's emergence on the European political and military scene for a century.

Creative Statesmanship

In domestic politics, Gustavus opted to work with the aristocracy which, in turn, resumed its long traditions of state service. His close partnership with the chancellor Axel Oxenstierna forms one of the great chapters in the history of creative statesmanship and led to the establishment of a new supreme court (1614) as well as a treasury and chancery (1618). The admiralty and the war office, which emerged later, were major departments of state and, by the time the general statute known as the Form of Government (1634) was issued, Sweden had been given a streamlined form of government unique in Europe with a bureaucracy of civil servants, most of whom were nobles working in the state's interests.

A reform of 1617 that turned the Riksdag into a four-chamber institution representing nobles and clergy, burghers and peasants, proved so successful that it lasted until 1866. At the same time the council of state became a permanent part of government and was therefore able to administer the country while Gustavus was away fighting his wars.

National Renewal of Education

Gustavus's national renewal also involved a thorough educational reform with a national scheme of *gymnasia* at secondary level, while his endowment of the university of Uppsala was on a magnificent scale. But although the king achieved his aims co-operatively, this remained a thoroughly princely form of rule, one centred on the dynamic personality of Gustavus himself with his superb gifts of inspirational public oratory and equally effective deftness in private conversation and negotiation.

War Against Poland Resumes

In 1621 the king resumed war against Poland: Sigismund was subsidizing internal Swedish dissidents and the elder Vasa dynastic line was still contesting Gustavus's legitimate right to rule as king of Sweden. This, however, was no mere family quarrel. The Thirty Years' War, central Europe's epic Catholic–Protestant conflict, was deepening in the 1620s and Gustavus conceived of his strategy on an imaginative and grandly international scale which earned him the right to be regarded as Europe's greatest Protestant prince. He was determined to keep his throne because he feared that a Catholic Sweden, having been defeated by Poland and allied inevitably to the Austrian Habsburgs who were the leaders of central European Catholicism, would then be able to close the Baltic to Dutch shipping.

The economic consequences of such a blockade would, he reasoned, undermine the United Provinces' protracted rebellion against Spanish rule. This Dutch cause was central to the survival of Protestantism right across the continent. It was the fear of a domino effect therefore which dictated Gustavus's initial, anti-Polish,

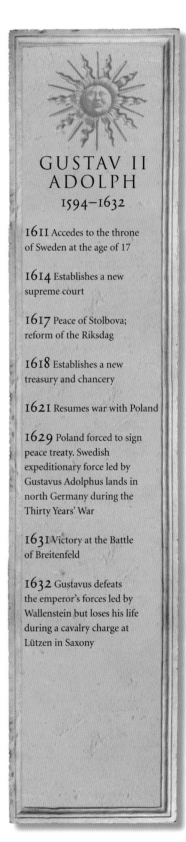

GUSTAV II ADOLPH
1594–1632

1611 Accedes to the throne of Sweden at the age of 17

1614 Establishes a new supreme court

1617 Peace of Stolbova; reform of the Riksdag

1618 Establishes a new treasury and chancery

1621 Resumes war with Poland

1629 Poland forced to sign peace treaty. Swedish expeditionary force led by Gustavus Adolphus lands in north Germany during the Thirty Years' War

1631 Victory at the Battle of Breitenfeld

1632 Gustavus defeats the emperor's forces led by Wallenstein but loses his life during a cavalry charge at Lützen in Saxony

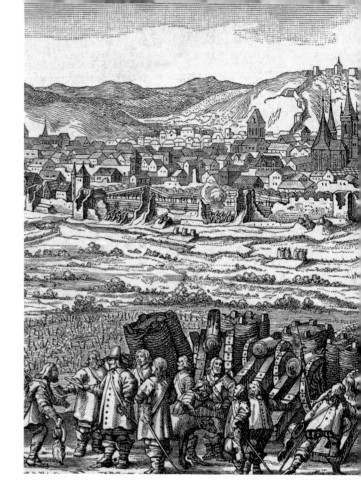

strategy and which led to the capture of Riga along with, eventually, the conquest of the whole of the previously Polish-controlled region of Livonia (Estonia and Latvia). By the time Poland was forced to sign the 1629 peace treaty its international authority had been dealt a decisive blow.

The Thirty Years' War

By the late 1620s, however, Gustavus had to turn his attention to northern Germany. Here the Protestant armies were being hammered by Tilly and Wallenstein, the generals commanding the Habsburg imperial forces which were now in occupation of Germany's Baltic coastline. Plans for a joint Habsburg-Polish navy threatened Sweden with invasion. Denmark and Sweden overcame their mutual hostility and in 1628 a joint force was sent to relieve Stralsund, the last remaining Protestant bastion in Pomerania. This was the prelude to the launch in 1630 of a Swedish expeditionary force which, led by Gustavus, landed in north Germany in an attempt to turn the tide of war. The next two years of campaigning before the king's early death would set the seal on Sweden's arrival as a major European power, and their impact would also shape the pattern of the continent's future.

Despite their parlous position the German Protestant princes were suspicious of Gustavus and his motives. But a treaty made with France in January 1631 strengthened his diplomatic position and, by the autumn of that year, both Brandenburg and Saxony were Swedish allies. Gustavus was in a dominant position militarily since he had reformed the Swedish army's organization with the same *élan* that he had shown in other areas of state building.

Innovative also in strategy, Gustavus was the first commander in history to introduce the light artillery whose easy manoeuvrability made for swiftness on the field of battle. He also reduced the size of the individual tactical unit, making it much more flexible and mobile along a line of battle which could now shift and regroup as opportunities for attack presented themselves. This gave his forces a clear advantage over the heavily massed forces of the enemy, which could regroup only with great difficulty.

'Lion of the North'

The Battle of Breitenfeld in September 1631 was a major victory over Tilly and in the winter of 1631–2 Gustavus's army swept all before it as this 'Lion of the North' advanced through central Germany. By 1632 he was contemplating organizing the incompetent German Protestant princes by getting them to

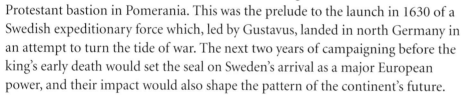

join a permanent Protestant League with himself as its military and political head.

A Swedish administration had already been imposed on the occupied territories and Gustavus was rewarding his generals and followers by bestowing conquered lands on them. Fears that Swedish domination might replace a Habsburg one restrained Gustavus's plans, however, and the league he did form in October 1632 covered only southern Germany – an area in which Protestantism was very exposed to Catholic threat. The king was now determined to conquer Bavaria and anticipated taking his campaign on to Vienna itself during the course of 1633.

Confronted by the prospect of a Swedish king establishing himself in the Hofburg, the emperor resorted to a crisis measure and recalled Wallenstein to command the imperial army despite having dismissed him just two years earlier. On 16 November 1632, at Lützen in Saxony, Gustavus and Wallenstein fought a complex battle, which lasted from dawn to dusk. The entire imperial artillery was seized and Wallenstein had to concede defeat. But the victory that was arguably Gustavus's greatest also claimed his own life and he died in the course of a cavalry charge.

Consequences of Gustavus's Reign

The European consequences of Gustavus Adolphus's reign were, and are, immense. His flair for leadership and practical intelligence built on the traditional resources of kingly power while also transplanting them to the modern world of organized government. His military genius changed the pattern of European warfare, and ambitious commanders who wished to use Gustavus's strategies now needed ever larger armies in order to implement those techniques. By the time of his death the Habsburgs had been denied their hegemonic goal and as a result there would be no centralizing Catholic and imperial power extending over central and eastern Europe.

Germany thereby was condemned to survive as a mere patchwork quilt of states until unity was imposed on her by Prussian war and diplomacy in 1871. This meant that Germany would be a European exception compared to countries such as France and England, Spain and the Scandinavian lands: areas in which kingship's powers had consolidated national territories and melded them into a greater unity. But the victories that Gustavus Adolphus won for Sweden, for Protestantism and for his view of kingly rule were also victories for a certain view of Europe. Diversity, whether in politics, culture or religion, would remain a key feature of the continent and a source of its future strength.

The Thirty Years' War marked a change in the nature of conflict from small wars to effectively total warfare. Civilian populations were affected directly as armies grew rapidly in size and often turned to living off the land to reduce sustenance costs. But successful armies such as those under Gustavus's command used smaller units of trained men, using artillery that enabled them to mount swift offensive campaigns.

179

POPE URBAN VIII (Maffeo Barberini), Bernini's Patron

R. 1623–1644

The rich, handsome aristocrat who had just been elected pope in 1623 was at the height of his powers. His diplomatic career had gained Maffeo Barberini an international reputation, but he also had cultivated tastes and the sculptor Gian Lorenzo Bernini, though many years his junior, was a friend of some standing. While Bernini was working on his sculpture *David*, Barberini had held a looking glass to the artist's face to provide a model for that look of intense concentration that had to characterize the features of the young hero emerging from the marble.

Both men believed that the function of art was not to entertain but to illustrate church doctrine through exalted imagery, so that the eye's delight might compel the mind's assent to Catholic belief. Both too were irascible. Bernini's visit to Versailles would result in Louis XIV's greatest portrait bust – but his independence of mind ensured a brief stay. This Neapolitan-born genius was invariably tactful though with Barberini, who considered him: '... a sublime artist, born by Divine Disposition and for the glory of Rome to illuminate the century'.

In the late summer of 1623 Urban summoned Bernini, then aged 24, and told him: 'It is your great fortune, Cavaliere, to see Maffeo Barberini made pope; yet our fortune is even greater, since Bernini lives in our pontificate'. Bernini, he said, should come and see him any time he wished. At their meetings Urban encouraged the idea that the sculptor should also evolve into an architect – a

Bernini began work on the tomb of his benefactor, Urban VIII, in 1628; the project was completed in 1647, three years after the pope's death. This detail from the elaborate gold, bronze and marble sculpture shows the pope extending his blessing.

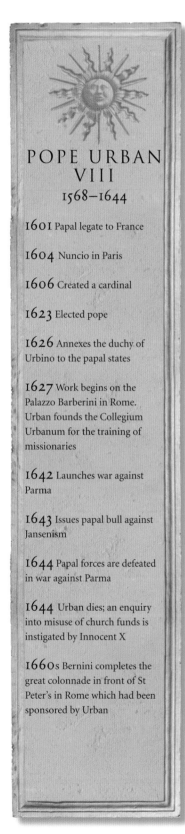

development which suited Urban whose plans for the future showed how, as a contemporary said, 'he wished to be seen as a prince'.

Urban Builds on the Legacy of Sixtus V

The legacy of Sixtus V (1585–90) included a sweeping reorganization of the curia, the papacy's central administrative apparatus, into 15 central departments or 'congregations', and he had also built up the papacy's fiscal reserves through new taxes and sale of offices. Banditry had been suppressed in the papal states and Sixtus was a vigorous civic planner: Rome's streets were widened and extensively re-routed, while the renovation of the underground pipes extending from Palestrina to the city had transformed the water supply. Rome emerged as a baroque capital and St Peter's dome was completed during Sixtus's pontificate. Urban's ambition built on this legacy and the supreme architectural expression of his policy came after his death. In the 1660s Bernini completed the colonnade whose embrace of the piazza in front of St Peter's was akin, said the artist, to the arms of the church enfolding the world.

Papal Patronage of Bernini

Sculptures whose flowing forms in the round made them look like three-dimensional pictures, new churches, fountains fed by the fresh water supply: all resulted from the papal patronage extended to Bernini, a policy initiated by Urban. He made only one demand of the artist: Bernini was to have no patron other than Urban. The supreme pontiff's powers of command are caught in Bernini's sculpture of Urban above the tomb he executed for the pope in St Peter's. The seated Urban extends his right arm and the gesture, though one of papal blessing, is also undeniably imperious. This papal possessiveness allowed but one exception. Cardinal Scipione Borghese, having helped to secure Urban's election, was allowed to employ Bernini; the end result, a bust which fixes that sensual power-broker in the eyes of all posterity, stands in the Villa Borghese. Urban might be an aesthete but he was also ruler of a sovereign state, the central figure of a great court and manager of an international diplomatic network: like any secular prince he needed to keep his friends very close to him.

The Barberini

The Barberini had played an important role in Florence's early 16th-century politics but their ambitions, along with their city's decline as a major political force, led them to move to Rome in the middle of the century. Here they became rich through their business interests and Francesco Barberini (1528–1600) was able to establish his family in dynastic style. In 1601 Maffeo was the papacy's legate in France and he then became the nuncio in Paris, before being made a cardinal in 1606. His election to the papacy was the result of years of careful cultivation of his reputation both in Rome itself and in the European courts. He was the last pope able to influence European diplomacy as a major force in his own right, and his decision to support French policy during the Thirty Years' War had a major consequence.

Urban's Political Policy

Urban's fear of a victorious Habsburg power advancing into Italy was broadly continuous with the medieval papacy's hostility towards the exercise of a German territorial power in the peninsula. He therefore decided to rule by dividing the two major Catholic powers from each other. French support meant papal opposition to Habsburg Austria, a power which might have expected some plaudits from Rome since it had declared a Catholic crusade against Protestantism in central Europe, while also opposing the Turks to the east. The Thirty Years' War could not be presented therefore as an anti-Protestant struggle maintained by a united Catholic civilization, and it became instead a struggle between European dynasties bent on asserting their territorial rights. The result of Urban's pro-French policy involved, from his own point of view, a major paradox: the pope had helped to secure the end of Europe's large-scale religious wars and their replacement by merely secular ones between nation states.

The Papal Court

Urban's loyalty to his own family, and the favours he showed them, was in the grandly dynastic tradition of European high politics. In the autumn after his election he named his nephew Francesco Barberini (1597–1679) a cardinal, and the honour was subsequently bestowed on two other members of his family, his brother Antonio the Elder (1569–1646) and Urban's nephew Antonio the Younger (1607–71). He also helped to secure his nephew Taddeo's marriage to the greatest of all Roman families, the Colonna. The family's Roman base was the Palazzo Barberini, work on which started in 1627, two years after Urban had acquired the site. Francesco Borromini – a master of complex form – worked on the project before Bernini, with his less involved designs, completed it. The end result was a princely monument and the palazzo's central architectural feature would be repeated across Europe, that of the symmetrical wings extending forward from the central block to form a *cour d'honneur*.

The papal policy of bestowing largesse and high office on favourites and relatives was no different from what happened in other European courts. But the frequent brevity of the pontificates meant that one set of courtiers displaced their predecessors with an equal rapidity. Nepotism therefore often involved lack of administrative continuity and this in turn meant that the papal states' policies lacked a long-term focus. But Urban was comparatively young when elected, and the fact that he reigned for 21 years meant that the political problems caused by

Bernini was the master of the portrait bust, to which he brought an informality of style that captured something of the personality of the sitter. In the late 1620s Urban commissioned a series of family portraits of this type, including this one of his brother, Antonio the Elder, made in c.1626–7.

Towering over the high altar at the centre of St Peter's is Bernini's Baldacchino, a huge bronze canopy almost 30 metres (100 ft) high. Completed in 1633, it was Bernini's first piece of work for St Peter's and a suitable tribute to Urban's papacy.

nepotism were obscured – until they re-emerged to undermine the papacy's effectiveness in international politics from the late 17th century onwards. Urban's annexation of the adjoining duchy of Urbino in 1626 turned the papal states into a substantial, well-consolidated, central Italian power. Civitavecchia was developed into an important port with a military harbour, the arsenal at Tivoli was expanded and the defensive citadel of Castel Sant'Angelo in Rome greatly strengthened.

Urban's Roman Domain

Popes were bishops of Rome and their spiritual authority was bound up with their right to rule in the papal states. The link between a ruler and his domain was therefore particularly acute in their case, forming as it did a necessary part of the papal claim to a universal authority as St Peter's successor. Urban's artistic projects were expensive and he also acquired Castel Gandolfo as a summer residence. But the expenditure was not of itself 'wasteful' as his opponents claimed. Magnificence, in this case, was a necessary and not an optional policy since it demonstrated the legitimacy and essence of his right to rule. His enemies – who included the Farnese family – accused him of unbridled dynasticism. But all aristocrats pursued such a policy if elected popes, as Farnese history showed: Paul III, a family member, had detached Parma and Piacenza from the papal dominions and bestowed them as independent duchies on Pier Luigi (1503–47), his son by an unknown woman, who then became the first duke of Parma.

Church Renewal

Urban's papacy, in order to be regarded as a success, in fact had to go beyond mere dynastic adventurism and nepotism. He therefore ruled as much more than just a Barberini, important though that was to him, and his papacy marks a high point in the history of the Catholic church's Counter-Reformation, the process which equipped it to meet the Protestant challenge spiritually, administratively and intellectually. Urban founded the Collegium Urbanum in 1627 for the training of missionaries and shortly afterwards he resumed the campaign for the Christianization of China and Japan. He approved St Vincent de Paul's foundation of the Vincentians, an order with a specific mission to the poor and an expertise in training seminarians, and he also encouraged the educational work of the Visitandines, an order of nuns founded by St Francis de Sales and St Jane de Chantal in 1610.

The spread of Jansenism, a French-based spiritual movement within the Catholic church, emphasized God's sovereignty and worried Urban greatly. Its account of God's foreknowledge seemed to him neo-Calvinist and he considered the associated downgrading of the role of free will positively dangerous. A major intellectual campaign was therefore directed against Jansenism after Urban issued the papal bull condemning its teachings in 1643.

The first major work Bernini executed for Urban was the great Baldacchino he designed for the high altar over St Peter's tomb in the basilica. Twisted columns of gilt bronze bring a sculptured animation to the otherwise massive architectural form and the occasional bee, a Barberini symbol, is carved onto the Baldacchino as the protégé's tribute to his prince. Bernini worked on his other major Barberini commission within the basilica, Urban's tomb, from 1628 to 1647.

Urban's Legacy

By then the entire family reputation was under assault. The war launched by Urban against Parma in 1642 ended in his defeat two years later and, once his predecessor was buried, Innocent X (1644–55) launched an official inquiry into charges that the Barberini had misappropriated church funds. Other great Roman families with papal connections, the Borghese, the Aldobrandini and Ludovisi, intrigued against the family and the two cardinals, Francesco and Antonio the Younger, fled to Paris. However, they were eventually allowed to return to Rome and to their great palazzo outside which, in the Piazza Barberini, they could see the Triton fountain whose sea god blows the waters through his conch just as Bernini had intended and as the greatest of their family had wished.

The Castel Sant'Angelo in Rome was originally built by Hadrian to house the ashes of the emperor and his successors, but over the centuries it was transformed into a fortress. In the early 17th century Urban VIII increased its fortifications and Bernini was commissioned to design the angels that now adorn the columns on the bridge leading to the castle.

LOUIS XIV, King of France

R. 1643–1715

'I think I am going to cry', said the king as death approached, 'Is there anyone else in the room? Not that it matters. No one would be surprised if I cried with you'. But during the 72 years of his reign it had mattered a great deal how Louis XIV appeared and behaved. He had maintained an iron self-discipline and only rarely was the mask of majesty disturbed by bad temper, extreme emotion or physical pain.

'Love of glory', according to Louis, meant that 'we must appear incapable of turmoils which could debase it'. Yet he was a sensual man. The autopsy revealed the enormous stomach and bowels which explained both his huge appetite and preservation of a good figure until the years caught up with him. Court portraitists paid due attention to the shapely legs and calves of which the king was inordinately proud. His last mistress, Madame de Maintenon, who was also his morganatic wife from, probably, 1683 complained to her confessor when she was 70 that the king, four years her junior, demanded his conjugal rights at least once a day. But for the public man, which was Louis's essence, self-possession was the key to kingship. Royal doctors barely detected a change in breathing patterns when he was operated on for an anal fistula on 18 November 1686, a gruesome occasion when he was cut up eight times with scissors and twice with a lancet.

Louis's Stoicism
The last years of his reign were melancholic. Earlier military successes had consolidated France's eastern boundary along the Rhine and gained large parts of the Spanish Netherlands (modern Belgium). But these triumphs gave way to a succession of military defeats inflicted by the anti-French 'Grand Alliance' of European powers during the War of the Spanish Succession (1701–14). Blenheim (1704), Ramillies (1706) and Oudenaarde (1708) were bloody blows. 'God seems

The embodiment of the absolute monarch ruling by divine right, Louis XIV was king of France for 72 years and a dominant figure in European cultural and political affairs. This portrait was painted in c.1701 by Hyacinthe Rigaud.

to have forgotten all that I have ever done for him', said the king ironically. A peace treaty allowed a junior branch of the French Bourbons to reign in Madrid, but the conflict ended France's European dominance and broke national finances. Louis had to melt his gold plate to help pay the bills and was reduced to eating off silver gilt. In 1711–12, within 11 months, he endured the deaths of three dauphins: his son, grandson and great-grandson. But even as these shadows encroached it was the king's stoic dignity which impressed observers.

Courtly Ritual at Versailles

No king in history either before or after Louis paid such precise attention to courtly ritual and he particularly enjoyed tinkering with etiquette in order to demonstrate his ultimate control. Versailles, which became the official seat of government on 6 May 1682, ran like clockwork. By the late 17th century a total of 20,000 courtiers and servants lived in the entire complex of buildings with some 5,000 of them living in the palace itself. The nobility were accommodated in the north wing and transported through the mêlée of the palace's crowded corridors in fleets of sedan chairs. In the town of Versailles, built to serve the palace's needs, there were about 40,000 inhabitants including the tradesmen, whose bills often embarrassed the courtiers. A culture of display meant that tailors and dressmakers thrived.

A few miles southwest of Paris lies the town of Versailles, where Louis built the largest, most magnificent palace in Europe and the greatest symbol of his power. An enormous workforce was employed to carry out many specialized tasks, including the building of a pumping station on the River Seine to supply water for the gardens' fountains. The palace was Louis's official residence and his seat of government from 1682.

This microcosm of France was astonishingly open to visitors: anyone could walk into the palace if dressed appropriately and bearing a sword as a sign of rank. It was especially crowded in winter when officers and soldiers returned at the end of the army's campaigning season. A rigid daily timetable governing ceremonies was therefore necessary if order was to be imposed on the throng, and the king was invariably punctual. He made *politesse* the prerogative of princes, raising his hat in the presence of all women including the humblest maidservant. Degrees of rank however dictated the height to which it was raised, and a duchess might also expect a kiss. Male courtiers were a different matter. A barely discernible levitation of the regal hat was strictly reserved for dukes of the most ancient lineage – the *ducs et pairs* who alone could sit in the king's presence and were thereby clearly distinguished from dukes of more recent lineage.

Kingship and the Government Fused

This reign elevated a novel idea of kingship that was summed up in Louis's apocryphal remark '*l'état, c'est moi*'. He wished, in other words, to be identified completely with his country's government and it was therefore the impersonality, rather than the egoism, of the king's authority that was striking. Versailles, extended first by Louis Le Vau as a result of Louis's 1668 commission and then by Jules Hardouin Mansart, became the king's own stage. Attracted to court, the French nobility stopped intriguing against the crown. Previous kings had had to travel around France in order to display, and so maintain, their authority. A new national stability made that itinerant procession redundant but in Versailles the king was on permanent display. His morning *lever* when he dressed, the *débotter* as he changed after hunting and the evening *coucher* while he prepared for bed: all were rituals attended by courtiers whose varying degrees of closeness to the king at such privileged moments showed the precise calculation of regal favour.

Versailles in fact contained many different courts quite apart from those of the king and queen. The 'children of France', consisting of the king and queen's children as well as the king's brothers and sisters, all had their own households, sharing as they did in the new, semi-sacred royal status. Service within this plurality of courts offered promotion to many, enabled some commoners to become nobles and could push the middling nobility to higher positions. The greatest court offices were hereditary but a large number of other jobs could be bought and sold with the king's permission. Many posts were thereby kept in the same family: the mole catchers at Versailles were always of the Liard family and five generations of the Bontemps were successive *valets de chambre* to the king from the reign of Louis XIII to that of Louis XV.

Louis Tames the Nobility

Behind Louis's resolve lay his troubled childhood memories of the Fronde, that series of revolts (1648–53) which showed how the nobility could lead whole

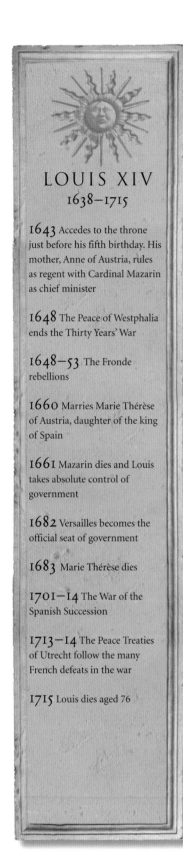

regions of France into rebellion. They now constituted his network of clients as they solicited an apartment at Versailles for the sake of prestige and as a demonstration of loyalty, asked his permission (only reluctantly granted) to visit Paris, or implored him to take them to his private retreat, the Château de Marly. Versailles also offered financial benefits to courtiers since government contracts were arranged here and courtiers could promote their favoured financiers for those business deals. Royal mistresses' influence on the king could be decisive here. Louise de la Vallière held the record for *placets*, requests for sinecures on behalf of friends which, if granted, earned the petitioner a percentage. Madame de Montespan, a successor in the royal bed until she put on weight, was granted a percentage on the meat and tobacco sold in Paris.

From 1661 onwards Louis governed without relying on a chief minister or royal favourite, a fact that makes him unique among French kings. Instead he used a cadre of ministers of his own choosing. Figures such as Colbert, the great reformer of finances, owed everything to the king's patronage and stood apart from the traditional courtly hierarchies. Louis's own family were excluded from government: the dauphin was never consulted and the king's brother, 'Monsieur' (the duc d'Orléans), concentrated his energies on jewels, boys and make-up, and also warfare – for which he had a flair.

Regal Patronage of the Arts

Culture also attracted the nobility to court. Louis's tournaments, concerts, plays, ballets and operas transformed the French arts by placing them at the service of a kingly patronage, which expected reciprocal recognition. After a performance of Corneille's *Racine* on 16 August 1674, during the war with the Dutch, the standards captured in battle were lowered before the king, while a plinth and obelisk topped by a representation of the sun were drawn along the Grand Canal, the great waterway built in the gardens. The new aestheticism was supplemented at court by a gallantry which redeployed Medieval chivalric traditions. Refinement and sociability expressed in speech and gesture showed that France had replaced Italy as the home of courtly values.

Brawls, duels and aristocratic scandals nonetheless persisted. The 'affair of the poisons' implicated a large number of female courtiers in the late 1670s and early 1680s. Olympe, comtesse de Soissons, was a former flame of Louis and fled to Brussels in 1680 when suspected of poisoning her husband. The unfortunate count had belonged to both the royal family of Savoy (an independent duchy) and to the Condé, a cadet branch of the Bourbons. Louis suspected that the son of this marriage, Prince Eugène, was homosexual on account of the prince's youthful cavorting with a group of young men who enjoyed dressing up as women. Relations between the two had always been cool therefore, and after Olympe's disgrace, Louis refused to allow Eugène's entry into the French army.

This proved a costly mistake since the prince turned out to be a soldier of genius and his generalship in the service of the 'Grand Alliance' helped to secure the French defeats of the 1700s.

The Sun King: Myth and Power

Louis plundered classical mythology to illustrate his achievements and was identified with Apollo. Sculptures of Apollo's chariot (traditionally associated with the sun) and of the god's mother, Latona, decorated the two great ornamental pools in the palace gardens. The idea that the monarch was like the sun had been expressed occasionally in earlier French culture. But Louis, through his artistic commissions, developed the notion into an insistent system of imagery and the French church, along with the Jesuits who were active as courtiers and educators, encouraged him to equate the king's 'glory' with that of the Christian God. Thereby privileged by the church, Louis could also be rebuked by it on account of his sexual conduct or foreign policy during the sermons preached before him at mass. Even here, however, the seating arrangements showed the sacred and social order. Only the king could face the altar and God. The congregation sat looking at the king.

The Parisian world regained the social initiative after Louis's death and the ideal of an urbane and witty refinement was claimed for the salons of Paris. For the French intelligentsia Versailles became a symbol of servility. Louis XV, overwhelmed by his palace, withdrew to his private apartment. It had taken Louis XIV's dedication to make Versailles work. Without the sun king's rays of inspiration the palace became a mausoleum both for a dynasty and a certain view of kingly duty whose time had passed.

This bronze statue of Neptune is one of a series of mythological figures surrounding the magnificent pool and fountains in front of the palace at Versailles. The 'bassin', or pool, was designed by the architect André Le Nôtre and completed in 1682.

K'ANG-HSI, Second Emperor of the Ch'ing Dynasty of China

R. 1661–1722

Concealed behind the imperial throne a group of young wrestlers awaited the arrival of an unsuspecting courtier. On the throne sat the 15-year-old emperor of China who had been born Hsuan-yeh and taken the name of K'ang-hsi ('heavenly harmony') to mark his reign. Smallpox had killed his father, the Shun-chich emperor, and the fact that Hsuan-yeh had recovered from the disease was one reason why he, rather than any of the emperor's other five sons, had been chosen to succeed seven years previously.

Now a teenager, his physical strength was already obvious as was his notable skill at archery. Since the accession, power had been exercised in K'ang-hsi's name by the four courtiers who ran the new Office of the Imperial Household as China's central government. This was an important innovation, replacing the rule of the Thirteen Offices, a structure dominated by eunuch administrators and, as such, something of a hangover from the reign of the previous Ming dynasty. For the Manchu people who now dominated China, eunuchs were a sign of inefficiency and mere intrigue. But, by 1669, of the original group of four it was Oboi who was not only dominant but also an actual threat to the throne. He was now set upon by the muscled wrestlers and arrested in the name of the emperor.

K'ang-hsi Consolidates China
Similar decisiveness marked K'ang-hsi's actions in 1673 when he decided to assert his authority over Wu San-kuei, whose southern vassal kingdom of Yunnan had become effectively independent. Wu had rebelled against the Ming and played a crucial role in establishing the Manchu succession. Other former Ming adherents

K'ang-hsi's 61-year reign was the longest in China's history. For the most part it was a period of peace and prosperity during which the emperor's outward-looking style of government encouraged international trade and permitted the observance of Christianity.

had also been given control over large areas of south and southwest China where they now joined him in revolt. This encouraged a northern rebellion by the Chahar Mongols, a tribe dominant within Inner Mongolia until it was conquered by the Manchu in 1635. K'ang-hsi kept his nerve in the face of initial southern defeats and by 1681, when his army marched into the Yunnan capital of Kunming, his dynasty was saved.

Recovery of Taiwan from the Cheng family two years later completed a process of internal consolidation. From their original base in the Fu-chien province of southeastern coastal China, the Cheng had for generations been running a large-scale trade monopoly over the South China seas. They had refused to accept Manchu authority and in 1662 expelled the Dutch from Taiwan which they now controlled. But in 1683 a family quarrel among the Cheng allowed K'ang-hsi's troops to intervene and the island was incorporated in Fu-chien. A reign of brilliant achievement now beckoned.

Origins of the Manchu

The people who called themselves Manchu by the 16th century had, since prehistoric times, been established in Manchuria, a region to the northeast of China's Great Wall. Originally a group of peoples called the Tungus, early Chinese written records refer to them as 'the eastern barbarians'. By the 12th century they were dominant in the region and, with a cultural solidarity re-enforced by their own Manchu language (written in a script derived from the Mongol alphabet), they reasserted regional control after the period of Mongol conquests in the 13th century.

Manchu Conquests

Ch'ing dynastic rule over the Manchu, dating from 1636, was a comparative novelty in the mid-17th century. Chinese officers garrisoned along the border established links with the Manchu, a fact which may explain the swift Manchu response when, in 1644, Ming dynastic officials requested military aid. Following a series of harvest shortfalls, Chinese social order had disintegrated and the bandit leader Li Tzu-ch'eng had seized Beijing. The military force that swept south consisted of Chinese and Mongols as well as Manchu and was organized in the distinctive Manchu system of the 'banner' – a military civilian unit including some 7,500 soldiers along with their households.

This army then seized Beijing and established Manchu dominance in the rest of China. Initially the Manchu sought to preserve their ethnic separation from the Chinese, and half of the senior officials were of Manchu origin. The distinctive Manchu braiding of hair worn in a pigtail was imposed on the Chinese population as a mark of loyalty, but the adoption of Ming methods of government was a method of pacifying the country. Chinese military leaders who surrendered were given noble rank and the entire army was organized in a new structure called the Army of the Green Standard, which was garrisoned throughout the country. Beijing itself was closely guarded by the Manchu Banner System troops.

With his domestic authority established, the emperor could move against Russian forces in Siberia. The region of Heilungkiang emerged as a conflict zone in the 17th century with gangs of Cossacks demanding tribute in furs from tribes living along the Amur river. In 1685 Ch'ing troops took the fort of Albazin built on the river's north bank by the Russians 35 years earlier. When the Russians regained it, a prolonged Chinese siege ensued. Negotiations between K'ang-hsi and Peter the Great led to the 1689 treaty which confirmed a new Sino-Russian border. As well as the Amur valley, Manchuria was also conceded by the Russians – a crucial point of prestige to the dynasty given its origins.

1696 marked the emperor's most audacious military enterprise yet when he moved against the Dzungar, a western Mongolian and nomadic people who had established dominance in Outer Mongolia and pushed the Khalka people, a predominant element in the Mongolian population, to the south where they sought imperial aid. At a site near Ulan Bator, the emperor led his forces to victory and then resettled the Khalka in Outer Mongolia, which now became part of the Chinese empire. Another Dzungar offensive in 1717 led to the invasion of Tibet and the occupation of its capital Lhasa. K'ang-hsi responded with his own invasion of Tibet which, after the expulsion of the Dzungar in 1720, was also incorporated within his empire.

K'ang-hsi and Chinese Government

K'ang-hsi's gifts as a tireless administrator touched all areas of Chinese government. He presided over one of history's greatest engineering projects, the embankment and the dredging of the Huang Ho (Yellow river), which regulated its flow so that the river no longer flooded over the northern China plain as it made its way from the Tibetan plateau to the northeastern Chinese coast. The great canal linking the Huang Ho with the Lower Yangtze river was also repaired, a crucial move since this enabled rice to be transported from the fertile south and its granaries to the north. National prosperity meant that there were large-scale tax remissions once authority was established by the 1680s, and war-ravaged areas gained tax exemptions.

As China benefited from political stability and economic prosperity under K'ang-hsi, the arts flourished and enjoyed royal patronage. Ch'ing ceramics, such as this plate with its design of charging cavalry, are noted for their elegance and refinement and were among items exported after the opening of four Chinese ports to international trade in 1684.

In 1711 the emperor announced that China's present head count should be the basis of future tax assessment, thereby exempting future population growth from taxation. Taiwan's recovery had been fundamental to this new prosperity and in 1684 K'ang-hsi lifted the previous ban on foreign trade. Four ports, including Canton, were opened to foreign ships and the result was an inflow of silver as merchants arrived from abroad to buy Chinese produce. An inter-regional and major international trade network developed in grain and chinaware, silks, cotton and tea, and China was increasingly integrated in a world economy.

The advent of a money economy, the rise of merchants and the spread of commercial attitudes constituted for many a threat to traditional values. This fear was counteracted by the state's urgent encouragement of Confucian values. The tributary system enforced China's cultural superiority and representatives of other nations wishing to trade had to approach the emperor as vassals. Korean vassalage was enforced especially rigorously and their rulers' choice of consorts and heirs had to be approved by the Chinese emperor. Japan regarded the Manchu as irredeemably barbarian and, issuing its own trade permits to Chinese traders, rejected the tributary system. Russian representatives however were treated with a notably greater degree of cultural respect.

A Philosopher-Emperor

With his simple personal tastes the emperor's court was a frugal affair staffed by only a few eunuchs and court ladies. But he was a splendid example of the Chinese philosopher-emperor and in 1677 he opened the Nan shufang, a special hall built by him inside the 'Forbidden City', as a location for his philosophical and historical discussions with leading scholars. This veneration for the national intellectual traditions gained him the respect and loyalty of the Chinese governing elite. In a similar mark of

The 'Forbidden City' in Beijing was home to emperors of the Ming and Ch'ing dynasties for about 500 years. It was within the walls of this city that K'ang-hsi engaged in intellectual discussions with leading scholars of the day, in a purpose-built hall known as Nan shufang.

respect for the country's Confucian traditions he resurrected the system of examinations, which governed entrance into the Chinese civil service.

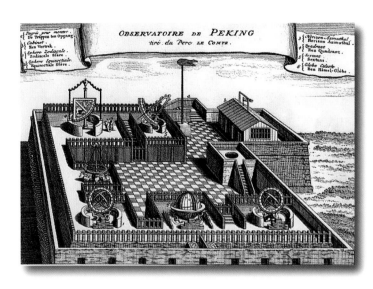

The emperor also established a new channel of entry by which the exceptionally talented could, on personal recommendation, enter his personal service. The fact that some of those admitted in this way worked on an officially sponsored history of the Ming dynasty shows K'ang-hsi's concern for Chinese continuity and his place within it. Moral guidance on the details of village life was offered in his official document of 1669, a work that followed the hierarchical pieties and was widely consulted by the Chinese peasantry until the end of the Manchu period in the early 20th century.

K'ang-hsi and the Jesuits

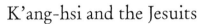

China's greater openness to the outside world during his reign was inspired by the emperor's own intellectual inquisitiveness and he was eager to learn from the Jesuit missionaries who had arrived in the country. The Dutch Jesuit Ferdinand Verbiest (1623–88) was a trained astronomer who taught the emperor geometry, compiled the official imperial calendar, advised on the construction of canonry needed to quell the south China revolts and acted as interpreter for the Chinese team during treaty negotiations with the Russians. His correspondence with such scholars and friends as Leibnitz inspired the European enlightenment's benign and admiring view of Chinese civilization. Other Jesuits were commissioned by K'ang-hsi to work on the trigonometric survey of his lands, which started in 1708 and was brought to a triumphant conclusion with the publication of the imperial atlas of 1717.

His respect for Jesuit scholarship led the emperor to issue a decree in 1692 allowing Catholicism to be propagated in China. But the other orders who arrived in the country, such as the Franciscans, Dominicans and Augustinians, lacked the subtlety of the Jesuits' approach and denounced Chinese cultural traditions such as ancestor worship. In 1706 the emperor expelled those Christian missionaries who would not follow the Jesuit line of cultural adaptability.

One mistake only marred his reign. K'ang hsi's three empresses and numerous concubines bore him 35 sons, and when in 1675 he nominated one of them to be his successor this caused immense conflict. He eventually reverted to the dynastic practice of maintaining his sons' equal rights of inheritance during the emperor's lifetime. But the institutional strength of Manchu China outlasted his reign for over a hundred years until the age of national disintegration and fragmentation in the 19th century.

The German Jesuit astronomer Johann Adam Schall von Bell spent 47 years in China and was invited by the emperor to build an observatory (illustrated above) within the royal palace at Beijing, complete with astrolabes, quadrants and an armillary sphere. Schall was responsible for reforming the Confucian calendar and plotting planetary movements. After Schall's death K'ang-hsi appointed Ferdinand Verbiest as his successor.

PETER I, '*The Great*', Tsar of Russia

R. 1682–1725

Seven years earlier he had ordered the execution of his rebellious son, the tsarevich Alexis. Now in 1725 the tsar himself was dead. Four bronze statues depicting the mourning figures of Russia and Europe, Mars and Hercules, surrounded Pyotr Alekseyevich's open coffin during the lying-in-state at St Petersburg.

His new city had been built on the banks of the Neva in the eastern Baltic lands seized from the Swedes, and the same spirit of creative novelty displayed by Peter in life now attended him even in death. Previous tsars, following Orthodox tradition, had been buried the day after they died, but it took a whole month to complete preparations for the funeral of a ruler who recast an entire civilization.

Peter's Funeral

Marshals and barons bearing the emperor's regalia accompanied the coffin to its burial in the cathedral of SS Peter and Paul, a light and airy structure begun just 13 years previously. Peter's princely predecessors were buried in Moscow inside the Kremlin whose fortification surrounding a central courtyard now seemed archaic and oriental compared to St Petersburg's Westernizing elegance. On the outskirts stood Peterhof, a palace whose design and scale rivalled Versailles, and the same classicism was evident in the city's Alexander Nevskii Monastery, named after the Russian Orthodox saint and ruler of 13th-century Novgorod. Muscovy had defeated Novgorod and abolished its sovereign independence in 1478. But Nevskii's victories over the Swedes made him a precursor of Peter in the new pantheon of Russian heroes, and his bones had been transferred to the monastery a year previously.

No patriarch presided at Peter's funeral since he had abolished the Moscow Patriarchate in 1721 and replaced it with the Holy Synod, a state body that

Portrait of Peter the Great during the Battle of Poltava, by the German artist J. G. Tannauer, from the 1710s. In this major engagement (1709) of the Great Northern War the Russian army defeated the Swedish army led by King Charles XII.

ensured ecclesiastical enforcement of Peter's autocracy. It was
therefore the pliant archbishop of Pskov, Feofan Prokopovich,
who delivered the funeral oration – itself an innovation for an
Orthodox funeral. He assured the new empress Catherine I,
the tsar's widow and chosen successor, that 'the female sex is
no hindrance to your being like Peter the Great'. Similarity to
Peter in character and ability was what mattered.

1462 – The First Tsar

Muscovy, already a distinct principality by the late 13th
century, had expanded on the disintegration of the Golden
Horde, the Mongol Tartar power to its east and south which
had been formed on the break-up of Genghis Khan's empire.
By the mid-15th century Muscovy was no longer paying tribute
money to the Mongol Tartars and, after Byzantium's final
collapse in 1453, it was the sole territorial protector of eastern
Orthodox civilization. Moscow had succeeded Constantinople
to become 'the third Rome' combining secular power with
spiritual authority. Grand Prince Ivan III (r. 1462–1505)
married Zoe, niece of the last Byzantine emperor, in a deal
brokered by a papacy keen to foster a united anti-Turkish front
and, fortified by this recognition, Ivan started to call himself
'tsar' in conscious recollection of the Caesars' Roman imperial
authority. 'Rex' was best avoided since that kingly title typified
the Latin Christendom of the West. Muscovy's new emblem of
the double-headed eagle was nonetheless Habsburg-inspired.
In 1480 Ivan proclaimed himself leader of 'all Rus' thus laying
claim to the lands of the Medieval state centred on Kiev. Much
of Kievan Rus now constituted the Ukraine and formed part of
Poland-Lithuania. The federation, first established dynastically
in 1386, had ensured the Catholicization of Lithuania, until then a pagan country.
Muscovy's aggressive fusion of nationalism with Orthodoxy was therefore a
cultural as well as a military threat.

The Romanovs

The Riurikid dynasty died out in 1598 and in 1613 the 'assembly of the land'
(*zemsky sobor*), representing the church, boyar nobles, landowners and urban
freemen, elected Mikhail Romanov to rule. Boyar factionalism during the
intervening 'time of troubles' had reduced Muscovy to chaos but the reign
of Tsar Alexis (1645–76), Mikhail's son and father to Peter, was marked by a
steady restoration of state authority and royal power. The legal code of 1649
systematized serfdom and by 1667 Russia had wrested the eastern Ukraine
(including Kiev) from Poland.

Built by Peter as his summer residence, Peterhof is an outstanding example of baroque architecture. Surrounded by parks and gardens adorned with fountains and gilded statues of classical gods and heroes, the palace housed major collections of sculpture, painting and other works of art .

Fedor III (r. 1676–82), Peter's sickly half-brother, succeeded their father Alexis. But the Miloslavskys, related to Fedor's mother, intrigued to ensure that Peter, although proclaimed tsar on Fedor's death, had to share the throne at first with his other half-brother, the equally delicate Ivan V (1682–96). Ivan's sister Sophia meanwhile ruled as regent and kept Peter away from court. Thus isolated, Peter pursued his precocious interests in mathematics and technology, ship-building, carpentry and joinery: accomplishments which he put to good use as he contemplated a solution to Russia's major strategic problem, the lack of maritime access.

Access to the Black Sea

The 17-year-old ruler hit his stride in 1689 when he banished Sophia to a convent after her involvement with the *streltsy* (the sovereign's personal musketeers) in an attempted coup against him. Construction of a large navy started soon afterwards, and the fleet which had sailed down the Don captured the port of Azov in 1696 from the Crimean Tartars who were vassals of Ottoman Turkey. Russia had gained an access to the Black Sea. The military parade held in Moscow to mark the victory included the novelty of Roman-style triumphal arches; Peter added a further twist by marching in the parade dressed as a bombardier rather than riding on horseback. Such gestures of ostentatious simplicity highlighted the authority of a ruler who could reject the conventional props of regal magnificence.

Peter Tours Western Europe

The Grand Embassy (1697–8) was a major diplomatic offensive comprising some 250 officials and the tsar travelled incognito as the expedition made its way to Prussia and Poland, the Dutch Republic and England. Its aim was to encourage an anti-Turkish coalition but it also gathered intelligence on Western technology and trade. Western rules of etiquette were also studied – an object of curiosity to the boyar nobility, since Medieval Muscovy had no knightly order and there was therefore no Russian chivalric tradition. Peter's creation in 1699 of a new Order of St Andrew (who was supposed to have visited Novgorod) tried to fill that gap

1682 Succeeds to the throne jointly with his sickly half-brother Ivan

1689 Banishes the regent Sophia after an attempted coup against him

1696 Ivan dies and Peter becomes tsar in his own right. Russian navy captures port of Azov and Russia gains access to Black Sea

1697–8 Peter tours western Europe

1699 Creates knightly Order of St Andrew

1700–21 Great Northern War between Russia and Sweden

1712 Peter moves capital from Moscow to St Petersburg

1721 Treaty of Nystadt incorporates eastern Baltic within Russia

1723 Persia cedes territories on the Caspian Sea to Russia

1725 Peter dies and is buried in the cathedral of SS Peter and Paul in St Petersburg

with its membership limited to a few magnates. But heavy drinking and physical violence remained key characteristics both of Peter's court and of his own personality. He enjoyed using his stick to beat even his closest friends, and his birthday celebrations in May 1723 were typically extreme with rough-grain vodka being drunk from noon until three o'clock the next morning.

Peter's 'All-Mad, All-Jesting, All-Drunken Assembly'

New national ceremonies, such as the 'victory days' marking anniversaries of great battles, were a feature of the reign but Peter also enjoyed the subversion of ceremonial as a way of demonstrating his power. The wedding of his niece Anna Ioannovna to the duke of Courland on 14 November 1710 in St Petersburg was followed a few days later by another wedding also planned by the tsar, that of his royal dwarf Iakim Volkov, with some 70 dwarves being rounded up to attend. Both wedding receptions were held in the Menshikov Palace and Peter himself held the wedding crown over the dwarf bride.

What he called his 'All-Mad, All-Jesting, All-Drunken Assembly' had its own select membership whose ceremonies mocked church liturgy, and from the 1690s onwards Peter also maintained a mock court headed by a 'prince Caesar' (whom Peter addressed as 'sire') and which parodied the real court. The fact that the 'prince Caesar' also headed the chancellery dealing with treason allegations was a deadly fact of real power.

The Great Northern War

Peter's major campaign was the Great Northern War of 1700–21, an epic conflict he launched against Sweden following his forces' occupation of Karelia, Ingria, Estonia and Livonia. Supported by Saxony and Denmark-Norway, he defeated Charles XII – himself one of the great military geniuses of the age – and the Treaty of Nystadt gave him the eastern Baltic. In celebration, the Russian Senate (a ten-man body chosen by himself and the new Russia's chief executive) gave him the title of emperor.

Two years later, and following a Russian invasion, Persia ceded its territories on the Caspian Sea's western and southern shores. An empire had been created from Archangel to the Caspian and from the Baltic to the Pacific. A state economy had also been built in order to supply the material means to achieve that goal, and Russia was consequently a major metallurgical and manufacturing power.

Military Means and Militant Aims

The right to buy peasant serf labour had created a new class of 'enlisted serfs' bound to the workshops; peasants conscripted for life and officers drawn from the nobility comprised a magnificent army which could be issued with Russian-made flintlock firearms, bayonets, cannon and mortar; the Baltic navy had some 50 battleships and countless galleys. Urban expansion was basic to these achievements and Peter allowed townspeople to elect their own municipalities. Merchants and professionals, artisans and tradesmen were enrolled in newly established urban guilds and townspeople generally were released from subjection to the provincial military governors. But militarism prevailed when Peter clamped down on the protests against his creation of 50 provinces each with its own sub-districts: he distributed army regiments to enforce his new structure and forced the localities to pay for the maintenance of these 'regimental districts'.

A Cultural Transformation

Military and naval personnel were educated in a new structure of state schools run on secular lines and Russia's culture generally had been transformed. The national calendars, instead of numbering the years from the supposed beginning of the world, now followed the western European system.

Russians looked different too, with the prescribed cutting of boyar beards and the desegregation of the sexes so that noblewomen had to expose their heads. Balls and dances, alien to Moscow's past, were a feature of secular St Petersburg. The nobility were major beneficiaries of Peter's reforms: during the reign's first half alone they were allocated some 40,500 hectares (100,000 acres) of land and 175,000 serfs in order to help them achieve Peter's goals, and the introduction of primogeniture protected their estates from breaking up.

This woodcut engraving shows a barber cutting the beard of a Russian noble by order of Peter the Great. On his return from touring western Europe (1697–8), Peter set out to outlaw the Russian fashion of growing long beards in the oriental style, believing the clean-shaven European look to be superior. He also ordered noblemen to abandon their long robes in favour of European clothing..

But this was also, in its own weird way, a meritocratic regime. The Table of Ranks (1722) made state service, rather than ancestry, the basis of nobility: junior army officers in rank 14, the lowest, qualified for hereditary nobility while civil servants, once they got to grade 8, had the same privilege.

The tsar might enjoy the company of the simple and the coarse but what he really favoured was ability: his private secretary Aleksei Makorov was of humble birth and his great favourite at court, the gifted general and administrator Alexander Menshikov, was an illiterate commoner raised to become the most titled noble of his day. He was Russia's effective ruler during the tsarina Catherine's reign (1725–7) after which charges of corruption secured his exile to Siberia. The Petrine autocracy had survived the tsar's death to become the standard by which all future rulers of Russia would be judged.

FREDERICK II, '*The Great*', King of Prussia

R. 1740–1786

'I am just off to Prussia', wrote Frederick to Voltaire on his accession in 1740, 'to receive homage without benefit of the flask of holy oil and those other useless and empty ceremonies introduced by ignorance'. Frederick refused coronation at Königsberg, the ancient capital of Prussia's kings, because what he wanted was the essence of power, and that was quite adequately expressed by acts of homage.

'Prussianism' – the application of militarist methods of order and discipline to civilian government – was already a European phenomenon before Frederick's time. But he developed those techniques in a way that presented kingship in a new light, since he based the legitimacy of his rule on the possession of a monopoly of force. The symbols and ceremonies that had given kingship its sacerdotal quality in the past were therefore entirely irrelevant to his purposes.

The 'Enlightenment' King

Frederick conformed to 18th-century views of 'enlightenment'. He paid a formal respect to the Lutheran Protestantism which had been Prussia's official state religion for over two centuries, but his personal convictions were those of a deist who believed in a conveniently remote deity, rejected any idea of supernatural agency, including miracles, and favoured religious toleration.

The king was an excellent flautist whose cultivated musical and literary tastes were evident at Sans Souci, the palace he built in a French rococo style at Potsdam near Berlin. Frederick was also a prolific writer; his *Histoire de Mon Temps* (1746) is a work of insight, though his poetry has few admirers. Littérateurs were gratified by Frederick's patronage, and his readiness to share in the sophisticated gibes and jokes about the folly of superstition – just like his preference for conversation in French rather than German – showed he was part of the educated consensus of salon society.

'Frederick the Great after the Battle of Kolin' by J. Schröder. During the Seven Years' War Frederick was defeated by a larger Austrian force at Kolín (Bohemia) and had to abandon his siege of Prague.

Built in the rococo style, Frederick's palace Sans Souci at Potsdam evokes the carefree purpose for which he envisaged the residence – as a retreat during summer months where he could indulge his artistic and intellectual interests as well as entertain private guests.

But when it came to the realities of war and power, Frederick's *machtpolitik* was indifferent to intelligentsia chatter about the virtues of peace. In this respect he was both an old-fashioned kind of European prince prepared to advance his kingdom's interests through war, as well as an innovative one who abandoned any pretence of moral constraint on his actions in the international arena. He interpreted the enlightenment cult of reason therefore according to his own domestic interests: rational and modern kingship meant a uniform administration intolerant of the independent institutions and individuals that might impede enforcement of the executive will and state law.

The Rise of Prussia

Prussia's militarist milieu had its roots in the region's conquest by the Order of Teutonic Knights in the 13th century and its subsequent forced conversion to Christianity. The last Grand Master of the Order, Albrecht von Hohenzollern, converted to Lutheranism, dissolved the Order, and turned the Teutonic state into a duchy which he ruled as a fiefdom of the kingdom of Poland. In 1618 the dukedom was inherited by that branch of the Hohenzollern dynasty which ruled Brandenburg. Frederick-William (r. 1640–88), the Great Elector, used his army to ensure the new state's sovereign independence from the Poles.

The introduction of a special excise tax in 1680 financed an army whose size was out of all proportion to the civilian population and which propelled this once obscure northern European territory into international greatness. Frederick III (r.1688–1713) sold his electoral vote to the Habsburgs in 1700 and received in return their recognition of his independent kingship. Frederick William I (r. 1713–40) conceded to the emperor Charles VI that his daughter, Maria Theresa, might be allowed to succeed him and was rewarded with the Austrian territories of Berg and Ravenstein. Adroit diplomacy brought Stettin and Western Pomerania into the Prussian kingdom as a result of Sweden's defeat in the Great Northern War (1700–21).

Frederick Inherits a Strong State and Army

The Prussian army with its characteristic goose-step march honed to perfection on the parade grounds became an object lesson in military precision. But there was more than just the spirit of the drill sergeant at work in the country, and Frederick's inheritance included a tradition of state support in education and culture. Public education was seen as an important aspect of maximizing the state's manpower potential and the establishment in Berlin of a Royal Academy of the Arts (1696) and a Royal Academy of the Sciences (1700) showed the Hohenzollern state's patronage of learning and scholarship.

Frederick burst upon the European scene to immediate effect after his accession in 1740 by seizing Silesia, among the most prosperous of Austrian possessions. His invasion on 16 December 1740 was done without any prior declaration of war and he had prepared his troops in secrecy, despite having written in friendly terms to Maria Theresa only days previously. The fact that Frederick had only recently condemned cynical power politics in his tract, *The Refutation of Machiavelli's Prince or Anti-Machiavel,* only deepened a European-wide sense of outrage.

A Tyrannical Father

The evasiveness that formed the king's personality may have been a legacy from Frederick's conflicts with his tyrannical father who, disappointed by his son's artistic interests, bullied and humiliated the young prince. In 1730 he was imprisoned in the fortress of Küstrin by Frederick William I after attempting to flee the country. Hans Hermann von Katte, Frederick's close friend and an accomplice in the plan, was executed in his presence. But, despite this inflicted trauma, Frederick's aims as a king would be strikingly similar to those of his father: the inculcation on a national scale of a Prussian ethos of hard work, thrift and discipline along with the elevation of the state's interests above those of any individual element within it.

Frederick's War Machine

The two wars waged over Silesia (1740–2, 1744–5) established Prussian rule in a territory whose resources were greater than those of any other Hohenzollern territory; this helped Frederick to build up his standing army from 83,000 to 190,000 during the reign. His state was a war machine dominating a country whose population was just 2.2 million in 1740 and the aim of his administration was to serve the army's needs in cash, resources and manpower, based on the forced recruitment of the Prussian peasantry. This assertion of state power was a necessity since the aggression that had won victory in Silesia had also isolated, and therefore endangered, Prussia. Frederick signed an agreement with Britain in January 1756 for the neutralization of Germany in the Franco-British conflict for maritime supremacy, which broke out in 1756. But this alienated France, his ostensible ally since 1741, and Frederick's overriding fear was of a joint Russian-Austrian attack supported by the French.

Frederick's solution to his dilemma was daring – a pre-emptive attack on Saxony in August 1756 followed by a march into Bohemia. By launching thereby the Seven Years' War the king ranged against him France and Sweden as well as

FREDERICK II
1712–1786

1740 Frederick accedes to the throne and invades Silesia

1746 Publishes *Histoire de Mon Temps*

1747 The palace of Sans Souci is completed

1756 Signs the Treaty of Westminster with the British and then invades Saxony, marking the start of the Seven Years' War

1759 Defeated by the Russians at the Battle of Kunersdorf and contemplates suicide

1763 Issues edict to extend universal primary education throughout the kingdom

1764 Agrees truce with Russia

1772 Arranges Poland's partition

1778–9 War of Bavarian Succession results in defeat for Joseph II of Austria

1786 Frederick dies

Austria and Russia. Subsidies from his British ally just about enabled Frederick to keep his army on the offensive, although he still had to debase the currency and stop paying civil servants their salaries. Defeat by the Russian army at Kunersdorf in August 1759 seemed to herald the end of Greater Prussia and the king contemplated suicide. By 1760 Brandenburg landowners were refusing to pay any more of the war's costs. The death of the Russian empress, Anna, in January 1762 saved Frederick since her successor Peter III had a despot's admiration for him and signed a peace treaty. From now on Frederick was intent on avoiding another Russo-Prussian conflict and the alliance he consequently signed in 1764 lasted until 1780.

By the end of the war in Germany in 1763 Frederick had lost some 180,000 men but Maria Theresa was forced to concede that Silesia was irrevocably lost. Nonetheless, the efforts of her son and successor, Joseph II, to gain part of Bavaria aroused Frederick's deepest fears of Habsburg penetration into Germany. The War of the Bavarian Succession (1778–9) ended in Joseph's defeat but Austro-Prussian enmity would be a long-lived factor in German history.

The Partition of Poland

Frederick's major diplomatic achievement, the first partition of Poland in 1772, was a classic example of his *raison d'état* at its most cynical. Prussia gained the Polish province of west Prussia while Austria and Russia, his erstwhile enemies, were persuaded by Frederick to join in the general dismemberment of the Polish kingdom. Brandenburg and Pomerania were now linked up with the previously isolated east Prussia and the new boundaries gave Prussia a greater territorial coherence. Nonetheless, this shift to the east also meant that Prussia became increasingly detached from western European cultural and political developments.

A Servant of the State

Frederick's conception of his kingly duty was awesome in its impersonality. He saw himself as a servant of the state and his view of Prussia's objective interests extended beyond the pursuit of a merely dynastic, Hohenzollern, power. He ruled his subjects, he said, according to law and above factions. And he spoke as his

The superiority of the Prussian army was demonstrated during Frederick's first battle, at Mollwitz on 10 April, 1741. Austrian forces failed to retake Silesia, and with Prussia's victory Europe saw the emergence of a new military power.

father's son when he emphasized how a ruler had to sacrifice his own feelings and subjective interests for the good of his people. But he was also clear that a system of personal rule by a prince who was 'the soul of the state' was the only way to achieve these kingly goals.

Prussia's government and civil service were certainly remarkably honest and efficient under Frederick – far more so than in other parts of *ancien régime* Europe. The judges of the higher courts had to pass a rigorous examination before appointment, judicial torture was abolished, and the codification of Prussia's laws – started during his reign – culminated in the 1794 issue of the Prussian Common Law – a landmark in legal history and proof that this was not a 'despotic' state.

Frederick's Legacy and Prussia's Decline

Prussia's 1763 edict aimed to extend universal primary education throughout the kingdom and a massive programme of resettlement brought in some 300,000 émigrés from other parts of Europe to restore Prussia's ruined countryside after the Seven Years' War. But a government machine so dependent on the ruler's creative leadership was bound to become stultified as the king aged. Serfdom, despite Frederick's personal antipathy to it, remained pivotal to Prussia's agricultural system because he needed the support of the landowning *Junker* nobles who, in turn, supplied him with his officer class, his officials and ministers.

Noble status, like noble lands, could not be acquired by those born outside the *Junker* class, since the nobility and its concept of honour was, for Frederick, the essence of his kingdom. Late 18th-century Prussia, with its system of state-sponsored manufacturing, was failing to respond creatively to new economic circumstances. And the new consciousness of German national identity, aroused to anger by the invasion of French revolutionary forces, was bypassing Prussia as a feudal anachronism. At the Battle of Jena on 14 October 1806 Napoleon ensured the capitulation of the old Prussian order which, needing *der alte Fritz* in order to make it work, had simply collapsed from within.

MARIA THERESA, Archduchess of Austria, Queen of Hungary and Bohemia, Holy Roman Empress

R. 1740–1780

That Austria had survived at all, let alone as a major power, was one of the more surprising facts of late 18th-century European politics. This fragmented entity was the dynastic possession of the house of Habsburg rather than a state with a national identity. Only the person of the ruler could impose any kind of cohesion and authority on it. Maria Theresa ruled Austria as its archduchess, while in Bohemia and Hungary her title was that of queen. Her possessions also included the Austrian Netherlands (modern Belgium), separated from Austria proper by the German territories. Hungary itself was a huge domain – extending from Croatia on the Adriatic coast to the eastern border with Poland.

Her father, Emperor Charles VI, had fought hard after the death of his only son to gain international recognition of the Pragmatic Sanction by which female heirs could be allowed rights of succession within the Habsburg territories. Hunger after those same lands inspired many European rulers, most of whom assented to the Sanction but few of whom could be relied upon to honour it on Charles's death. Maria Theresa's reign coincided with that of two rulers who combined cleverness with ruthlessness: Frederick II of Prussia and Catherine II of Russia. But this Austrian ruler would show how integrity, bravery and force of character could count as much as cleverness and wit when it came to preserving a dynasty.

Maria Theresa's marriage in 1736 to Francis Stephen, duke of Lorraine, aroused French objections to a near neighbour contracting an Austrian Habsburg alliance.

*The only female ruler in the history of the Habsburg dynasty
and sole surviving heir of Charles VI, Maria Theresa came to
the throne in 1740. This portrait by Gabriel Mathei was painted
before her accession.*

As part of a Franco-Austrian deal, Francis had to give up Lorraine, which was transferred to Stanislaw Leszczynski, the unsuccessful French candidate for the crown of Poland. The French could therefore conclude the War of the Polish Succession (1733–8) with some honour preserved. Francis was allowed to succeed the childless Gian Gastone, last of the Medici grand dukes of Tuscany, and when Maria Theresa succeeded her father in 1740 she appointed her husband as co-regent in Austria. Despite Francis's affairs this was an affectionate alliance producing 16 children, ten of whom survived to adulthood.

A Threat to Austria

Frederick's invasion of Silesia in 1740 started the War of the Austrian Succession, which lasted until 1748 and included within it the Habsburg struggle to regain Silesia. France, Bavaria, Spain and Saxony joined Frederick's campaign and hoped to dismember Austria in its entirety. Participation in the Polish war as well as in a conflict of 1737–9 against the Turks had wrecked Austrian finances and led to the defeatism of advisers surrounding the young monarch. Appearing before the estates of Hungary, a normally fractious body of representatives, Maria Theresa displayed courage in making her plea for a mass levy of troops to wage war, and her request was granted.

The decision of Charles Albert, elector of Bavaria, to support Frederick was unsurprising. Although he had signed up to the Pragmatic Sanction, he had himself some claim to Austria through Bavaria's reigning Wittelsbach dynasty and by the end of 1741 Bavarian as well as French troops were occupying Prague. But the Bavarian ruler's election as Holy Roman Emperor to succeed her father dismayed Maria Theresa. Her sex, she knew, disbarred her but she had proposed Francis as an alternative. Habsburgs had been Holy Roman Emperors since the 15th century and the break in tradition hit her hard. The fact that Austrian troops were marching into Munich even as Charles Albert was being crowned an emperor in Frankfurt in February 1742 proved consoling.

Charles Albert was restored to his Bavarian throne in 1744 with French and Prussian help but on his death, months later, Maria Theresa secured the imperial dignity for her husband. An initial secession of part of Silesia to Frederick in 1741 had given her breathing space during the war and although the 1748 Treaty of Aix-la-Chapelle confirmed the subsequent secession of the whole of Silesia, her territories mostly survived intact. Austria had survived. Now she had to advance.

Reforms of the Austrian Army

Army reform was basic to Maria Theresa's reforms which were intended to strengthen the Habsburg system of government generally. She had reacted to Prussian militarism by proposing a 60,000 increase in the standing army to a total of 110,000 and she created a new military academy, the Theresianum, in order to

train and encourage the nobility in traditions of military service.

She was spectacularly lucky in her choice of reforming ministers. Friedrich Wilhelm, Count von Haugwitz, had fled Silesia in 1741 after Frederick's invasion and therefore brought a personal edge to the revival of Habsburg power and finances. He carried through the proposal that the imperial diets, bodies representing nobles, clergy and towns, should meet only once every ten years rather than annually as in the past. They would continue to negotiate on the amount of taxation to be voted to the government, but the ten-yearly interval guaranteed a steady income to the state and also inevitably led to a diminution of the diets' political standing with a corresponding increase in the crown's authority.

A contemporary engraving of Maria Theresa and minister of state Wenzel Anton, Count von Kaunitz. As part of Maria Theresa's foreign policy reforms, von Kaunitz abandoned Austria's traditional alignment with Britain in favour of alliances with France and Russia designed to isolate Prussia.

The Hungarian diets, however, were excluded from these reforms and their notorious independence of mind would remain to plague the monarchy until 1867, when that year's *ausgleich* created the compromise of a dual Austro-Hungarian monarchy with effective Hungarian internal autonomy.

Meanwhile Wenzel Anton, Count von Kaunitz, worked on that 'reversal of alliances' in 1756 by which Austria could resume its campaign for Silesia's recovery: since Britain and France on the one hand were irreconcilable enemies, and Austria and Prussia on the other hand were necessarily and equally opposed to each other, it made sense for Austria to abandon its British alliance in favour of the French, while Prussia would jettison France in favour of Britain. The aim was Frederick's continental isolation. But not even Austria allied with France and Russia could break the Prussian will and, at the war's end in 1763, Silesia remained Prussian territory with immense consequences for German history. Not just sentiment but also economics had dictated the stubborn Austrian campaign for Silesia. With its reserves of coal, iron ore, lead and zinc, Silesia would be a major source of German industrial power.

Creative Government in Vienna

The need to pay war debts proved a creative challenge which led Austria's government to a thorough revamping that pre-figured many other 19th-century developments. Labour productivity became the aim of state economic development policies: foreign workers and artisans were imported from Italy, the Low Countries and German territories to encourage manufacturing, and foreign farmers were encouraged to migrate to depopulated lands, especially in Hungary.

The 1775 customs union embracing all the monarchy's lands (except Hungary) was a progressive measure encouraging trade expansion. Hungary's serfs

benefited from the law of 1767 which, imposed by Maria Theresa on the country's nobility, regulated the rights and treatment of the peasantry. A similar law of 1775 did the same for the Bohemian peasantry. Her concern for public education was absolutist in style and reflected her fears that illiteracy would undermine public order. The General School Regulation for Austrian lands of 1774 established a system of elementary and secondary schools as well as teacher training colleges. By 1789 there were some 500 state schools.

The Partition of Poland

Territorially Austria expanded through the dismemberment of Poland. As a highly traditionalist dynastic ruler who believed in observing other countries' territorial integrity Maria Theresa had profound reservations about the successive partitions of the Polish kingdom. She had been appalled by Frederick's flouting of this principle in Silesia and had a deep instinct that international disorder was the necessary consequence if other rulers imitated him. She also feared, rightly, accusations of hypocrisy given her views on Frederick. But Russia was now spreading south to imperil the Ottoman empire and Kaunitz had proposed that she ally herself with the Turks to forestall the emergent Russian threat.

This deeply Catholic monarch was affronted by the idea of an Islamic alliance. Frederick's solution was the option forced on her: the Ottomans would be allowed their European possessions while the three great eastern European powers could, through mutual amity, break up Poland. Besides which Kaunitz insisted, rightly, that Austria would only be weakened by standing aside while allowing Russia and Prussia to gain advantage.

By the first partition of 1772 therefore Austria gained Galicia from Poland. In 1775 Austria also gained the Bukovina from the Ottomans and hence a corridor linking Galicia with Hungarian Transylvania. Kaunitz's further initiative, aided by Maria Theresa's son Joseph, proposed exchanging the Austrian Netherlands for Bavaria, a scheme accepted by Bavaria's new ruler, the Elector Palatine. This would have created an alternative German power block to Prussia and was opposed by a panicky Frederick, who declared war in July 1778. Maria Theresa intervened, negotiated with Frederick and frustrated the official Austrian war aims.

Maria Theresa's Successors

Joseph had been Holy Roman Emperor and co-ruler with his mother since Francis's death in 1765, but Maria Theresa's strict maintenance of her rights as ruler led to frequent clashes. When Joseph succeeded his mother in 1780 he began a policy of repressive centralization, which showed some of the contradictions of 'enlightened' Habsburg policy by this stage. Maria Theresa, although personally pious, had restricted the number of religious holidays and stopped those under 24 from taking religious vows, believing this would increase economic productivity.

A portrait of Maria Theresa and her family by Heinrich Fuger shows the empress in later life. Her 16 children included the emperors Joseph II and Leopold II, Marie Caroline of Naples, and Marie Antoinette of France.

Joseph went further: he thought that a third of the monasteries did no productive work in education, health care or agriculture, and he therefore dissolved them.

A 1781 edict established toleration and equality between religious denominations while Joseph's abolition of serfdom, although not universally implemented, amounted to a social revolution. He also gave peasants the right to travel, marry and choose trades without having to ask their lords' permission. But when in 1781 he eased official censorship (an important feature of his mother's reign), he discovered widespread popular discontent against his authoritarian brand of liberalism. Censorship was re-imposed and the Austrian secret police were active monitors of public opinion from the mid-1780s onwards.

Maria Theresa's other son, Leopold II (r. 1790–2), succeeded Joseph and witnessed the initial impact of the French revolution, which would lead to the execution of his sister Marie Antoinette whom their mother had married to Louis XVI. The 19th-century's liberal nationalist challenge would undermine the Austrian Habsburgs and establish their reputation for repression. By then the creaking imperial bureaucracy was more than tinged with absurdity, fantasy and grandiosity. But the dynasty, ensconced in Vienna at the Schönbrunn palace reconstructed by Maria Theresa in all its baroque glory, retained its Austrian Habsburg titles and residual authority until the collapse of 1918.

CATHERINE II, 'The Great', Empress of Russia
R. 1762–1796

St Petersburg was the city chosen by Yekaterina Alekseyevna as the best place to launch the coup of 9 July 1762, which installed her on the imperial throne of Russia. 'I am an aristocrat', she had once said, 'it is my profession'. But the glory she now sought would elevate her beyond the ranks of other nobles and she had prepared the ground with typical efficiency.

Count Grigory Orlov, whose portrait by Andrey Ivanovich Cherny hangs in the State Hermitage Museum in St Petersburg, was one of the protagonists in the coup that placed Catherine on the throne of Russia in 1762.

She knew that the regiments stationed in the city would back her, and the military officer who was her lover, Grigory Orlov, had been placed in charge of the coup's military details. Public opinion too, as represented in the courts of both St Petersburg and Moscow, had warmed to the style, cultivation and intelligence of this German-born princess.

Her husband Tsar Peter III, also German by birth and upbringing, had succeeded the empress Elizabeth in the previous year, but had never concealed his dislike of Russia and hankered after his native land. His open admiration of Prussia's Frederick II was calculated to enrage, since this was the national enemy opposed by Russian forces during the Seven Years' War (1756–63). Highly strung, a near alcoholic and probably impotent, Peter was clearly getting ready to set his wife aside. But it was equally clear that this tsar was incapable of effective rule. Placing herself at the head of a military force, Catherine advanced to the city's Kazan cathedral where she was proclaimed empress and sole ruler of Russia. Peter III was forced to abdicate and then assassinated by his wife's followers eight days later. At Moscow, two months afterwards, Catherine was crowned empress.

Catherine's Upbringing and Marriage
Sophie Friederike Auguste von Anhalt-Zerbst was born the daughter of a minor German prince but through her mother she was related to the far

Catherine's attempts at framing a constitution for her adopted country were abandoned, but her later reforms and foreign policies were more successful. This 1783 portrait by Dmitrij Grigorevic Levickij depicts her as legislatress in the temple of the goddess of justice.

more significant ducal house of Holstein. When she was just 14 she was chosen to be the future wife of Karl Ulrich, duke of Holstein-Gottorp, who was Peter the Great's grandson. In 1744 she joined the duke in Russia where, as the grand duke Peter, he was heir to the throne; the two cousins were married in the following year. The young German who had now become the grand duchess Yekaterina (Catherine) Alekseyevna was bored and lonely in an alien culture. Grand Duke Peter's indifference to his wife was immediately apparent, as was his readiness to humiliate her.

She sought refuge in books and her absorption in the literature of the age would gain her the admiration of enlightened Europe's thinkers and writers. But this was also reading with a pragmatic purpose. Catherine's programme of self-education was intended to equip her for her future role, and as she surveyed the Russian scene it is unlikely that this tough-minded woman thought for long that her role would be merely that of a decorative tsarina.

Sex provided another distraction. Great charm of manner and tremendous physical energy overcame the disadvantage of her plain features, and her campaigns of sexual conquest were markedly successful. During the 18 years of her unhappy marriage she had at least three lovers. She was quite happy for the suspicion to spread that none of her three children, including Paul the imperial heir, had been fathered by her husband. The ambitions she had shown both intellectually and sexually acquired a political focus as she established herself as a figure in her own right, one with ambitions for a distinctive model of Russian enlightenment and national advance.

The Russian Court of the Empress Elizabeth

The Russian court to which Catherine had been transplanted was that of the empress Elizabeth, daughter of Peter the Great, and its milieu was much more cultivated than that of the Petrine autocracy. Nonetheless, it was another St Petersburg coup that had propelled the high-spirited and clever Elizabeth to the throne. Her palace revolution of 6 December 1741 had disposed of the year-long regency of Anna Leopoldovna, exercised on behalf of Anna's son the emperor Ivan VI, and it had also despatched the regent's clique of German advisers. Elizabeth was guided by those who wanted a pro-French foreign policy in order to diminish the German influence on Russian affairs. Russia had therefore allied itself with France and Austria during its struggle against Prussia in the Seven Years' War and it had also annexed part of southern Finland as a result of the war waged against Sweden in 1741–3. Peter's unpopular decision to break the anti-Prussian policy by making peace with Frederick II had been a decisive nail in his coffin.

The Winter Palace

As the founder of Moscow University and of the St Petersburg Academy of Arts, Elizabeth was an immensely significant patron of Russian art and culture. She had also commissioned the Italian architect Bartolomeo Rastrelli to build the Winter Palace in the Russian baroque style which now came to typify St Petersburg's buildings. This principal residence of the tsars was the fifth such palace to be built. In the year of Catherine's coup it had only just been finished, complete with golden stucco mouldings, white columns against a green background and 176 sculptured figures adorning the roof. But if life at court was increasingly sophisticated it had also become intrigue-ridden, as Catherine's scheming against her husband demonstrated. Elizabeth could not match the control methods of her father and, being preoccupied with the planning and execution of magnificent court and church ceremonial, she left the details of Russian government to favourites and advisers drawn from the country's nobility whose factionalism diminished the tsardom's institutional authority.

Catherine's Anti-clerical Measures

The fact that the Russian treasury was empty as a result both of war and Elizabeth's palace expenditure gave Catherine her first challenge. Within months of her accession she had therefore secularized and gained state control over the properties owned by the Russian clergy, who possessed a third of all the country's land and serfs. Peter the Great's reforms had already secured the ideological

The Winter Palace was commissioned by Empress Elizabeth with the intention of outshining even the most sumptuous of European royal palaces. It was here that Catherine established her official residence and began a tradition of collecting works of art which continued for over 300 years. Today the building forms part of the State Hermitage Museum, one of the world's greatest art collections.

submission of the Russian Orthodox church, and Catherine's measures ensured that the clergy were now reduced to the level of state-paid officials. Such an anti-clerical measure suited Catherine's status as an 'enlightened' ruler inspired by the writings of her personal friends Voltaire and Diderot. But her attempt at implementing a reform of Russian law quickly came up against the facts of Russian life as lived by a vast, illiterate and backward population.

In 1767 Catherine convened a commission with the aim of producing a Russian constitution and filled it with delegates from the imperial provinces along with representatives of all social classes apart from the serfs. The *Instruction* that she wrote and presented to the commission was a model of progressive liberalism and drew on her reading of Montesquieu and Rousseau. It urged equality under the law and the extension of legal rights while at the same time condemning torture, capital punishment and the institution of serfdom as undermining of human dignity. The document also showed that enlightenment's rays had to fall from above: absolutist government would be preserved and, in order to be effective, the ruler had to stand above the law. After debating for a whole year the commission adjourned, having failed to agree on how to reform Russian government and law. It would never be reconvened. Catherine's *Instruction*, although a stimulus to the Russian liberalism of the future, proved irrelevant to the Russia of her time and to the empress's own mode of rule.

Famed for their horsemanship and feared for their military skills, Cossack troops led by Pugachov staged a rebellion against Catherine in 1773.

The Pugachov Rebellion

Serfdom under Catherine not only remained but was also greatly extended as the basis of the state. She needed the support of the serf-owning nobility for her other projects and she distributed crown lands among her favourites and ministers in order to ensure their loyalty. The large-scale rebellion which broke out in 1773 led by Yemelyan Pugachov, a former Cossack officer who claimed to be her dead husband and therefore Russia's rightful ruler, confirmed Catherine in her view that Western liberalism was irrelevant to Russia, a land in which anarchy was forever incipient even when not immediately apparent. Spreading from the Urals and across the southeast, the rebellion's mostly Cossack forces were getting ready to march on Moscow by the summer of 1774, at which point it took some crack regiments to reassert order.

Catherine's Foreign Policy

In foreign policy the empress was initially cautious with regard to Prussia and maintained the Russian alliances with Austria and France. Poland, visibly decaying internally, provided a ploy for her diplomacy and in 1764 she installed Stanislaw Poniatowski, a former lover, as its king. Throughout the 18th century Russia's main foreign policy goal had been the push against Turkey in order to gain access to the Aegean and the Mediterranean through the Black Sea. Catherine's resumption of that campaign aroused national enthusiasm and projected her as a Russian patriot.

Here the influence of Grigory Potemkin, her minister, field marshal, former lover and possibly morganatic husband, was paramount. He had been to the fore in Russia's successful war against Turkey in 1768–74. In 1783 he annexed the Crimea from the Ottomans, thereby gaining for Russia territories extending from the Caucasus to Russia's southwest and including the Black Sea's northern coast where, at the harbour in Sevastopol, Potemkin developed the new Russian fleet and its naval base. Istanbul and the Bosphorus were now within striking distance. Catherine brought further pressure to bear on the Turks by strengthening the alliance with Austria, their historic enemy.

The Partition of Poland and Annexation of the Crimea

Celebratory scenes were carefully choreographed by Potemkin as the empress travelled across the Crimea to take possession of her new province in 1787. She had by now renounced her Prussian and British alliances, both countries having become alarmed by Russia's southward expansion. But she showed herself to be a careful ruler in managing the West's fears, and the reign avoided any Russian involvement in European wars. Great power consolidation was cemented by the Second Partition of Poland in 1793, with Catherine annexing the western Ukraine while Prussia absorbed most of western Poland, and by 1795 the Polish kingdom had vanished from the map of Europe.

Death of an Imperialist

By the time Catherine died of an unexpected stroke, French revolutionary and democratic ideas were undermining her style of dynastic power. Ironically, those notions of a politically liberal enlightenment she had been drawn to in her youth were now winning the day. She was apprehensive of her dynasty's future and wanted her grandson Alexander to succeed her rather than her feeble son Paul, but not even Catherine could bypass the laws of dynastic inheritance. By strengthening the nobility's powers and prerogatives she bequeathed a substantial problem to tsarist Russia. But the 200,000 square miles (520,000 sq. km) of land to the south and west which were now Russian-ruled constituted Catherine's greater legacy and ensured for her the admiring regard of Russia's rulers and people long after the end of Romanov rule in 1917.

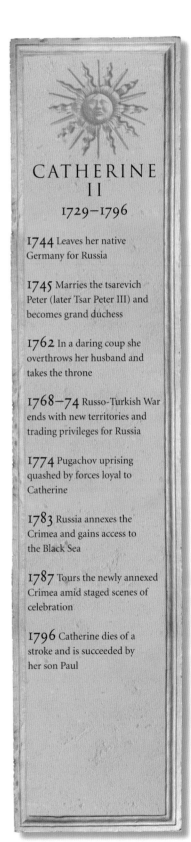

CATHERINE II
1729–1796

1744 Leaves her native Germany for Russia

1745 Marries the tsarevich Peter (later Tsar Peter III) and becomes grand duchess

1762 In a daring coup she overthrows her husband and takes the throne

1768–74 Russo-Turkish War ends with new territories and trading privileges for Russia

1774 Pugachov uprising quashed by forces loyal to Catherine

1783 Russia annexes the Crimea and gains access to the Black Sea

1787 Tours the newly annexed Crimea amid staged scenes of celebration

1796 Catherine dies of a stroke and is succeeded by her son Paul

NAPOLEON BONAPARTE, Emperor of France
R. 1804–1814, 1815

'My policy is to govern men as most of them want to be governed. That I think is the way to recognize popular sovereignty'. Napoleon's statement of aims showed how he was both the last of the 18th century's enlightened despots and also the first of the modern European totalitarians. His mental baggage consisted of enlightenment clichés about 'reason', the need for 'progress' and the wickedness of the past. He also understood how a reputation for culture could be turned to political effect by cultivating an aura of profundity. A mobile library mounted on a gun carriage therefore accompanied him when he went on campaign.

Imagery was always important to Napoleon and his patronage of the artists David and Ingres produced propagandist portraits, which glorified the ruler in a stylized iconography whose intensity of power worship had not been seen in Europe since the reign of Louis XIV. Rootless and lacking any real aim except endless war, Napoleon had both a low view of human nature and an acute understanding of flattery's power. Humanity, he said, was 'led by baubles', which is why he founded the Légion d'Honneur and distributed its medals with such prodigality.

A Corsican's View of the French
The fact that he was born in Corsica partly explains Napoleon's outsider view of the French and the ease with which he dismissed the enormous casualties (totalling some 1.4 million) that he inflicted on them during 17 years of war. 'A single night in the brothels of Paris will replace that lot', he once said after sustaining heavy losses in battle. But as a public policy he allied himself with a new French nationalism as first the republic and then the Napoleonic empire defended itself against its enemies. He ran a conscript army but one which was both in awe of Napoleon (*'le petit caporal'*, as his men called him admiringly) and also identified itself strongly with the cause of the *'patrie'*.

*Jacques-Louis David's portrait (1800–1) commemorates Napoleon's
crossing of the Alps at the St Bernard Pass in May 1800 while
leading his army into northern Italy, where he cut off the Austrian
army from its home base. David's painting compares the emperor to
Hannibal and Charlemagne whose names are carved alongside
Napoleon's in the rocks beneath the horse's hooves.*

Napoleon's crucial insight was that the French were weary of revolutionary disorder but liked other elements of the 1789 legacy. The coup he launched on 9 November 1799 therefore closed down French democracy but safeguarded the abolition of feudalism, the sale of church lands, equality under the law and a rationalized administration. His regime internally was hardly one of terror, and the total number of political prisoners was only about 2500. No questions were asked of former royalists or former revolutionaries as long as they obeyed the new regime. Napoleon knew his people and their weakness for a 'strong man' at the top. They allowed him to become the latest of a long line of French rulers who sought personal glory by extending national boundaries. The difference between Napoleon and his predecessors, however, was that he pursued those goals more efficiently and more successfully.

Had he been born a few years earlier, Napoleone di Buonaparte would not have been French, since Corsica was only ceded from Genoa to France in 1768. His cynical opportunism about the role of chance owes much to his recognition of that crucial accident of birth. A scion of the local minor nobility, he was sent to the military academy near Troyes where he was clever and solitary, studious at mathematics and sometimes bullied. He then entered the elite ranks of the École Royale Militaire in Paris, where he specialized in the artillery techniques that became one of the hallmarks of his generalship.

Napoleon's Early Successes and Fame

At the time of her marriage to Napoleon in 1796 at the age of 33, Joséphine de Beauharnais was already divorced and had two children. Her union with Napoleon would last until 1809, when he divorced her and married Marie Louise of Austria, who later bore him a son.

Fame arrived early when he launched a successful attack on the British and royalist-occupied city of Toulon in 1793. The Directory, a cabal that governed France from 1795 to 1799, rewarded him financially after he had quelled with memorable brutality an insurrection in Paris during the autumn of 1795. With money and fame came sex: Napoleon became the lover and then the husband of Joséphine de Beauharnais, formerly the mistress of Barras who was a leading figure in the Directory regime. The Italian campaign of 1796–7 established him on a European stage with his first wave of military successes over the Austrians in Lombardy and a defeat of the army of the Papal States. By now most of northern Italy, the Rhineland and the Low Countries were under French control.

The fact that so many of his ordinary soldiers thought that Napoleon knew their names was important in establishing his magnetism as a military leader. But so also was his mastery of spying and counter-intelligence techniques using informants based within the enemy camp. Italy is also where Napoleon showed his talent as a propagandizing journalist: he published two newspapers for distribution among his troops and these also circulated in France while a third was printed in Paris. All cemented his own reputation as a coming man, while the Directory sank into inefficiency and corruption.

The subsequent Egyptian campaign of 1798–9, launched to cut England's links with India across this decrepit province of the Ottoman empire, saw Napoleon in the role of savant. He included in his expedition a team of scholars whose investigations of the ancient sites, subsequently published, laid the foundations of modern Egyptology. Past rulers of France had been patrons of scholarship and so Napoleon, a ruler in waiting, decided to imitate them. His removal of an enormous number of Egyptian artefacts to France as he retreated following a rare defeat constituted looting on a grand scale.

Rule of the First Consul

On his return Napoleon launched the coup that made him First Consul – a title adopted because idealization of Roman republican virtue had become a powerful sentiment among French revolutionaries. Napoleon however went on to give France a better, more unified government than any achieved by the revolution's leaders. Whether in taxation or transportation, higher education or banking systems, the reforms bore the inspirational imprint of the mind of a clever soldier bringing centralized order out of chaos. He regimented France just as he had regimented his army. Having little time, and even less aptitude, for the dull deals and closet intrigues of conventional civilian politics, he therefore abolished it.

The *Code Napoléon*, a code of civil laws drafted by jurists and presided over by the ruler, was influential not just in France but in all countries influenced by her revolution and its aftermath. Other Napoleonic legal codes did the same for criminal and commercial law, while his division of France into regional *départements* each run by a *préfet* taking his orders from Paris constituted a lasting legacy.

Emperor Napoleon and Dynastic Succession

Victory at Marengo over the Austrians (1800) was the prelude to a respite from war during the Peace of Amiens (1802–3) and Napoleon now started to plan the security of a dynastic succession. Proclaimed emperor of the French on 18 May 1804, he was crowned in Paris in the presence of a pliant pope on 2 December. A second coronation in Milan on 26 May 1805 made him king of Italy.

The resumption of war brought Napoleon the victories at Austerlitz, Jena and Friedland, which led to the establishment of a French empire stretching from the

NAPOLEON BONAPARTE
1769–1821

1769 Born in Corsica

1795 Quells an insurrection in Paris

1796 Marries Joséphine de Beauharnais; then leads French campaign into Italy

1798–9 Egyptian campaign

1799 Launches a coup and proclaims himself First Consul

1800 Victory over Austria at the Battle of Marengo

1804 Crowned emperor

1805 Crowned king of Italy

1808 Deposition of Bourbon king and attempted occupation of Spain

1812 Disastrous retreat from Russia after his invasion

1814 Exiled to Elba

1815 Escapes from Elba, is briefly restored as emperor, but is defeated at the Battle of Waterloo and then exiled to St Helena

1821 Dies on St Helena

1861 Napoleon's remains are interred in Les Invalides in Paris

Baltic to the Adriatic with client states in place in Germany, Warsaw and Italy. This also entailed an extension of Napoleonic dynasticism, with the emperor placing his brothers on several new thrones. Jerome was king of Westphalia in northwest Germany, Louis became king of Holland, while Joseph first emerged as king of Naples and Sicily before being transferred to the throne of Spain.

Napoleon's sister Elisa, imposed on Lucca as its duchess, was a rare success story. She proved to be a good administrator who doubled silk production in three years and developed the marble quarries at Carrara. Pauline, meanwhile, had married Prince Camillo Borghese and scandalized Roman society by posing as a nude Venus for the sculptor Canova, whose marble record of her sinuous form is perhaps the most substantial legacy of this period's dynastic adventurism.

Napoleon's mother Letizia had left Corsica in 1793 and was now ensconced at the new court in Paris where she was given the title of Imperial Highness and known as 'Madame Mère de l'Empereur'. 'Pourvou que cela doure' ('If only it lasts'), she was heard to say in her rough Corsican French as she surveyed this giddy division of the spoils among her brood.

The Battle of Eylau was fought on 7–8 February, 1807 in east Prussia between Napoleon's forces and Russian troops. An enormous loss of life resulted on both sides and, although the French gained possession of the battlefield, they failed to destroy the Russian army. The battle is depicted in this painting from 1808 by Antoine-Jean Gros.

Napoleon on the Defensive

Economics, other countries' nationalism and the Royal Navy wrecked Napoleonic dynasticism. Of the two powers on Europe's periphery he was prepared to negotiate with Russia but never with Britain, which he regarded as 'Carthage' to his Rome and as a sordidly commercial power. The abandonment of the invasion of Britain – a plan paid for, foolishly, by the sale of the French colony of Louisiana – increased his ire. Presiding over a shattered French economy, he tried to revive it from 1806 onwards by imposing a protectionist system and forcing the Napoleonic empire to use French exports.

This 'Continental System' was another example of the Napoleonic empire's sterile survival strategies which invariably involved leeching off the defeated. Austria in defeat was forced to pay 125 million francs, Saxony 25 million and Prussia had to commit the proceeds of 16 years' taxation. Britain, however, used her empire as a trading opportunity in direct contrast to the futile carnage of Napoleonic 'glory'.

The emperor was forced on the defensive by the wave of Spanish nationalism provoked by his deposition of the Bourbon dynasty in 1808, and attempted occupation of a country whose people he despised as superstitious peasants but who, nonetheless, proved to be murderously effective guerrillas. Russia, having made peace in 1807, was alienated by the selfishly French economics of the Continental System and provided his nemesis after the 1812 invasion. Half a million troops and some of Napoleon's best cavalry were sacrificed during his retreat from Moscow.

Glorious Defeat and Exile

The fall of Paris to the allies on 31 March 1814; Napoleon's exile to Elba and subsequent escape to the French mainland; the '100 days' of recovered *élan* leading to final defeat by the British-Prussian force at Waterloo and a permanent exile at St Helena: all nonetheless ministered to the subsequent Napoleonic mythology.

The emperor's doom was used by romantic writers such as Victor Hugo to represent the idea of a glorious defeat and of nobility frustrated by fate. This would be a politically powerful legacy in subsequent French history. Napoleon also proved an inspiration to later dictators. His technocratic nephew, Napoleon III, resumed family business with a coup d'état in 1851, which made him emperor, and was present when his uncle's remains were placed in an ornate sarcophagus under the dome of the Invalides on 2 April 1861. And in December 1940, after the fall of France, Adolf Hitler ordered that the remains of Napoleon II (1811–32) – the emperor's son by his second marriage to the archduchess Marie Louise of Austria and whom he had named 'king of Italy' – should be brought back from Vienna and laid to rest close to his father's tomb.

VICTORIA, Queen of the United Kingdom of Great Britain and Ireland, and Empress of India

R. 1837–1901

The 'Victorians' had a vivid sense of the difference between themselves and their 18th-century predecessors. By the time of the queen's funeral in 1901, energetic capitalism and social change had obscured so much of the British past that Georgian England seemed as remote as the age of the first Elizabeth. Victoria provided a rare link with the country's recent history while also symbolizing a new British self-confidence and conviction about moral progress.

This miniature painting of Albert by William Charles Ross was created in 1840, the year of his marriage to Victoria. Only five days after Albert's arrival at the English court in 1839, Victoria proposed to him; they were married four months later.

Prone to self-pity, egomania and morbidity, often hysterical in speech and manner, manically eager to offer unsolicited opinions to both her family and ministers, Victoria nonetheless achieved a close identification with the Britain of her reign. Longevity helps to explain this success. A highly developed regal manner compensated for her obvious physical disadvantages. Very short, plain and red-faced, Victoria seemed the image of George III even when she was young.

Victoria's Doubtful Parentage

But it is doubtful whether her father was in fact the duke of Kent, George III's son who, at 50, had married as a match of convenience Victoire, princess of the ducal house of Saxe-Coburg and a widow of the prince of Leiningen, another minor German title. The duke had died when Victoria was less than a year old and her mother would continue a relationship with the Irish adventurer Sir John Conroy, a member of her household who may well have been the queen's natural father.

As a child Victoria was brought up in Kensington Palace, her mother having been appointed by parliament to be her guardian and then regent, in the event of her acceding to the throne while still a minor. But the duchess was disliked by the English royal family, and Victoria's early years were spent in isolation from the

*This engraving is from a flattering portrait of Victoria by George
Howard, ninth earl of Carlisle, made in c.1865. In reality
the queen was short and inclined to fat, with the distinctive
Hanoverian nose and a ruddy complexion.*

royal household. She therefore came to the throne knowing little of her predecessors and had seen very little of her uncle William IV.

The Queen and Lord Melbourne

As a child she was educated by Baroness Lehzen, a governess from Hanover; the prime minister Lord Melbourne instructed the young queen in English history and politics. From the beginning, however, she showed an instinctive sense of public style, and at her first court function she adopted the innovation of wearing a black dress with the insignia of the Garter in order to set off the splendour of the chivalric regalia.

There were early dangers, however. Melbourne, a substitute father figure, captured her for the Whigs and his was a precarious premiership dependent on a tiny majority. The scheming of her mother and Conroy to have the duchess declared a regent, despite the fact that Victoria was already 18 when William IV died, threatened to undermine the queen. Lady Flora Hastings, the duchess's lady-in-waiting, provided an early Victorian moral scandal when wrongly accused of having had an affair with the egregious Conroy. Victoria's censoriousness surfaced and she used the affair both to distance herself from her mother and to establish her own authority at court. She was equally stubborn, and very stupid, in dealing with the leader of the Conservatives, Robert Peel, when he tried to form a ministry in 1839 after Melbourne had lost a parliamentary vote of confidence. Peel, well within his rights, asked that some of the Whig noblewomen holding positions in the royal household as ladies of the bedchamber be replaced by Tory ladies. The queen refused, and Melbourne's Whigs returned to office for another two years. Such episodes showed the truth of the diarist Creevey's remark: 'The Queen is a resolute little tit'.

Marriage to Albert

The idea that Victoria should marry her cousin Albert was a long-cherished scheme of her mother and uncle. Albert's promiscuous and syphilitic father, Duke Ernest I of Saxe-Coburg, was the duchess's younger brother. His mother Louise, separated from her husband, had proved to be energetically unfaithful before her early death when Albert was 12. Many suspected that Albert's real father was in fact Baron von Mayern, the Jewish chamberlain at the Coburg court. Certainly there was a profound difference between the cultured refinement of the young prince and the sensual boorishness of the rest of his family. Moreover, unlike his brother Ernest, Albert proved not to be a carrier of syphilis.

The arrival of an unknown German was controversial, and parliament reduced his annual allowance from a proposed £50,000 to £30,000. But Albert made an immediate impact on Victoria. The fact that they were both physically tiny seemed the only similarity between this reserved intellectual aesthete and his

VICTORIA
1819–1901

1820 Victoria's father dies and her mother is appointed to be her guardian

1837 Accedes to the British throne aged 18

1840 Marries Prince Albert of Saxe-Coburg-Gotha who becomes her prince consort

1861 Death of Prince Albert and withdrawal from public life

1864 Victoria's support for Prussia in the Schleswig-Holstein dispute earns her a rebuke from the prime minister and marks the end of royal interference in foreign affairs

1876 Victoria is proclaimed empress of India

1901 Victoria dies and is succeeded by Edward VII. She is buried at Frogmore alongside Albert

noisy, ill-educated cousin. He was, however, handsome and Victoria was highly sexed, informing Melbourne of the 'gratifying and bewildering night' she had enjoyed after the wedding. A dynastic arrangement became a romance whose undoubted ardour and sincerity helped to shape powerful Victorian sentiment about family life.

A Move to the Countryside

Albert was a countryman whose aesthetic sense was formed by the beauties of the south German landscape and he turned Victoria, previously a full-time Londoner, into a countrywoman. They acquired two homes, Osborne on the Isle of Wight and Balmoral in Scotland. Albert's architectural design and decoration of Osborne showed the expert taste of a connoisseur of the Italian renaissance style. Balmoral they bought and left to stand as an exercise in the grim manner of Scottish baronial architecture. Both places provided an escape from the tedious gossip and card games of the courtiers at Buckingham Palace.

Victoria's Relationship with Her Subjects

But even at court in London the queen could withdraw regularly from her royal household to spend time in private with her family. This domesticity was something new in British monarchy and the royal family also needed to guard its privacy more than in the past. Eighteenth-century English kings could move quite easily and familiarly among their subjects. But the hectic pace of urban population growth created a new phenomenon – that of the large, often unruly, and invariably inquisitive crowd. Royalty now needed greater protection from the population. Mingling therefore the formality of set state occasions with the luxury of domesticity, the British crown adopted its annual ritual of changing residence with the seasons.

Albert also educated the queen in the politics of her constitutional role, teaching her to accept a Tory government as a democratic necessity, and the need to distance herself from the Whigs. His wider plans to elevate the court into a centre of intellectual and cultural life were frustrated – almost inevitably so given the predominantly philistine nature of the modern British royal household.

A European Network of Royalty

Victoria was at the centre of a great European network of gossip through her various relatives. She wrote weekly to her mother's other brother, uncle Leopold, king of the Belgians. Until the revolution of 1848, she was linked to the reigning French royal

Victoria and Albert bought Osborne House and its estate on the Isle of Wight in 1845. The original house was demolished and this three-storey pavilion was built in the style of an Italian villa. The seaside residence gave the royal family some privacy and seclusion from public life.

family, since Leopold's second wife was daughter to King Louis-Philippe. Her eldest daughter married the crown prince of Prussia and Albert's German contacts were naturally very strong. By the end of her reign the British royal family was linked to the thrones of Russia, Greece, Romania, Norway and Spain.

Unsurprisingly, the queen was tediously well informed on the finer details of various dynastic claims to territories right across Europe. The strength of her attachment to dynastic rights set her at odds with the liberal nationalism of her own time – a cause traditionally supported by most British governments during her reign. But her beliefs were largely immaterial. Despite its surface majesty, British royalism had become politically irrelevant.

As foreign secretary from 1846 and then as prime minister, the third viscount Palmerston (1784–1865) was a leading advocate of the rights of nationalities against unrepresentative and reactionary dynasties. He was also entirely indifferent to Victoria and Albert's views on these matters. They gained an important concession in ensuring that despatches on foreign affairs had to be sent to the queen before they went abroad, and could not be altered after she had seen them. Palmerston's refusal to follow this rule led to his dismissal as foreign secretary in 1851. But four years later he was in office as prime minister, with the queen's bestowal of the Garter following a year later.

The Dilemma of Constitutional Monarchy

Both queen and consort showed the difficulty faced by constitutional monarchy in a democratic age. They demonstrated a strong attachment to hard work and public affairs and they understood that monarchy could not afford to be seen as just an antiquarian survival. But in engaging with questions of policy they could be seen as partisan and the sole result of such meddling was to reveal, rather brutally, their lack of power compared with democratically elected governments.

The Grieving Widow

Albert's early death at the age of 42 left the widowed queen with eight unmarried children to raise – progeny she had spent little time with previously. She now abandoned herself to an orgy of grief, withdrew from public view for over ten years, and turned Albert's memory into the centre of a weirdly neo-religious familial cult. Albert's dressing gown would be placed in her funeral casket.

She continued to work on state papers, often expressing her thoughts in bizarrely infantile capital letters and insistent underlinings. But on affairs of state Victoria, after Albert, really had nothing interesting to say. Whereas his memoranda to ministers had been informed and well argued, her comments were mostly vapid. And without Albert's guidance she got things badly wrong. The queen had invariably been pro-Prussian and anti-French. But her support for the Prussian seizure of the previously Danish-ruled duchies of Schleswig and Holstein in 1864 was incautiously obvious, earned her a rebuke from Palmerston and proved to be the last time the English crown tried to shape British foreign policy.

Victoria appears (front, centre) in this 1894 family photograph with her children and grandchildren. (Kaiser Willhelm II of Prussia is pictured at left in the front row.) Victoria and Albert's nine children, many of whom married into other European royal families, were born between 1840 and 1857.

Victoria's Withdrawal from Public Life

She explained her absence from public life as a horror at 'the spectacle of a poor, broken-hearted widow, nervous and shrinking, ALONE in STATE as a show'. But this withdrawal encouraged the spread of republican views because, for many, an absent monarchy seemed a pointless and expensive institution. Paid £400,000 a year from the civil list to be head of state and using that money to build up her private fortune, the queen refused public duties such as the state opening of parliament. She only agreed to do so in 1871 because parliament was set to debate royal allowances; in the next 30 years she opened parliament four more times.

Benjamin Disraeli was the politician who understood her best. 'The crisis has begun', he once informed her, 'and I shall need all your Majesty's support'. Flattery kept her quiet and, by making her empress of India, Disraeli turned the queen into a symbol for the brash expansion of late 19th-century British imperialism.

Regina Imperatrix now lies next to the prince consort at Frogmore, the specially constructed royal mausoleum within Windsor's Home Park whose cold marmoreal splendour distances both Victoria and Victorianism from modernity.

LUDWIG II, King of Bavaria

R. 1864–1886

Handsome and introspective, passionate about the arts and an extravagant spender, Ludwig was the last European ruler to be inspired by the idea of kingly and absolutist rule. The castles he commissioned and helped to design in a profusion of styles constitute his greatest legacy.

The Ruler as Aesthete

Neuschwanstein, a Romanesque building with Byzantine and Gothic interiors, was raised next to Hohenschwangau, which was the castle of Ludwig's father, King Maximilian II. It therefore represents the son's claim to individuality and independence. It is also an important religious building whose wall paintings use Christian iconography to depict the idea of chaste love and chivalric idealism. Linderhof was an exercise in the rococo style, with its formal grounds containing a grotto in which operas were staged on an underground lake lit by the electricity that was the age's 'high-tech' delight. Herrenchiemsee, Ludwig's tribute to Louis XIV, on the other hand, is an imitation Versailles built on an island in the middle of the Chiemsee. With the assistance of the stage designer Christian Jank, Ludwig had created a string of theatrical confections where the king of a diminished Bavaria could act out a role.

The Wittelsbach Dynasty

Monarchs in the western Europe of Ludwig's time, if they were to survive, had to accommodate themselves to an age whose politics were being shaped by mass democracy, whose governments were adopting the centralizing methods of an ordered bureaucracy and whose economies were being recast by heavy industry.

Ludwig resisted these prosaic facts. The past glories of the Wittelsbach dynasty were real enough: they had ruled Bavaria first as dukes from 1180 onwards and then, from 1805, as kings. From 1623 onwards the reigning Wittelsbach had also been electors of the Holy Roman Empire. Occupation by the French

Amid a romantic setting of mountains and lakes in southwest Bavaria stands Neuschwanstein Castle, one of Ludwig II's lavish building projects. It is named after the Swan Knight, Lohengrin, the hero of Wagner's opera of the same name.

234

revolutionary army led to Bavaria becoming an ally of France in 1801 and under
the Treaty of Pressburg (1805) it acquired some Austrian-ruled territories and
its present boundaries. As a member of the Confederation of the Rhine, the
country's foreign policy was controlled by Napoleon, but it also enjoyed full
sovereignty internally, and the political regime of early 19th-century Bavaria
embraced the Napoleonic ideal of a centralized and anti-clerical state.

The constitution of 1808 abolished serfdom, proclaimed equality under the
law and introduced universal liability to pay taxation. This constitutionalism
survived the end of the Napoleonic empire in the form of a two-chamber
parliament. Ludwig was therefore at odds with a well-established political
system of constitutional monarchy.

Patronage of Wagner

The castles would become part of modern Bavarian *kitsch*. But Ludwig's
patronage of Richard Wagner, whom he rescued from poverty and debt,
was the last substantial legacy of German kingship in the arts and it enabled

the composer to finish work on his opera cycle *The Ring of the Nibelung*. Wagner had become embroiled in the wave of liberal-nationalist revolutions that swept Germany in 1848–9 and was then forced into exile before an amnesty of 1861 allowed him to return to Germany. His political ideals were hardly those of the frustrated autocrat. But as a youth Ludwig had been entranced by a concert performance of *Lohengrin* (1850) and identified with its central figure of the lonely knight. Wagner's re-creation of German mythology stirred Ludwig's imagination and he projected a future in which the king and the composer would lead a revival of German culture.

In one of his first acts as king, Ludwig summoned Wagner from Stuttgart to work in Munich. The entire cycle of the *Ring* was first performed triumphantly in 1876 at the Bayreuth *festspielhaus*, partly paid for by Ludwig. *Parsifal* (1882), Wagner's last opera, is also the result of Ludwig's patronage. Its theme of sexual indulgence and renunciation, of innocence and suffering, forms an inescapable part of Ludwig's own life story.

Homosexual Love at Court

A strain of romantic recklessness ran in the family: Ludwig's grandfather, Ludwig I, was forced to abdicate because of his affair with the Irish-Spanish actress Lola Montez. But the young Ludwig found himself subjected to the strict disciplinary regime deemed appropriate to a crown prince and future ruler. He reacted by embarking on a series of homosexual infatuations in a pattern which persisted throughout his life. Although a rebel against political constraints, in his affairs Ludwig followed conventions well established in princely courts.

His closest companions and lovers were mostly aristocratic and frequently they were young army officers who then became his equerries. Ludwig's lovers may well have included Paul Maximilian Lamoral von Thurn und Taxis (a member of an aristocratic family of legendary wealth), Richard Hornig who stayed by the king's side as his equerry for many years, as well as the Hungarian actor Josef Kainz. But however deep their intimacy with the king, these men also had to play the role of courtiers.

Bavaria meanwhile was counting for less and less in the new politics of Germany. The state of Prussia, guided by the tactical genius of its chancellor, Otto von Bismarck, was setting the pace in the 1860s for the unification of Germany. A new country – a second *reich* – would emerge dominated by Prussia's army and by her politicians, by Prussian industry and high finance. This German federation would be continental Europe's greatest power. Ludwig's reaction involved dressing up as Louis XIV. If the master of Versailles had been the Sun King then, declared Ludwig, he would be the Moon King in a pale but real reflection of the absolutist style.

'The Death of Siegfried' (1899) by the Belgian Symbolist painter Henri de Groux depicts a scene from 'Nibelungenlied', the epic poem made famous by Wagner in his 'Ring' cycle of operas. At a young age Ludwig had been fascinated by Wagner's work and later became a friend and major benefactor of the German composer.

Ludwig Flirts with Marriage

On 22 January 1867 Ludwig announced his engagement to his cousin, Princess Sophie of Austria. Behind this improbable event lay the facts of war, something which also doomed it from the start. In a strategically brilliant 'Seven Weeks' War' during the summer of 1866 Prussia had fought, and defeated Austria. Ludwig's Bavaria had been allied to Austria and therefore, like the other German states which had also been Austria's allies, Bavaria had to accept the fact of Prussian dominance. Ludwig was no longer the king of a truly independent country. In these circumstances what was the point of a marriage that would mean an alliance with Austria which was merely another defeated power? Ludwig, under pressure to produce an heir, flirted with the idea of marriage in that winter of 1866–7. But circumstances both emotional and diplomatic highlighted the pointlessness of marriage and in October 1867 the engagement was cancelled.

Bavaria Comes under Prussian Control

Ludwig had to make another announcement in 1867: from now on Bavaria would be allied to Prussia under the terms of a so-called 'mutual defence' treaty. Bavaria therefore had to support Prussia in the war against France which broke out in 1870 and which ended in the humiliation of the French army at the Battle of Sedan in September. In the same month Ludwig, instructed by Bismarck, had to issue a public declaration calling for the creation of a new German empire. The autonomy granted by Prussia to Bavaria under the German constitution of 1871 amounted to little more than local control of its postal and telegraph service as well as of its railways. This residual element of autonomy nonetheless proved important in determining Ludwig's fate.

Was Ludwig Really Insane?

In the 1870s Ludwig was communicating with his rump government back in Munich almost exclusively through intermediaries, messengers and telegrams. It proved easy enough therefore to intrigue against such an isolated figure, and a psychiatric team was appointed by the government to produce a report on his mental state. It concluded, conveniently, that the king suffered from paranoia. On 10 June 1886 Ludwig was officially declared insane by the government and it was announced that his uncle, Prince Luitpold, would be regent. It was a classic coup. Ludwig's telegrams to friends and newspapers asking for help were intercepted. The king was seized at Neuschwanstein in the early morning of 12 June and taken into custody at Berg Castle south of Munich.

Was Ludwig really insane? Bismarck, who was hardly a figure likely to indulge a lunatic, managed to get a message through to Ludwig sometime between 10 and 12 June and urged him to escape to Munich where he could then show himself to his people. Despite all his years of isolation the king was still personally popular and a large force of Bavarian peasants had tried to get through to

Neuschwanstein in order to rescue him and take him across the border.

A Myth in His Own Time

The fact that he became a myth in his own time also contributed to his appeal. Ludwig's night-time rides on 18th-century sleighs (accompanied by servants dressed in the correct period livery) often included impromptu stops when he visited the local peasantry in their homes. Stories of these graciously *de haut en bas* encounters only grew in the telling. The grandiose building projects had also in fact been popular. They were very successful public work projects employing a large number of the Bavarian population and, as great tourist attractions, they had brought visitors and money to a country whose economy was mostly rural and poor compared to the booming economy of an industrializing Prussia. The politicians in Munich claimed that Ludwig was bankrupting the state finances. Ludwig's supporters said that he paid for his buildings out of his own personal fortune. But whichever claim was true, Ludwig had become an anachronism, a reclusive king devoid of kingly power.

Ludwig's eccentric behaviour and reclusive nature led to the circulation of countless myths during his lifetime, which only increased after his mysterious death by drowning.

Suicide or Murder?

In the early evening of 13 June Ludwig asked to go for a walk by the shores of Lake Starnberg near Berg Castle. Professor Bernhard von Gudden, the psychiatrist who had headed the medical team examining the king, went with him and told the guards there was no need to accompany them. The bodies of both men were found dead in the water close to the lake shore just before midnight. Although the official autopsy found no water in Ludwig's lungs he was officially declared to have committed suicide by drowning. The fact that he was a strong swimmer adds to the mystery and has fed the conspiracy theories suggesting murder.

The final act in the life of this aesthete-king, though so murky and melancholic, is surely also somehow appropriate. Love of beauty and a fateful obsession with death: these had always been themes linked together in German romantic art, literature and music. And they are present *par excellence* in the leitmotifs of the operas of Richard Wagner. The waters of the Rhine are evoked as a central symbol in the *Ring* whose harmonies protest against the power of modern materialism and preach the message that those who wish to love must give up the search for power. These themes were there too in the life of Ludwig II and must have hovered over the waters of Lake Berg on that summer's evening as night's shadows spread over the dead body of a broken king.

THE LAST OF THE SUN KINGS
The Twentieth Century

Representative democracy and nationalist assertion, forces unleashed during the previous century, ensured that monarchical power in its dynastic form either disappeared completely or became at best marginal in the course of the 20th century.

Scandinavian kingship adapted swiftly and members of the royal houses in Denmark, Norway and Sweden became in effect the 'first citizens' of their countries' democracies. The house of Orange-Nassau provided the Netherlands with a monarchy which was absorbed within the country's traditionally liberal political culture. Kingship in Belgium, a country sharply divided on cultural lines between the speakers of French and Flemish, had few powers but played an important symbolic role in reconciling the two communities. Morocco's king was exceptional in the sweeping range of his executive powers but even in Nepal, that anomalous survival of absolute kingship in the Himalayas, the throne had been forced by 2006 to relinquish its sovereignty and transfer it to a parliamentary body. Totalitarianism, however, had proved to be the most distinctive political ideology of the early 20th century in both Europe and Asia with new authoritarian rulers inheriting the role of previous Sun Kings in providing a focus for national identity. Nowhere was this truer than in the case of China on its tempestuous journey from an imperial past to a Maoist future.

Henry P'u-i, last emperor of China from 1908–12, pictured here in 1940, at which time he was the Japanese puppet emperor of Manchuria.

An Emperor Becomes a Citizen

Sometime in November 1925 the historian Steven Runciman, then a young man aged 22, met the last emperor of China. Henry P'u-i (1906–67), as he now called himself, had been dethroned in 1912 at the age of six by the Chinese republican government which had come to power the previous year. Initially, he had been allowed to stay on in Beijing's Forbidden City, the enclosure that had housed his imperial forebears. His guardians then moved him to the port town of Tientsin, where international treaty arrangements allowed each of the Great Powers to have their own quarter, or concession, areas which were self-governing under a consul-general. A house was found for P'u-i in the Japanese concession and it was here that he lived with the remnants of his imperial household.

One day a message arrived at the British consulate-general where Runciman was staying. Did he play the piano and, if so, would he join the former emperor in practising duets? After some playing which revealed that the ex-emperor was unlikely to earn a living as a concert pianist, Runciman and P'u-i settled down to drinking cups of jasmine tea. The historian later recalled a 'frail etiolated youth, not at all good-looking' but with a graceful air, 'suitable for the last head of an old dynasty'.

P'u-i revealed that he had adopted the name Henry because of his admiration for England's King Henry VIII. He called his chief wife, of whom, thought Runciman, 'he was clearly not fond', Mary after the monarch dubbed 'Bloody Mary' because of her persecutory attempts at England's re-conversion to Catholicism. P'u-i's chief concubine was called Elizabeth I, which possibly indicated a greater fondness on the former emperor's part.

P'u-i's Manchu dynasty had ruled China for 267 years but his own life was among the most pathos-ridden of all those who have ruled, or attempted to reign, as Sun Kings. From 1934 to 1945 he was emperor of the Japanese puppet state of Manchuria and, in his middle years, the Chinese communist government allowed him to work in the mechanical repair shop of a botanical garden in Beijing. Shortly before her death in 1965, Queen Elisabeth of the Belgians, accompanied by her daughter, Marie-José, formerly queen of Italy, visited Beijing and Chairman Mao asked P'u-i to show the two monarchs around the Forbidden City which had once been his home. 'Henry' had invariably performed the role expected of him and proved to be, apparently, an excellent guide, well informed on the various treasures that he displayed with pride and happy to talk about his old life – although he struck the regal tourists as being wistful and sad. But it is surely a pleasing irony that one of history's dominant communist leaders should have provided P'u-i with an opportunity to enjoy once again the company of what Runciman called 'ladies of his old exalted class'.

Dynasticism as an element of government was disappearing swiftly in the Europe and Asia of the 1920s. The end of the First World War saw the dethronement of the Hohenzollerns in Berlin, of the Romanovs in St Petersburg and of the Habsburgs in Vienna. The rule of Italy's House of Savoy came to an end after a national referendum held in 1946 voted for a republic, and on 1 January in that year Japan's emperor Hirohito renounced his divinity, an attribute which had been fundamental to his dynasty's authority.

Leopold II, king of the Belgians from 1865–1909.

As the idea of hereditary rule by monarchs and emperors became ever more irrelevant to industrialized democracies, so too did the notion that some of these rulers might be considered the supreme embodiments of their countries and nations as 'Sun Kings'. Some of the more recent examples of that idea had indeed brought shame to their countries.

Kingship in Africa: Genocide and Massacre

Leopold II (1835–1909), king of the Belgians, headed a group of European investors formed in 1877 in order to exploit the trading riches of the Congo River Basin recently explored by Europeans. By 1884 the *Association Internationale du Congo* had signed treaties with some 450 of the area's independent African rulers and chiefs. On that basis it claimed to rule the entire territory as an independent state, and the Berlin West Africa Conference of 1884–5 recognized the sovereignty of the 'Congo Free State' with Leopold as its sovereign ruler. This was a private business masquerading as a state and Leopold's title was held separately from that of his kingship in Belgium. As, in effect, its chief executive he ran the business with a rapacity remarkable even in the history of European colonialism in Africa, and the king extended military control over his country's interior in the 1890s.

Leopold was certainly the Congo Free State personified and his administration allowed forced labour, mutilation and beatings for minor crimes. Quotas for rubber production had been imposed on villages, and their inhabitants could be taken as hostages to ensure those targets were met. The state's population of 20 to 30 million may have been reduced to as few as eight million by the time a scandalized European public opinion forced Leopold to give up this personal possession of his in 1908. The Congo Free State was then abolished and replaced by the Belgian Congo, a colony that was run as part of Belgium's empire.

The Central African empire run by Jean-Bédel Bokassa (1921–96) showed how a degenerate local elite was capable of developing the idea of kingly and imperial rule to the ruination of its unfortunate subjects. Bokassa had been president of the then Central African Republic for ten years when, in December 1976, he assumed the title of Bokassa I. A year later, in a clichéd imitation of Napoleon I, he was crowned in a ceremony whose expense further undermined the already struggling national finances. He was financially improvident, as well as capricious in his cruelty and was personally involved in his imperial guard's massacre of 100 schoolchildren. The French republic, embarrassed by its association with the tyrant, sent in its paratroopers in the military coup of 1979 which restored the republic, deprived Bokassa of his title and sent the ex-emperor into exile.

The Rise and Fall of the Ethiopian Crown

Ethiopian kingship had deep Judaeo-Christian roots in the Horn of Africa and the conquering 'Lion of Judah' which appeared on the national flag was a symbolic assertion that Menelik I, the country's mythical early ruler, had been the son of the queen of Sheba and the biblical King Solomon.

Jean-Bédel Bokassa, emperor of the Central African Republic from 1977–9, seen here at his flamboyant coronation ceremony.

The rulers belonging to the Solomonid dynasty (1268–1854) claimed to be Solomon's direct descendants and this genealogy, however spurious, was used to legitimize their authority. Ethiopia's Christianity together with its Amharic language provided the cultural basis of the national unity established by the dynasty's rulers before the onset of some 150 years of feudal anarchy in the early 18th century. Menelik II (1844–1913) was ruler (1865–89) of the regional kingdom of Shewa, whose princes claimed to be related to the Solomonid dynasty, and from his capital at Addis Abbaba Menilek re-established Ethiopia's unity as its emperor (1889–1913). Tafari Makonnen (1892–1975), Menelik's relative, ruled Ethiopia from 1916 onwards and, following the period when he had been regent to the empress Zauditu, he became emperor in his own right in 1930 as Haile Selassie I.

Tafari's title signified 'Might of the Trinity' in the theological dynastic style but he was also intent on his country's transformation into a modern state. Haile Selassie retained the royal prerogative, which he merely delegated to the country's two-chamber parliament, an institution consisting of appointees and of indirectly elected members. But his programmes of public works, abolition of slavery, and reforms of a tax regime previously run on feudal lines boosted the country's economy, and exports of coffee, the major Ethiopian trade, soared. The Italian colonies in neighbouring Eritrea and Somaliland were undermined by

Ethiopia's trading prosperity and, in 1935, Mussolini provoked the seven-month war which resulted in Ethiopia's incorporation into a new Italian East African empire. Haile Selassie, a dynast unseated by a totalitarian, fled the country.

The emperor regained his throne in 1941, but by the 1960s the former progressivist was an increasingly reactionary and isolated figure. He had proclaimed a revised constitution in 1955 and as a result there was now an elected lower house with parliament being allowed to question the emperor's ministers and express disapproval of his decrees. But the imperial power to rule by such decrees as well as Haile Selassie's right to nominate his own government remained unaffected. The reforms therefore guaranteed an endemic instability that became especially acute since Haile Selassie manipulated different political factions against each other as a way of buttressing his own power.

Following a failed military coup in 1961 against him, the emperor retreated into his own milieu of aristocratic landowners at a time when land reform was becoming a major domestic issue. By now he was heavily dependent on US support and therefore vulnerable to that Marxist-Nationalist fusion which was so effective an anti-colonial force in post-war Africa. The United States and its wartime allies had backed Haile Selassie's scheme for an Ethiopian-Eritrean federation, which, having been formed in 1952, proved only the prelude to Eritrea's annexation in 1962 as a province of the 'Ethiopian empire'.

From the early 1960s Eritrean nationalism, fed by local Muslim resentment at the country's incorporation within an Ethiopian Christian culture, began a struggle for independence that lasted three decades. Rebellion also broke out in the Ethiopian region of Ogaden whose Somali population identified with the state of Somalia, which became independent in 1960 following a post-war period of rule by British and Italian protectorates. With a large body of radicalized opinion in Ethiopia demanding a limitation to individual land-holdings, Haile Selassie's power base had dwindled to a precarious oligarchy. The 1974 military coup exploited the country's economic crisis and famine, deposed the emperor and installed the Marxist-Leninist regime whose agents, in all probability, strangled him to death in 1975.

Haile Selassie I, emperor of Ethiopia from 1930–6, 1941–74, pictured in his coronation robes in 1930.

Fascism and Communism: Totalitarian Styles

Both fascism and communism, variants on a totalitarian theme in Europe between the two world wars, showed that 'Sun Kings' did not have to be dynasts and that anti-democratic movements could produce leaders who also claimed to represent the soul of the people. The authority of Stalin (1878–1953) as Russian leader was not solely buttressed by his position as secretary general of the Russian Communist Party (1922–53) or the mass murders and show trials that disfigured his regime. As a 'red tsar' he claimed to represent, despite his Georgian nationality, an ancient and vigorous Russian nationalism which was greatly strengthened by the country's invasion by the Wehrmacht in the summer of 1941.

Hitlerian fascism was even more consumed than Stalinism by a cult of the leader as embodiment of the national spirit. German history from the first Reich of 800 onwards was used and abused in order to present national socialism as the supreme expression of the nation and the *führer* as the collectivity's personalized apotheosis. History and personality combined to similar effect in the figure of Benito Mussolini (1883–1945) whose inspired insights, as *duce*, were supposed to justify his movement's strategic goals. Mussolini, a former journalist, used his propagandist gifts to portray Italian fascism as a revival of ancient Roman imperialism. His goals therefore included the restoration of Italian naval hegemony so that the Mediterranean Sea might once again be *mare nostrum*, and the country's colonization of Libya became a major imperial enterprise of the inter-war years.

Fascism in all its forms elevated the visionary leader while also encouraging the politics of mass identity which brought the people together through rituals, parades and marches. The Sun King in his dynastic form had invariably appreciated the role that such rituals could play in the consolidation of his power. Fascist leaders were his eager pupils in this regard and Nazi Germany proved particularly adept at reviving grotesque forms of pagan religiosity as part of its consistently anti-Christian ideology. Spanish fascism, however, was different and it exploited the country's long tradition of a national-minded Christian monarchy even though the Spanish throne was kept empty during Francisco Franco's authoritarian regime.

Juan Carlos, king of Spain from 1975 to the present, pictured here on the left with General Francisco Franco in 1970.

Spain: Democracy and Monarchy Restored

The monarchy that had been restored in 1874, together with the parliamentary democracy enshrined in the constitution of 1876, had given Spain an unusually long period of stability. But the reign of the pro-clerical reactionary Alfonso XIII (1902–31) saw the return of political instability partly as a result of his own actions since he intervened in the political process in order to secure a regular rotation of governments whose episodic nature might, he thought, increase his own kingly authority.

The successful coup d'état launched by General Miguel Primo de Rivera in 1923 overthrew parliamentary democracy, replacing it with a regime pledged to support 'Country, Religion, Monarchy'. At first this programme appeared to suit Alfonso's interests and the king was closely associated with the government's attempts at ruling Spain. But the de Rivera regime was also fiscally incompetent and its consequent unpopularity led to its defeat in the election which Alfonso was forced to call in 1931. In April of that year he was compelled to leave Spain by the country's newly elected republican-socialist government and the administration also demanded the king's abdication. Eventually, Alfonso abdicated his rights in favour of his third son, Don Juan, the father of Juan Carlos, the present king of Spain.

Generalissimo Franco led the nationalist forces in the civil war (1936–9) which subverted Spain's democratic republic and in 1969 he bypassed Don Juan's senior claim to the throne by designating Juan Carlos as his official heir, although retaining his own full powers in the meantime. Franco's intentions for Spain's future during a period of long illness from the late 1960s onwards are uncertain but what is indisputable is that he set the scene for contemporary Europe's most surprising royal restoration. Juan Carlos (b.1938) presided over a swift dismantling of Franco's system on his death in 1975, encouraged the revival of political parties and declared an amnesty for political prisoners. He resolved on a personal identification with the principles of the new democracy and in 1981 the king took the lead in opposing the military coup which had attempted a restoration of authoritarian rule.

Monarchy in Britain: An Enduring Influence

Europe's most enduring monarchy was less closely associated with its country's evolution by the end of the 20th century. The House of Windsor had survived the inter-war period and the abdication crisis of 1936 caused by Edward VIII's desire to marry an American divorcée, Wallis Simpson. The claim to be 'supreme governor' of the Church of England remained an integral feature of English kingship and the 'national church' did not at that time allow the re-marriage of divorced persons. Edward's consequent abdication brought to the throne his brother who reigned as George VI, and during the years of the Second World War the English crown became symbolically associated with the cause of the United Kingdom's survival as an independent country.

Elizabeth II, queen of the United Kingdom from 1952 to the present, pictured here at the 1967 State Opening of Parliament.

During a long reign, Elizabeth II (b.1926) has proved to be an exemplary and self-effacing constitutional monarch as well as a devoutly Christian sovereign. Her coronation in Westminster Abbey was filmed and televised but the queen has always refused permission to broadcast the section in the film recording her anointment with holy oil, since she regarded that rite as the ceremony's most sacred element.

A constitutional monarchy, however, of its very essence, cannot afford to draw attention to itself through those acts of spectacular self-definition, opulence and patronage which define a 'Sun King'. In the public arena therefore the House of Windsor has confined itself to charitable works, public platitudes and the performance of its ceremonial duties on those national occasions at which a royal presence is required. It has also proved particularly averse to using its riches in order to patronize the arts, previously a powerful source of kingly prestige.

The monarch has maintained the set pattern of the royal progress, which moves the household according to the seasons of the year between Balmoral, Windsor Castle, Buckingham Palace and Sandringham. This annual progress is reminiscent of European kingship at its most powerful but the royal house's senior members have calculated that ostentation would undermine both themselves and their institution. A reputation for sober dutifulness is part of the unwritten contract that allows the English monarchy to survive and royalty performs the role allotted to it under this dispensation.

Pope John XXIII, pope
of the Roman Catholic
Church from 1958–63,
seen here at his coronation.

The Papacy: a Kingly Survival

Kingship at the height of its influence had invariably been associated with sacral authority and the endorsement by so numinous a source had lent monarchies not only their legitimacy but also their stability. The fact that Europe became an increasingly secular continent in the course of the 20th century contributed therefore to the displacement of kingship in its classic form, and those royal houses that did survive had to maintain their mystique by seeking the approval of the media, a necessarily transient and unstable source of authority.

In the early 21st century, however, the spiritual power of the papacy still retains its connections with many features of monarchical government despite the fact that it has always been an elective institution. The personnel surrounding the supreme pontiff in his curia and who transact papal business are the last survivors of Europe's *ancien régime* courts, and popes also continue to be temporal rulers – albeit only of the Vatican City with its 44 hectares (109 acres). The courtly rituals of papal coronations were still celebrated on a magnificent scale until the reforms of the second Vatican Council (1962–5) started to discourage the idea that popes were also earthly monarchs.

When Pope Pius XII (1876–1958) was crowned in 1939 the ceremony would have been very familiar to his Renaissance predecessors: Pius was carried under a processional canopy on the portable throne, the *sedia gestatoria*, which was raised aloft by his attendants. Twin peacock-feather fans were raised behind him, symbols of imperial rule which had their origins in the court ceremonial of Byzantine emperors. These external forms of authority became less favoured in papal circles during the late 20th century but the long papacy of John Paul II (1978–2005) saw a striking reaffirmation of the pope's personal role as guardian of orthodoxy in a world church organized on hierarchical lines.

A Court at the White House: the Kennedy Presidency

It was a politician raised as a Catholic who showed how the world's most powerful 20th-century democracy could produce a president with many of the attributes of a 'Sun King'. John Fitzgerald Kennedy (1917–63) was born into a family with a pronounced dynastic style and one whose members operated as a political clan to their mutual advantage. As president of the United States he surrounded himself with advisers and close confidants – just as his predecessors had done in the White House. But his personal elegance, literary turn of phrase and telegenic appearance established Kennedy as a new kind of American leader, and the circle who surrounded him were both appreciative of his personal charms and shared his ambition to create a re-energized United States.

These were Kennedy's 'courtiers' and, as the self-proclaimed leader of a younger generation, his rhetoric talked of the need to extend America's 'New Frontier' – a metaphor that evoked the appeal of the country's culture and also re-expressed, in a Cold War context, the ideals of liberty enshrined in the US Declaration of Independence. The famous analogy with Camelot, coined by the American journalist Theodore White, popularized the idea that a court had been established in the White House and the notion was founded on Kennedy's fondness for, and use of, the educated and cultured as well as the beautiful and ambitious.

As with many ruling dynasties, the sources of the Kennedy power were murky. Boston's local Democratic Party provided the family with its political base and their much-invoked Irish origins were key to the Kennedy appeal in a party and city strongly influenced by their fellow immigrants. JFK's father, Joseph P. Kennedy, wished and expected his children to become politically powerful and used the fortune he had amassed by stock-exchange speculation before the 1929 Great Crash in order to achieve that goal. He may well have also traded in illegal liquor during the 1920s, when the sale and manufacture of alcohol was legally prohibited in the United States. Appointed US ambassador to Britain in 1937, Joseph Kennedy decided that Britain was doomed to defeat in the increasingly inevitable conflict with Germany and in 1940, urging American isolationism, he resigned his position. His son John, however, served in the Second World War as a naval officer and during his political career became an active proponent of US involvement in international relations.

Kennedy sustained serious injuries while commanding a patrol torpedo boat and he may have become addicted to the amphetamines that he injected to relieve the pain he subsequently suffered. Heroism in action nonetheless contributed to his mystique as leader and the suffering, borne with grace, was part of Kennedy's appeal to his inner circle. *Profiles in Courage* (1956), a study of eight American politicians who had obeyed their consciences rather than conventional opinion, won Kennedy the Pulitzer Prize and, although mostly written by his researcher Theodore Sorensen, the book helped to establish him as a politician with national ambitions. Having served three terms in the House of Representatives (1947–53), Kennedy was elected a Massachusetts senator and edged his family into American high society by marrying Jacqueline Lee Bouvier in 1953.

John Fitzgerald Kennedy, 35th president of the United States, from 1961–3, pictured here in 1962.

Idealism combined with realism informed Kennedy's ambition. Another Irish-American Democrat, Senator Joseph McCarthy of Wisconsin, was running a demagogic campaign in the early 1950s against supposed communist sympathizers holding public office, and his intimidatory techniques had outraged liberal opinion. Kennedy disapproved of this associate of his father's but, knowing that 'half my people in Massachusetts look on McCarthy as a hero', he was cautious in expressing his views. But the position in foreign affairs he expressed in 1959–60 when running for the Democratic nomination to the presidency, and then as the party's candidate for that office, could not be clearer. The preceding Eisenhower administration had been negligent in allowing a 'missile gap' to develop between the Soviets and the United States, and a Kennedy administration would make good this deficiency in nuclear armed missiles.

Kennedy's vigorous and focused electioneering virtually established the style of the modern American presidential election. Newspapers concentrated on the candidate's personality as well as discussing his views and Kennedy understood exactly how to use the new medium of television to heighten the aura of leadership and command. He was the first Catholic to be elected to the US presidency as well as the youngest president in the country's history – although the margin of his victory was slim – and Jo Kennedy probably used his influence with Chicago's mayor to gain a crucial victory in the state of Illinois by fraudulent means. Kennedy survived the disaster in Cuba's 'Bay of Pigs' when CIA-backed Cubans attempted to retake the island from communist control and were shot down on landing in April 1961. He secured the withdrawal of Russian intermediate-range nuclear missiles from the island in October 1962 and took the first steps in building up the US military involvement in defence of South Vietnam against the communist North. But as president he also came to appreciate that the survival of the new America that he personified required not only a readiness to display strength but also a sophisticated willingness to negotiate with those who were not her natural allies.

Kennedy's numerous infidelities showed him capable of the sexual licence characteristic of many a dynastic ruler running a court, while rumours of his toleration of organized crime syndicates showed that he was, in this respect at least, his father's son. The major civil rights legislation that he promoted was only passed after his death, but it was imagery that provided much of the substance of this iconic presidency – not least the television footage recording his assassination by shooting while being driven in a motorcade in Dallas, Texas on 22 November, 1963.

America's involvement in the Vietnam War following Kennedy's death and its inability to defeat the guerrilla armies of the communist-inspired Vietcong, was the nemesis of the country's foreign policy in Southeast Asia. But the war also undermined one of the region's longest-established dynasties – that of Cambodia, a country that was drawn into the war as Vietnam's neighbour.

Cambodian Kingship: a Study in Catastrophe
Norodom Sihanouk (b.1922) first succeeded to the throne in 1941 when his country was still a French protectorate. At first he was little more than a figurehead ruler. Towards the end of the Second World War, however, the Japanese forces that were then occupying Cambodia encouraged the young king to declare his country's independence of France. This proved a premature step and the French civilian and military administration returned to rule the country.

But Sihanouk had gained a taste of power and demonstrated the close link that existed at that time between the king and his loyal subjects. He therefore bided his time until the French colonial regime in Indochina collapsed in 1954, and then founded the People's Socialist Community (*Sangkum Reastr Niyum*), a mass movement whose members were not permitted to join other political parties and which contested the first national elections held in the newly independent state in 1955. Sihanouk's party won every seat amidst widespread reports of electoral abuses encouraged by his police force and, having abdicated in favour of his father, he became Cambodia's prime minister as well as its foreign minister.

Following his father's death five years later, Sihanouk accepted the role of head of state and, until the mid-1960s, he enjoyed an extraordinary dominance over his country's affairs. A flair for diplomatic manoeuvring enabled him to preserve Cambodian neutrality, and the North Vietnamese were allowed to operate in secret from the country's eastern border area in return for their recognition of Cambodia's borders. Meanwhile Sihanouk rejected American offers of military aid and saw America's allies, Thailand and South Vietnam, as a regional threat. By the late 1960s, however, he was using severely repressive measures in order to enforce his will and he was ousted in 1970 in a coup led by anti-communist elements in the Cambodian military who were supported by the United States.

The new regime allowed US and South Vietnamese forces to train on Cambodian soil and pursue communist forces within the country and this dragged the country into the Vietnam War. When Cambodia's communists refused to abide by the peace agreements of 1973 which ended the war between North and South Vietnam, Cambodia was subjected to massive aerial bombardment by the United States. The radical communist Khmer Rouge seized power in 1975 and allowed Sihanouk to return from his exile in Beijing, but placed him under house arrest shortly afterwards.

From 1975 onwards the Khmer Rouge presided over one of the 20th century's greatest series of genocidal atrocities but in 1979, with Vietnamese forces making headway into the country, the Khmer decided to release Sihanouk and hoped that he would represent their case as the country's UN ambassador. Sihanouk first denounced the Vietnamese and then disassociated himself from the Khmer Rouge but subsequently set up his own government in exile, which consisted not just of his own neutralist party, but also the Khmer Rouge.

The Vietnamese had established a puppet regime in Phnom Penh which mostly consisted of those Cambodian communists opposed to Pol Pot, the Khmer Rouge leader. In 1993, however, under UN-sponsored elections, the country's national assembly voted to restore the monarchy and Sihanouk once again ascended the throne. Until his abdication in 2004 Sihanouk reigned over a country that struggled to deal with the legacy of one of the 20th century's bloodiest civil wars, a conflict in which he himself had played an ignoble role.

Iran: Death of a Dynasty

The Middle East, the region that had given birth to kingship, witnessed some of the most historically significant examples of the institution's survival, revival and decline in the 20th century. Iran's Pahlavi dynasty, a 20th-century creation, tried to assert its continuity with the rulers of ancient Persia by adopting the historic title of *shahanshah*, or 'king of kings'. Reza Khan, the army officer who led the 1921 coup that toppled the Qajar dynasty, was

Norodom Sihanouk, king of Cambodia, 1941–55, 1993–2004, holds his joined hands behind his cap in Buddhist fashion in a ceremony in Phnom Penh, 1952.

*Mohammad Reza
Pahlavi, last shah
of Iran, 1941–79,
photographed
in 1960.*

elected shah by the country's constituent assembly in 1925 and was a notably modernizing monarch. Women were required to discard their Islamic veils, the education system was reformed on Western lines and the shah's foreign policy aimed to reduce Iran's financial and diplomatic dependence on foreign powers. His *realpolitik* attempted a balancing act between Britain and the USSR, both countries with a long history of Iranian involvement. But this policy came unstuck as a result of the British-Russian alliance formed in 1941 and, in that year, the two powers occupied Iran to secure the supplies required in order to maintain the Soviet army's resistance to the German invasion of Russia. Reza Shah abdicated in humiliating circumstances and in September 1941 he was succeeded by his son, Mohammad (1919–80). Iranian nationalism became a powerful movement during Mohammad Reza's reign and it was his failure to ally himself with that body of opinion which destroyed his *parvenu* dynasty.

In 1951 Mohammad Mossaddeq, a member of Iran's *Majles*, or parliament, forced through a measure nationalizing the installations and concessions owned by the Anglo-Iranian Oil Company, a British-owned business, and the shah was forced to appoint him as premier. Two years later Mohammad Reza tried to dismiss Mossaddeq who was, however, a popular figure with a gift for self-publicity, and nationalist forces drove the shah into temporary exile. Nonetheless, the US government was supportive of Mohammad Reza and he was swiftly restored to his throne. Mossaddeq's government was then toppled in a coup and the Anglo-Iranian Oil Company, now part of a consortium formed with other businesses, was allowed to renew its oil concessions. But a powerful sentiment had been unleashed and Iranian national feeling became increasingly identified with Shi'ite Islamic militancy. The shah was criticized not just on account of his autocratic style of government but also because of his secularity and clear dependence on Western interests.

Iran was predominant among those Middle Eastern countries that benefited from the huge rise in oil prices as a result of the embargoes, cuts in production and reduction in exports imposed in 1973 by the Organization of Petroleum Exporting Countries (OPEC). Enormous disparities of wealth had emerged in Iran, and the religious leader Ayatollah Ruhollah Khomeini, exiled to Paris because of his opposition to the shah, became the embodiment of Iranian national feeling and anti-Western resentment. The Iranian Islamic revolution of 1978–9 transformed the politics of the Middle East while also changing the balance of power between the region and the West.

It destroyed the shah, who was sent into exile and died shortly afterwards in Cairo. Middle Eastern dynastic monarchs who retained their wealth and power, as in the case of Saudi Arabia's King Fahd (r. 1982–2005), became vulnerable to an Islamic critique which condemned them for their subservience to Western interests. Arab nationalism added its own, often more secular, voice to these protests. The movement acquired its greatest modern leader in 1952 when Gamal Abdel Nasser led the coup which deprived Egypt's corrupt and incompetent Farouk I (r. 1936–52) of his throne and abolished the Egyptian monarchy.

Jordan's Precarious King: Middle Eastern Conclusions

Hussein ibn Talal (1935–99), who succeeded to the throne of Jordan in 1953 as King Hussein of the Hashimite dynasty, was particularly exposed to the destabilizing effects of Arab nationalism, since it was his former territory on the West Bank of the River Jordan that had been seized by the Israeli military in June 1967. As a Hashimite, the king belonged to the family of those claiming to be the direct descendants of the prophet – Muhammad was a member of the house of Hashim which formed part of the Quraysh tribe. But the Hashimites were also central to the politics of the 20th-century Middle East, for the hereditary emirs of Mecca belonged to the same lineage.

Faysal and 'Abd Allah, sons of Husayn ibn 'Ali who ruled as Mecca's emir from 1916 to 1924, became respectively kings of Iraq and of Jordan as a result of the Western powers' re-drawing of the region's national boundaries after the Ottoman empire's collapse at the end of the First World War. Hussein's greatest supporters were the Bedouin tribesmen, but his Palestinian subjects, many of whom had emigrated to Jordan after the foundation of the state of Israel in 1948, felt they owed him little allegiance. As a result, Hussein was forced to rely on a large military establishment in order to enforce his rule and his close relationship with the West, and especially the United States, was a fertile source of Arab resentment.

The Arab-Israeli war of 1967 produced a further wave of Palestinian refugees fleeing from the West Bank into Hussein's territorially diminished kingdom and the Palestinian Liberation Organisation (PLO), operating from its base within Jordan, organized guerrilla warfare against Israel while also threatening Hussein's own authority as ruler. Three years later military conflict for control of Jordan erupted between the PLO and Hussein's army, and in 1971 the organization was expelled from the country.

For the rest of his reign Hussein maintained one of the most difficult balancing acts in the Middle East. He remained a close ally of the United States, retained strong British connections and avoided any military campaigning against Israel. But Hussein also re-established good relations with the PLO and, in 1988, he allowed the organization to assume Jordan's former claim to the West Bank. Meanwhile, the need to protect his throne and secure his financial base forced him to become increasingly intimate with Saudi Arabia, another ally of the West, and in 1994 he signed a peace agreement normalizing relations between Jordan and Israel.

Hussein's life was one of precarious kingship and, by the time of his death, Middle Eastern sentiment and Arab awareness had demonstrated for over two generations their capacity either to cast dynasticism aside or undermine it from within. The first Sun Kings known to history had emerged in these lands, but their late 20th-century heirs and successors had shallow roots in the region, and the very idea that dynasts might claim to be the supreme expression of a nation's identity was being obscured by the sands of time.

Hussein Ibn Talal, king of Jordan from 1953–99, seen here in military uniform in 1960.

Index

Picture acknowledgements

akg-images
2 Erich Lessing.

Ancient Art & Architecture Collection Ltd.
118 Kadakawa; 112 R. Sheridan.

Corbis
4 © Gianni Dagli Orti/Corbis (top); 4 © Ali Meyer/Corbis (bottom right); 5 © Bettmann/Corbis (top); 5 © Fine Art Photographic Library/Corbis (bottom left); 5 © Arte & Immagini srl/Corbis (bottom right); 11© Stapleton Collection/ Corbis; 12-13 © Roger Wood/Corbis; 14 © Alinari Archives/ Corbis; 15 © Summerfield Press/Corbis; 17 © Alinari Archives/Corbis; 21 © Francis G. Mayer/Corbis; 22 © Bettmann/Corbis; 27 © Archivo Iconographico, S.A./Corbis; 31 © Dave Bartruff/Corbis; 33 © Araldo de Luca/Corbis; 41 © Bettmann/Corbis; 43 © Araldo de Luca/Corbis; 45 © Charles & Josette Lenard/Corbis; 49 © Bettmann/Corbis; 51 © Kraus, Johansen/Archivo Iconographico, S.A./Corbis; 55 © Araldo de Luca/Corbis; 59 © Burstein Collection/Corbis; 60 © Bettmann/Corbis; 63 © Burstein Collection/Corbis; 65 © Angelo Hornak/Corbis; 66-67© Brooklyn Museum/Corbis; 69 © Ali Meyer/Corbis; 70-71© Adam Woolfitt/Corbis; 73 © Gianni Dagli Orti/Corbis; 75 © Christie's Images/Corbis; 77 © Christophe Boisvieux/Corbis; 78 © Bettmann/Corbis; 81 © Archivo Iconographico, S.A./Corbis; 85 © Werner Forman/Corbis; 87 © Archivo Iconographico, S.A./Corbis; 89 © Austrian Archives/Corbis; 91 © Bettmann/Corbis; 93 © Jon Hicks/Corbis; 95 © Archivo Iconographico, S.A./Corbis; 96 © Historical Picture Archive/Corbis; 101 © Mimmo Jodice/Corbis; 102-103 © Ruggero Vanni/Corbis; 104 © Archivo Iconografico, S.A./Corbis; 113 © Archivo Iconographico, S.A./Corbis; 114-115 © Gianni Dagli Orti/Corbis; 117 © Sandro Vannini/Corbis; 119 © Pierre Colombel/Corbis; 123 © Archivo Iconographico, S.A./Corbis; 125 © Brooklyn Museum/Corbis; 126 © Bettmann/Corbis; 128 © Chris Hellier/Corbis; 133 © Sigit Pamungkas/Reuters/ Corbis; 135 © Summerfield Press/ Corbis; 136 © Archivo Iconographico, S.A./Corbis; 139 © Alinari Archives/Corbis; 141 © Archivo Iconographico, S.A./Corbis; 142 © Bettmann/ Corbis; 145 © Richard A. Cooke/Corbis; 147 © Bettmann/ Corbis; 149 © Archivo Iconographico, S.A./Corbis; 151 © Francis G.Mayer/Corbis; 153 © Gianni Dagli Orti/Corbis; 154 © Hulton-Deutsch Collection/Corbis; 158 © Ali Meyer/Corbis; 160 © Historical Picture Archive/Corbis; 1 63 © Stapleton Collection/Corbis; 164 © Stapleton Collection/ Corbis; 169 © Fine Art Photographic Library/Corbis; 171 © Stapleton Collection/Corbis; 172-173 © Stapleton Collection/Corbis; 175 © Krause, Johansen/Archivo Iconographico, S.A./Corbis; 176 © Bettmann/Corbis; 178 © Bettmann/Corbis; 181 © Araldo de Luca/Corbis; 183 © Araldo de Luca/Corbis; 188 © Archivo Iconographico, S.A./Corbis; 193 © Pierre Colombel/Corbis; 195 © Arte & Immagini srl/Corbis; 197 © Christel Gerstenberg/Corbis; 199 © The State Russian Museum/Corbis; 203 © Bettmann/ Corbis; 205 © Bettmann/Corbis; 208-209 © Bettmann/ Corbis; 211 © Arte & Immagini srl/Corbis; 213 © Corbis; 215 © Ali Meyer/Corbis; 216 © Reproduced by permission of The State Hermitage Museum, St. Petersburg, Russia/ Corbis; 217 © The State Russian Museum/Corbis; 220 © Hulton-Deutsch Collection/Corbis; 223 © Francis G. Mayer/Corbis; 225 © Bettmann/Corbis; 226 © Archivo Iconografico S.A./Corbis; 228 © National Gallery Collection; by kind permission of the Trustees of the National Gallery, London/Corbis; 229 © Stapleton Collection/Corbis; 232 © Bettmann/Corbis; 236 © Christie's Images/Corbis; 239 © Hulton-Deutsch Collection/Corbis; 240 © Corbis; 241 © Stapleton Collection/Corbis; 242 © Yann Arthus-Bertrand/Corbis; 243 © Hulton-Deutsch Collection/Corbis; 244 © Bettmann/Corbis; 245 © Hulton-Deutsch Collection/ Corbis; 246 © Reuters/Corbis; 247 © Bettmann/Corbis; 249 © Bettmann/Corbis; 250 © Bettmann/Corbis; 251 © Bettmann/Corbis.

Shutterstock
4 Vova Pomortzeff (bottom left); 8 Vova Pomortzeff; 9 C.J. Photography; 19 Nir Levy; 24-25 John Said; 28 Paul Picone; 29 Styve Reineck; 35 Taolmor; 36 Maza; 39 Alfio Ferlito; 44 Jack Cronkhite; 46 Holger Mette; 52 Pippa West; 57 Vova Pomortzeff; 58 W.H. Chow; 79 Brandus Dan Lucian; 82-83 Vadym Andrushchenko; 88 Nadejada Ivanova; 98-99 May Lane; 107 Alex James Bramwell; 108 Vova Pomortzeff; 109 Vova Pomortzeff; 110 Connors Bros.; 121 Louise Shumbris; 129 David Wardhaugh; 130-131 Yanto Hung; 157 Philip Lange; 159 Jamo Gonzalez Zarraonandia; 162 Holly Jahangiri; 166-167 Dennis Albert Richardson; 184 iofoto; 185 Khirman Vladimir; 190 Salamanderman; 196 Michel Stevelmans; 200-201 Dainis Derics; 206 Dainis Derics; 218-219 Marek Slusarczyk; 231 Ronfromyork; 235 Ryan Klos.

Quercus Publishing has made every effort to trace copyright holders of the pictures used in this book. Anyone having claims to ownership not identified above is invited to contact Quercus Publishing.

For John Harrison

Author acknowledgements

My literary agent Georgina Capel, along with her assistants Rosie Apponyi and Abi Fellows, provided me with greatly valued encouragement while writing this book whose conception owes much to the inspirational figure of my publisher Anthony Cheetham. Wayne Davies was a courteous and vigilant editor. I am also grateful to Victoria Huxley for the accurate work she has done as copy editor, and to Graham Bateman, Steve McCurdy and Virginia Carter at BCS Publishing for their expertise in designing the book's layout and researching its accompanying illustrations.

I have benefited from the work of many other historians who have written on the subject of kingship. Among medievalists I wish to note in particular my indebtedness to the writings of David Abulafia, Richard Fletcher, Jacques Le Goff, Karl Leyser, Walter Ullmann and J.M. Wallace-Hadrill. Those whose works have guided me in the later history of the subject include: John Adamson, T.C.W. Blanning, Norbert Elias, J.H.Elliott, R.J.W.Evans, and H.R.Trevor-Roper. Although having learnt so much from their achievements the author assumes responsibility for any contestable interpretations contained in this book.

Raymond and Granwen Williams, and Dewi Rhys Williams, provided me with mental and social refreshment on my visits to their republican-minded domains in west Wales for which I am correspondingly grateful. The dedication records my admiration for a schoolmaster whose enthused and informed teaching of history has inspired so many of his pupils.

HYWEL WILLIAMS.

Fall River Press, 122 Fifth Avenue, New York, NY 10011

ISBN 978-0-7607-9460-9

Printed and bound in China

3 5 7 9 10 8 6 4 2